Birds of Passage

Studies in Environmental Anthropology and Ethnobiology

General Editor: **Roy Ellen**, FBA

Professor of Anthropology, University of Kent at Canterbury
Interest in environmental anthropology has grown steadily in recent years, reflecting national and international concern about the environment and developing research priorities. This major new international series, which continues a series first published by Harwood and Routledge, is a vehicle for publishing up-to-date monographs and edited works on particular issues, themes, places or peoples which focus on the interrelationship between society, culture and environment. Relevant areas include human ecology, the perception and representation of the environment, ethno-ecological knowledge, the human dimension of biodiversity conservation and the ethnography of environmental problems. While the underlying ethos of the series will be anthropological, the approach is interdisciplinary.

Recent volumes:

For a full volume listing, please see the series page on our website:
https://berghahnbooks.com/series/environmental-anthropology-and-ethnobiology

Birds of Passage

Hunting and Conservation in Malta

Mark-Anthony Falzon

berghahn

NEW YORK · OXFORD

www.berghahnbooks.com

First published in 2020 by
Berghahn Books
www.berghahnbooks.com

Library of Congress Cataloging-in-Publication Data
A C.I.P. cataloging record is available from the Library of Congress
Library of Congress Cataloging in Publication Control Number: 2020016087

British Library Cataloguing in Publication Data
A catalogue record for this book is available from the British Library

ISBN 978-1-78920-766-8 hardback
ISBN 978-1-80073-909-3 paperback
ISBN 978-1-78920-767-5 ebook

https://doi.org/10.3167/781789207668

For Federico

Contents

Illustrations

Figures

Table

Acknowledgements

This book would not have been possible without the direct or indirect help of many people. As far as my academic formation is concerned, my greatest debt is to James Laidlaw, the William Wyse Professor of Social Anthropology at the University of Cambridge. Also at Cambridge, Matei Candea was generous with his time and knowledge, King's College provided exquisite accommodation during my study trips, and the Department of Social Anthropology hosted me for a seminar on hunting in Malta that helped me shape my ideas.

The University of Malta's research infrastructure made possible access to generous resources. My colleague Paul Sant Cassia gave me liberally of his wisdom, as did the late Paul M Clough, Dominic Fenech and Gillian M Martin. Giuliana Fenech read and commented on a version of Chapter 2. The Italian government funded a research trip to Lampedusa and Linosa. Vahdet Ünal of Ege University discussed aspects of fish conservation and suggested key scholarly sources with me. Alicia Said, too, recommended sources on fisheries. Edwin Lanfranco's botanical knowledge helped me get the names of plants right.

The list of hunters who helped me is long, but Andrew Buhagiar, Raymond Cordina and Paul Debattista stand out. Victor Falzon is not a relative, but he still took the trouble to prepare the map. Raymond Galea and Aron Tanti generously provided original photographs from their impressive portfolios. I also wish to thank Joe Perici Calascione (FKNK), the late and fondly remembered Joe Sultana (BirdLife Malta), Axel Hirschfeld (CABS), Sergei Golovkin (formerly WBRU) and Joseph Lia (WBRU).

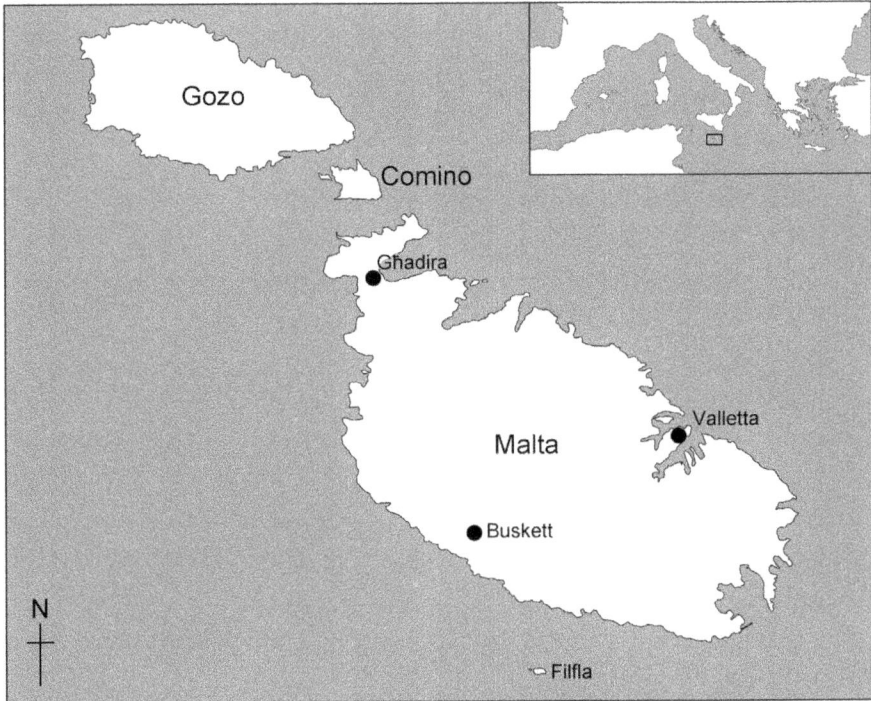

The Maltese archipelago. Map created by Victor Falzon, published with permission.

Introduction

Birds fascinate because they appear to be fundamentally alien forms of life – removed from our environment and from our concerns, free to float above us and forever out of reach. They leave no tracks, and their journeys are for the most part invisible.

—Jon Day, *Homing: On Pigeons, Dwellings and Why We Return*[1]

Among the earliest known animal images are small carvings of flying swans. Found at Mal'ta, an Upper Paleolithic site in Siberia, they are made from mammoth ivory and are thought to date back at least 15,000 years. Wonderfully stylized and designed to be worn as pendants, they tell of a timeless human fascination with bird flight and migration. They also suggest that swans in particular have long been spellbinding and talismanic (see Cocker 2013). In antiquity, they were associated with Venus and Apollo on account of the unsullied whiteness of their plumage. In a passage in the *Aeneid*, the sudden appearance of swans is read as an auspicious sign (Impelluso 2004). The examples are many and as well-travelled as the birds themselves.

The mute swan is the best-known species of its kind in Europe. In flight, its stately and self-assured presence on lakes and ponds is transformed into over 2 metres of beating wingspan. The mute swan is fully migratory and freezing temperatures can displace it off the normal routes and wintering sites. So it was that a flock of swans appeared at St Thomas Bay in Malta, an island in the Mediterranean, on 20 January 2002. For the small crowd that congregated on shore, it was to be a short-lived charm. Within minutes of the swans' arrival, a speedboat was in hot pursuit. On board, like demented Lohengrins, three hunters. Swans are powerful flyers, but their tremendous weight makes take-off a laborious process. A barrage of shots drowned out whatever wistful swansong there may have been. At least six birds were killed, three of which were quickly bundled into the boat, which then made off at great speed.

In Malta, swans are fully protected occasional migrants. The shooting, which was hailed as an outrage and a national embarrassment domestically, was also widely reported in the British press and international news channels.[2] As it turned out, the grainy photographs taken from shore by onlookers were enough for the police to arrest and charge three young hunters, who were eventually convicted and sent to prison. The incident remains etched in the memory as one of the darkest episodes in the history of bird conservation in Malta. There are more personal scars too. Ten years later, I happened to be talking about birds and hunting with builders who were doing some work at my house and who were all themselves hunters. When the conversation touched on swans, one of the men, whom I shall call Salvu, suddenly appeared upset and sullen. Later, one of his colleagues took me aside and told me never to bring up the swans story again when Salvu was around. The convicted hunters were close relatives of his and the matter had shamed the family. Tellingly, the shame was greatest in hunting circles: by their reckless and brazen action, the swan killers had done great damage to the public image of hunters in Malta. As we shall see, it had also come at the worst possible time.

'Path-building', Georg Simmel assures us in a celebrated essay, 'is a specifically human achievement; the animal too continuously overcomes a separation and often in the cleverest and most ingenious of ways, but its beginning and end remain unconnected, it does not accomplish the miracle of the road: freezing movement into a solid structure that commences from it and in which it terminates' (Simmel 1994: 6). Be that as it may, the path-building projects of humans and animals do in fact intersect in many ways. Take the protagonists of this book. Birds, like other migratory animals such as fish and insects, are good to think with: to draw battle lines and contest accessibility over, to align social divisions (both internal and external), to precipitate contesting notions of 'culture' and 'value', to embody different elaborations of aesthetics, to establish transnational alliances and to highlight that the hegemony and legitimation of scientific enquiry are contestable.

They also set up a perfect domain where anthropological enquiry can be applied fruitfully. What follows is first and foremost an ethnography of hunting and conservation in what bird protectionists widely regard as one of the darkest corners (Malta) of a black spot (the Mediterranean) for migrating birds. The case is lent complexity in that the number and variety of birds shot and trapped in Malta has declined sharply in recent years, and especially following the country's accession to the European Union (EU). In this sense, the book is a study of conservation outcomes at a time when global issues like bushmeat, the Anthropocene and the 'sixth extinction' (Kolbert 2014) have become particularly pressing for conservationists and ecologists. Besides, and because migration journeys cut across geographical, political and social boundaries, the exploitation and conservation of migratory species bring into play a number of unique features and challenges. Beyond the specifics of the case study, this book can be located within a number of scholarly fields. First, it is a study of human–nonhuman interactions, and of some of the practices and feelings that pattern and nourish them. Second, it sheds light on the politics of hunting and conservation, and the ways in which it is played out in national, supranational (mainly the EU) and international political spaces. Third, it is a study of how local environmentalist movements are made and of how they embed themselves in broader discourses of science and rationality. Fourth, it offers a look at how supranational regulations and legislation are translated into practice in specific local contexts. These are some of the arguments that are dealt with in the chapters that follow.

In Chapter 1 I first describe the setting and its birds, with an emphasis on the transience of migration. I then describe the twin practices of hunting and trapping. It turns out that they have emerged as one of the most vitriolic issues in the country, aligning individuals and groups, precipitating national referendums, leveraging political parties as well as being leveraged by them, and becoming a *cause célèbre* in perceptions of, and state interactions with, the EU. Finally, I discuss my fieldwork in Malta and locate it within the hunting-conservation dynamic. The main argument of Chapter 2 is that an in-depth understanding of hunting requires us to pay attention to both emotion and practice. I look at how hunters are made and at what sustains their urge to hunt. The anatomy of the emotions that hunters feel is explored in terms of the characteristics of nature generally and birds specifically. (It is also here that the vagaries of migration matter.) I then discuss the ways in which the hunting experience intersects with notions of modernity, masculinity and Mediterranean alterity. In Chapter 3, I turn my attention to the relations between hunters and conservationists. I first trace the rise of bird protection organizations in Malta and their location within global models and trajectories of conservation. I then discuss politics and the various political spaces within which bird protection is embedded; in particular, the transition from national politics to multilevel governance is explored. I also look at some of the ways in which hunting emerged as a contested field. In the final part of the chapter I focus on a single set of events that took place in 2015, when a national referendum was held on whether or not spring hunting should be banned. It turns out that the fate of long-distance migrants is also shaped by local and national circumstances. Chapter 4 takes up the theme of physical places to explore some of the many and complex relations between Maltese hunters and their environment, focusing in particular on hunting as spatial experience ('being-in-the-field'), as well as access to, and transformations of, the 'pulling' land that attracts migrating birds. These transformations are often vigorously opposed by conservationists and it is to this aspect that I then turn in the second part of the chapter. In Chapter 5, I look at how bird protectionists attempt literally to make place for conservation. This includes fenced bird reserves, sites of 'special scientific interest' and internationally recognized 'important bird areas'. I also describe and discuss the rise of field surveillance by Maltese and international activists, and its crucial role in bird conservation. Hunting in Malta offers an excellent case study of the intersection between science, numbers and conservation, and Chapter 6 looks at bird protectionists as producers of scientific data generally and numbers in particular. I discuss some of the ways in which hunters contest these data and seek to set up a discourse of sustainability in a context where the species concerned breed elsewhere. In the last section I trace the development of an enumerative modality in the context of Malta's accession to the EU. It turns out that Malta is a fine testing ground for anthropological understandings of human–wildlife interactions, conservation and environmental governance.

Notes

1. See Day 2019: 7.
2. See, for instance, 'Outrage at Maltese Massacre of Swans', *The Telegraph*, 24 February 2002.

CHAPTER 1

Troubled Journeys

Malta's population stands in excess of 350,000 people, a number which is
swollen by hoards [*sic*] of visitors during a long tourist season. They come
to soak up the sun; to enjoy peaceful tranquillity and clear unpolluted
waters; to eat well thanks to the farmers who ensure agricultural self-
sufficiency for the island; and to savour the George Cross spirit of
the people. Malta is a paradise, except for one vice of some 5% of her
population who at regular intervals down the tools of their various trades
to shoot and trap more than four million wild birds every year.
  —David Bellamy, 'Foreword', in Natalino Fenech, *Fatal Flight*[1]

The nation-state of Malta consists of a group of islands in the central
Mediterranean. The nearest land is another island, Sicily, which lies
about 90 km to the north. The northern coast of Libya is 360 km to the
south, and the easternmost and westernmost points of the Mediterranean
are roughly equidistant. By far the largest island of the group is Malta
itself, followed by Gozo, Comino and Filfla, in that order; there are also
a number of tiny offshore islets and rocks. In all, the country covers an
area of just 316 km² and is the smallest EU Member State as well as
one of the world's smallest sovereign states. It is also one of the most
densely populated. The current figure is about half a million, most of
whom live on Malta; about 37,000 people live on Gozo and three people
on Comino.
  The islands consist of various layers of sedimentary limestone that
often give rise to rugged features, especially in coastal areas. There are no
mountains, but a number of hilly ridges are prominent in the north and
west of Malta, and practically in the whole of Gozo. There are high sea
cliffs in the western parts of Malta and Gozo, as well as gentler ones in the
south of Malta and on Comino. In many places, the friable limestone cliffs
constantly calve boulders to form screes and a rugged coast. Among the
key topographical features are the various *widien* (valleys), most of which
lead from the higher areas in the west towards the sea; a handful of these
contain year-round watercourses, but there are no rivers or lakes.

Figure 1.1. The rugged west coast. Photograph by the author.

The dearth of freshwater and the rocky terrain conspire to make the islands look very bare, especially in summer. The overall impression of the Maltese landscape is that of a lacework of rubble walls that strain to contain a shallow reddish soil and that are interspersed with rocky areas and criss-crossed by the relatively verdant *widien*. About a third of the country is under crops and about 5 per cent (the lowest rate among the countries of the EU) is forested.[2] The rest of the unbuilt landscape is made up of a number of ecological types. The most common of these is a kind of low shrubland known as garrigue (*xagħri*). Garrigue may look very barren at a distance, and especially so in summer, but it is in fact characterized by a large variety of evergreen or deciduous shrubs (usually lower than 50 cm), the actual range of which depends on factors such as human disturbance and exposure. Especially along the sides of valleys and around ridges, garrigue is often replaced by maquis, a Mediterranean community that is dominated by small evergreen trees (up to about 10 m high) and medium to large evergreen shrubs (typically 1–5 m). A type that is as species-rich as garrigue is that of dry grasslands or steppes, which are usually dominated by herbaceous species and notably grasses. In Malta, steppe often rubs shoulders with garrigue, and it is also found on abandoned fields and in a specialized form on coastal clay slopes. The fourth main kind of community is the Mediterranean evergreen wood. Historically, deforestation has meant that naturally occurring woods are all but absent in Malta and are represented solely by a few scattered so-called 'remnant' stands; however, afforestation has in recent decades created significant pockets of woodland. In addition to these four types, there are a number of small and uncommon communities, such as coastal cliffs, coastal halophytic shrublands, saline marshes, sand dunes, riparian woodlands and riparian shrublands (Lanfranco 2015).

Not surprisingly for a miniscule island country with a relatively large population, Malta has by far the highest proportion of built-up area in Europe. About a third of the main island of Malta (but considerably less in the case of Gozo) is taken up by houses, roads, industrial areas, tourism- and recreation-linked development and infrastructure. The most densely built-up zone is clustered around the capital, Valletta, a walled city that sits on a peninsula that overlooks a deep-water harbour on either side. The harbour to the south is hemmed in by a further three separately walled maritime cities, and that to the north by a more recent and dense conurbation. The harbour area aside, there are a few dozen towns and villages scattered across the country. Until the 1970s or so, each settlement was surrounded with countryside, but intensive building has meant that many of them, especially those in the eastern side of the country, have merged into a more or less continuous whole. As will be seen in the course of this book, the dense population and shrinking countryside are very relevant to the hunting and conservation issue.

Politically, Malta became an independent nation-state in 1964. Its history before that was one of a succession of foreign rulers, the last being the British, who added the islands to their Mediterranean possessions in 1800 (formally in 1814).[3] Since independence, the country has functioned as a parliamentary democracy, with the Labour Party (PL) and the Nationalist Party (PN) swapping roles in government and opposition every few years. The Green Party (Alternattiva Demokratika (AD)) was

Figure 1.2. Flatter agricultural land and villages in the south. Photograph by the author.

set up in 1989, but has never managed to win a seat in parliament. The intense bipartisan rivalry that prevails and the slim majorities by which parties typically win elections[4] are important factors to bear in mind when analysing the politics of hunting and conservation. One should add that politics in Malta is strongly centralized and that political processes and contestations are located squarely within the space of a national imaginary. There are, to be sure, sixty-eight local councils, but their power is limited to things like waste collection and minor roadworks. Equally relevant to the arguments of this book is Malta's accession to the EU in 2004, following a hotly contested national referendum held in 2003 in which a narrow 53.6 per cent of voters opted for the country to join.

With respect to the economy and society, historically the most important factor was that the islands offered an excellent harbour in a strategic geographical location. The maritime and military activities it enabled made Malta an attractive place to occupy, and they also made possible the relatively high population. Today, the mainstays of the economy are transshipment, manufacture for export, financial and other services, and tourism. The last of these accounts for a good chunk of the country's livelihood. Perhaps unwittingly, the millions[5] of tourists who visit Malta every year have proved a significant player in the hunting and conservation dynamic.

The vast majority of Maltese people are Roman Catholic and religion is conspicuously part of the sensory landscape in the form of churches, street niches, place and person names, local festivals and so on. The national language, and one of the official languages of the EU, is Maltese, which consists of a Semitic infrastructure that goes back to the Arab period (ca. 870–1091) and a lexical element that draws on later influences and especially that of Romance languages. The majority of Maltese understand and to some extent speak English, which is in fact the second official language. Although English is by and large the prestige language, there is considerable code-switching and hybridization between the two languages in everyday conversations.

Birds of a Small Island

At first glance, a small and densely populated island might not seem a tremendous prospect ornithologically. Indeed, the list of species that breed regularly in Malta stands at a paltry twenty-one. Four of these are seabirds that breed in inaccessible sea cliffs and on offshore rocks, and the rest mainly small passerines or species that are localized and restricted to bird reserves (Raine et al. 2009; Sultana et al. 2011). At least as far as hunters are concerned, none of the regular breeders are considered to be particularly desirable, and in any case most are fully protected by law (the EU Birds Directive) and may not be shot or trapped at any time of the year.

This lean situation changes dramatically when migration (*il-passa* in Maltese) is brought into the equation. The volume, diversity and magicality of bird migration between Europe and Africa has been described as an 'extraordinary . . . enormous . . . twice-yearly transference of biomass from one hemisphere to another' (Merritt 2016: 48) and 'strong seasonal compulsions that draw creatures between regions, from one hemisphere to another' (Macfarlane 2007: 292). More prosaically, it has been estimated that 5 billion individuals of ninety-seven species of landbird migrate from Eurasian high-latitude areas to lower latitudes around the Mediterranean basin and into Africa (Newton 2007); every autumn, approximately 2.1 billion songbirds and near-passerines alone migrate from Europe to Africa (Hahn and Bauer 2009). Malta's geographical position matters, because the islands are situated on the central Mediterranean route favoured by a number of species. Of the 400 or so bird species that have been recorded in Malta, about 120 are more-or-less regular migrants that fly over and sometimes stop to rest or feed on the islands. Another fifty migrate over Malta and sometimes spend the winter there, in varying proportions. The handful of breeders aside, the rest of the 400 is made up of vagrants and occasional migrants (see, for instance, Sultana and Gauci 1982). The point is that migration seasonally and regularly transforms the islands from something of an ornithological outpost (even if the resident seabird colonies are considered to be of ecological importance internationally) into a substantially significant place on the map of ornithological value and possibility. As Raine (2011: 17) puts it of Comino, 'during peak migration periods it can appear as if every available sprig of vegetation has a passerine perching on it'.

Migration being such a key part of the workings of this book, it makes sense to briefly go through the rhythms and protagonists. The two main migration seasons are spring, when birds fly north from their wintering grounds in Africa to breed in Europe, and autumn, when the direction is reversed. The first migrants of spring usually trickle in around late February and include hirundines, harriers and smallish passerines such as wheatears. Influxes of thrushes and larks, as well as offshore duck passages, also sometimes occur around this time. The number and variety of migrants increase in late March and reach their peak in April and early May, when it is possible, on a good day, to record fifty species or more. These may include birds of prey, herons, waders, passerines and colourful non-passerines such as hoopoes and bee-eaters. The

Figure 1.3. A Montagu's harrier on spring migration in Malta. Photograph by Aron Tanti, published with permission.

spring migration peters out in May, and summer is largely a quiet season, although there is a significant movement of waders and some passerines. The first autumn migrants begin to appear around mid-August and reach a peak in September. The spring and autumn migrations are not exactly the same species-wise – for example, autumn is remarkable for its concentrated and large-scale movements of birds of prey. October and November bring thrushes, skylarks, woodcock and finches, among others, and early winter plovers and ducks. This is also the time when many birds migrate that eventually winter in Malta; the list includes chats, wagtails and starlings.

Given that there are so few resident and so many migrant species, the number and diversity of birds that are around on any given day vary immensely. Even during the peak migration periods, it is quite possible to see a handful of birds one day and to wake up to a countryside teeming with birds the next. Although bird migration is not fully understood, it is known to be related to variables like moon phase, cloud cover, wind strength and direction, low pressure fronts, thermal air currents and so on (Baker 1984). To further complicate matters, the migration behaviours of different species vary widely and different places in Malta tend to experience different things at any one time. Especially on a small island with limited opportunities for birds to stop over, the infinite number of ways in which these variables come together mean that bird migration contains an element of unpredictability. There are patterns, to be sure, but there is no fixed formula or anything approaching it.[6] Thus, for example, a heavy passage of turtle doves on 14 April 2007 left both hunters and birdwatchers gasping – it was too early in the season, there was not a cloud in sight, and the strong northwesterly wind was all wrong (turtle dove passages usually occur on overcast days with easterly winds). On another occasion I was in the field one morning in September and saw a steady stream of quail making landfall on the eastern coast of Gozo. A hunter who happened to be there shot incessantly, but there was no sign of either quail or hunters a few hundred metres inland. This dialogic, and largely unpredictable, relationship between fleeting presence and absence is possibly the key defining feature of bird migration, and of its appropriation by hunters and birdwatchers, in Malta.

The Practice of Bird Hunting

As practised today, the taking of wild migrating birds in Malta includes a number of different and sometimes overlapping types. The first is that of shooting with three-shot (the legal limit) semi-automatic shotguns, although a small number of old-timers and nostalgics use two-shot double-barrel weapons. The Romance-derived Maltese word for this kind of hunting is *kaċċa* and that for hunter the masculine *kaċċatur* (pl. *kaċċaturi*). This kind of shooting is practised using two different methods. The first involves roaming and walking-up ('flushing', usually with trained dogs) birds, or shooting them as they happen to otherwise present themselves in the field. The second is to stay put and wait for migratory birds to come into range. Hunters sit in places that they consider to be vantage points and usually but not necessarily conceal themselves in purpose-built hides (*dura*, pl. *duri*). Decoys and bird-callers (nowadays mostly of the electronic type or calls that are downloaded from the internet and played back on mobile phones or portable wireless speakers) are a staple of this second type of hunting, regardless of the legislation that prohibits their use. In practice, a typical hunting session will often include both types – hunters usually sit in hides during the first hours of the day or in the event of a steady stream of migrating birds, but they will also at some point roam to pick up any stragglers. Whichever of the two methods they choose, hunters nowadays often wear some sort of camouflage when in the field.

The second way in which birds are taken in Malta is that of live capture or trapping. The Maltese word for this practice, which has deeper

Figure 1.4. An elevated shooting hide (*dura*) overlooks a clump of planted acacia and eucalyptus trees. Photograph by the author.

historical roots (guns only became widely available in the nineteenth century), is the Semitic-derived *insib*; the word for trapper is the masculine *nassab* and that for a trapping site *mansab*. (That there is a word for the place itself indicates that trapping is more strongly sited and linked to specific places.) The most commonly used technique is that of

Figure 1.5. A trapping site (*mansab*). Photograph by the author.

clap-netting in which birds are lured by means of live decoys (*tat-taħrik*) and call-birds (*tal-għajjat*) to a small rectangular patch where they can be netted with a pair of horizontally laid-out and sprung panel nets operated by means of a pull-cord (*gbid*) by the trapper, who sits in a hide (also called *dura*) a few metres away. Clap-netting has a worldwide distribution and its design has remained virtually unchanged since ancient Egyptian times; for example, a 1678 diagram in Ray's *The Ornithology of Francis Willughby of Middleton* (as shown in Shrubb (2013)) shows an arrangement that is identical, down to the smallest detail, to a *mansab* in Malta today.

Clap-netting is an effective means of catching a variety of birds. The trapping of turtle doves (*insib tal-gamiem*) is now outlawed, but was used until recently to take birds in spring, a few of which would be kept in aviaries to be used as decoys and the rest consumed. Turtle dove trapping was widespread and the subject of much technical knowledge and lore. Especially in places that were renowned for their strategic location, trapping sites were often ingeniously constructed in ways that maximized their catching potential. The best sites were prized cultural objects whose reputation extended well beyond the immediate place where they were found. Today, *insib tal-gamiem* typically evokes much elegiac discourse among hunters, trappers and rural people generally: a small book on the subject published in 2014 consistently uses the past tense and opens with the words 'as turtle dove trappers, we can say farewell to our practice' (Deguara 2014: 1, my translation).

The other trapping techniques that are occasionally (and illegally) used include cage traps as well as a kind of horizontal net traditionally used to capture quail. Unlike in many other Mediterranean countries, snares and bird lime have not in recent history been used to trap birds in Malta. The reason is that trapping is aimed at procuring birds that are intended to be kept alive and that should therefore be unharmed by the trapping process – so much so that trappers emphasize the special attraction of catching and keeping birds alive (*taqbdu ħaj*), as opposed to shooting them.

In recent years, and in various ways, Malta has applied derogations from EU law to allow the trapping of three kinds of birds in autumn: plovers, song thrush and seven species of finches. The trapping of plovers is a specialized type that requires open terrain, the availability of live decoys (although plastic ones have been found effective when coupled with electronic bird calls) and a measure of technical skill. The plovers that are caught are kept in aviaries and valued for their plaintive calls. This kind of trapping used to be rare, but has increased in recent years, in part due to the outlawing of other kinds of trapping. Thrush trapping, on the other hand, is practised by relatively few people. It is not generally considered to offer as much sport as the other kinds of trapping.

The one form of trapping that is as highly valued as it is widely popular and hotly contested is finch trapping. In Malta, finches (*tal-għana*) are commonly kept and valued for their appearance and song. Although it has a longer history, finch trapping became ubiquitous in the twentieth century. It makes use of live decoys that are used to attract migrating birds to an area where they can be clap-netted. It also involves a large volume of technical knowledge about migration patterns, weather variables, the selection of decoy birds, actual catching methods and so on, the details of which are beyond the scope of the present work.

Apart from these main types of hunting and trapping, there are three more that are specialized and less common. The first two, which are regulated by law, are the offshore hunting of migrating ducks from seacraft and the hunting of wild rabbits; rabbits are the largest terrestrial mammals in Malta (there are no deer, foxes or boars). The third type, which is illegal, is the trapping, by means of clap-nets set over artificial ponds, of migrating waders. This is a practice that started about twenty years ago and has gained considerable traction in spite of protectionists' efforts to the contrary.

The different types of legal hunting and trapping usually require special licences, and a good number of practitioners hold multiple licences.

The reason for this is that although each kind of trapping or hunting is associated with a particular set of motivations and knowledge, many people practise more than one type (and sometimes several). Thus, a man might shoot turtle doves and quail in spring, rabbits in summer and autumn migrants in October, and trap finches in November and December. He might also join friends on a sea hunt for ducks. (It is common for hunters and trappers to join relatives or friends in the field.)

There are two further points to be made in this brief description: both are embedded in politics and subject to much contestation, and are therefore crucial to what follows in this book. First, hunters in Malta are entirely dependent on migration and its apparent whims. The word and conceptual category *kaċċa* (which also means 'game birds') carries no connotations of gamekeeping or breeding for shooting purposes (as 'game' does with grouse and pheasant on shooting estates in Britain, for example). In Malta, a hunter is someone who shoots migrating birds, while a trapper is someone who traps them.

Second, even as hunters and trappers cast their practices as 'traditional', they constantly seek to innovate. It follows that the above descriptions are intended to provide a general outline of what in fact is a set of practices in constant flux. A few examples will suffice to make the point. It was only from the mid-twentieth century that trappers realized that there was a return passage of finches in early spring – prior to that, the birds were thought to migrate only in autumn. The discovery led to the development of large-scale trapping in March and early April, to the extent that the *gojjin ta' Marzu* (March linnet) quickly became one of the most desirable target species. Hunting at sea was all but unknown until the last decades of the twentieth century, when the wide availability of powerful seacraft and the discovery that ducks and other kinds of birds migrated along the coast in large numbers encouraged substantial numbers of hunters to spend their days at sea chasing flocks of ducks, herons, seabirds and so on; at its peak in the mid-1990s, hunting at sea had become a major conservation issue in places such as the channel that separates Malta from Gozo. Mechanical lark mirrors (*alwettiera*) were once widely used to attract migrating skylarks by mimicking pools of water. They are now no longer in use; instead, electronic callers are used that appear to do the job just as well. The trapping of plovers at night, a practice unknown until recently, now involves the use of night-vision devices, electronic callers, monitors installed in hides and remote-controlled clap-nets. At the time of writing, hunters continue to innovate.

If these changes are located at the intersection of technology and knowledge of bird behaviour, there is another factor that is just as significant:

legislation and conservation effort. For example, robins were, until the 1990s, illegally trapped in their thousands, usually by boys, by means of simple cage traps (*trabokk*) that could be bought openly at markets and ironmongeries. However, successive and focused campaigns by bird protection organizations, as well as the increasing law enforcement that followed, meant that the practice had all but died out by the turn of the century.[7] In general, hunting and trapping practices experienced the effects of a growing conservation movement that in turn led to rafts of legislation and enforcement that had to do with open seasons, huntable areas and protected species.

Finally in this section, a word on terminology. There are regional differences in the meaning of the words 'hunting' and 'trapping'. In Britain, the word used for the taking of game birds is 'shooting'. 'Hunting' means the taking of wild deer or other mammals, usually with the help of dogs (hounds) and sometimes on horseback; 'stalking' is used specifically for a kind of deer hunting in which the hunter spots and closes in on the quarry on foot. In North America, 'hunting' is a broader term that includes all of these practices, including the taking of wild birds. In both contexts, 'trapping' refers to the taking of animals (usually mammals) using a variety of traps and snares, for purposes that include pest control and the procurement of meat or fur. In the wider context and in scholarly sources that are not specific to Britain, the English word used for the taking of wild animals (including birds) for food or recreation is 'hunting'. Thus, in Malta, the word 'shooting' is not used, except in a disparaging sense by opponents keen to emphasize trigger-happiness; rather, the word used in the English-language press and elsewhere is 'hunting'. The English word used for the live capture of wild birds for recreation (and food in the past) is 'trapping', although 'live capture' is increasingly used in technical circles in order to avoid unfavourable associations with the types of trapping practised elsewhere in which the quarry is killed. In this book, I shall use the word 'hunting' somewhat generically to refer to the practice of taking wild birds by shooting or trapping them; I shall be more specific in the case of descriptions and arguments that require a distinction between hunting and trapping. Much, but by no means all, of what follows can be applied generically to all forms of hunting in Malta, including trapping.

A Contested Practice

The extent to which hunting is a high-profile and controversial topic in Malta cannot be overemphasized. The present number of hunters is about 13,500, which means that there are at least seventy hunters per square kilometre of huntable land.[8] Although the figure is impressive and certainly a major clue as to why the practice creates such friction, density alone cannot offer a satisfactory explanation.

The first indications that the practice was going to attract flak gathered pace in mid-twentieth-century accounts by foreign observers.[9] Writing in 1954 in a book on the birds of Malta, Roberts despaired about the multitude of 'so-called sportsmen who roam all over the Island mercilessly slaughtering or maiming everything in feathers'; he thought that the extensive trapping that took place was 'an even greater evil' (Roberts 1954: xv). In an essay on Malta, Brockman lamented that no 'official action' seemed possible to reduce the 'indiscriminate slaughter by gun and trap' that went on (Brockman 1961: 73). As late as 2013, Mark Cocker's landmark book on birds and people claimed that Malta had a 'sophisticated attachment to bird trapping and hunting'; indeed, it was the most notorious place for turtle dove hunting (Cocker 2013: 245).

Not that the exceptionalist language of 'indiscriminate slaughter', 'black spots' and 'massacre' of migratory birds was a prerogative of outsiders. Indeed, it probably reached its high point in Natalino Fenech's *Fatal Flight*, published in 1992. Fenech is a Maltese bird protection activist and self-taught ornithologist. In a moment of national self-revelation, he subtitled his book 'The Maltese Obsession with Killing Birds'. By the time *Fatal Flight* was published, the attack on hunting as an unsustainable, pathological and cruel practice had gone from murmur to chorus. The main bird protection environmental nongovernmental organization (ENGO), the Malta Ornithological Society (MOS – later BirdLife Malta), had grown into a well-organized group with interests in education, the setting up of nature reserves, ornithology and campaigning. It had cast (notably in the media) bird hunting as a major negative presence and politicized it to a remarkable extent. Especially during the migration seasons of spring and autumn, hardly a day passed when the press did not fall over each other to give a blow-by-blow rendition of shot birds and near-misses. The outcomes included new legislation – if only rarely its enforcement – in 1980 that greatly reduced the list of huntable birds (prior to that date, only twenty-two species were protected) and established a comprehensive set of other regulations, as well as the setting up of a nature reserve in the same year.

At first, hunters were slow to realize that what must at the time have seemed like a ragtag opposition – 'a couple of people with binoculars', as described by the president of the hunters' association in 1983[10] – had metamorphosed into something that was not merely a nuisance. It was only from the 1980s that the main hunting organization (later the Federazzjoni Kaċċaturi Nassaba Konservazzjonisti (FKNK) – the Federation of Hunters, Trappers and Conservationists) got its act together and became the significant force it is today. The first large public demonstration by hunters was held in September 1983 and was a reaction to the new legislation as well as demonstrations that had been held by the MOS. The years that followed saw constant and bitter sparring and the consolidation of a Manichean template in which the lines of good and evil and hunter and protectionist were drawn in a steady hand. The crystallization of the two sides into formidable adversaries reached new levels when Malta joined the EU in 2004. Since then, the relations between hunters and conservationists, and indeed the dynamics of conservation itself, have been played out in a political space that goes beyond that of the nation-state. So contentious is hunting that in 2015, a national referendum was held on Malta's right to derogate for the spring hunting of turtle doves and quail. This was only the third national referendum in decades – the other two were about EU accession (2003) and the introduction of divorce (2011).

It is crucial to note that a lot has changed since the national obsession with killing birds was diagnosed in 1992. The last two decades have seen three main transformations. First, there is now a raft of laws that regulate hunting in all its aspects and in minute detail. Second, there has been a shift away from a situation in which the hunting laws existed mostly in the breach to one in which there is significant enforcement. Third, a growing number of hunters have come to realize that not all birds are legitimate targets at law and that there are places where and times of year when hunting cannot be practised. Arguably, the result of these changes is nothing short of profound. As little as twenty years ago, any bird that was larger – and often smaller – than a sparrow was shot on sight, and it was not possible to walk anywhere in the countryside without seeing all kinds of birds being shot. That scenario is now a receding memory as protected birds are largely left alone and closed seasons and protected areas are broadly respected. Even if there are many exceptions – for example, large and rare birds are still sometimes shot, turtle doves are commonly targeted in spring and the illegal use of electronic bird callers is rampant – the rule is that the obsession has been considerably tamed. The manner of that transformation, its hits and misses and its many and contested readings, makes up a substantial part of this book. It is the story of a long and ongoing process of conservation and its outcomes.

Hunting in the Mediterranean

The Mediterranean is nothing if not extremely blue. You can spend a very pleasant week here, driving the modern roads and drinking the good local beer, without suspecting that the area harbors the most intensive songbird-killing operations in the European Union.
—Jonathan Franzen, 'Emptying the Skies'[11]

Any work on hunting in Malta must locate the practice within its Mediterranean context. The point has often been made that the region, which is a flyway for wild migrating birds, is especially prone to their widespread and indiscriminate taking. This is thought to apply to the historical *longue durée* as much as to the present. For instance, Woldhek estimated that hundreds of millions of birds were taken annually in the Mediterranean.[12] Magnin put that figure at 1000 million for illegally taken birds alone.[13] The figure of 'millions' of illegally hunted migratory birds was put forward again by Schneider-Jacoby and Spangenberg (2010). Most recently, Brochet et al. (2016) estimated that 11–36 million birds belonging to 375 species are taken illegally in the region annually, many of them on migration. The point is that the Mediterranean is generally thought by bird conservationists to be a particularly problematic region. Among the more significant recent outcomes was the adoption in 2014 of a resolution by the Convention on the Conservation of Migratory Species of Wild Animals (CMS) that established an intergovernmental task force on the illegal killing, taking and trade of migratory birds in the Mediterranean (MIKT). The task force brings together governmental representatives of CMS parties around the Mediterranean, including the EU and other interested parties; representatives from non-CMS parties as well as relevant international organizations and networks are also part of MIKT as observers. The mission statement says that 'the Mediterranean basin is currently a hotspot for illegal killing and trapping and MIKT is the first pan Mediterranean Task Force to be developed, having a distinctly regional focus and aiming to be replicated for other parts of the world'.[14] (Malta is one of the parties to MIKT.)

The intensity with which birds were and are hunted in the Mediterranean raises a number of questions. The first is that there may be a fundamental distinction between northern and southern European approaches to hunting and conservation. Hell (1996) argues that two divergent hunting cultures coexist in contemporary Europe. The first, which spans a vast geographical area including all the regions where German dialects are spoken as well as a number of central European countries, is based on a notion of hunting as 'harvesting', in which the hunter is responsible for the management of animal populations. By

Figure 1.6. Trappers' hides (*duri*) positioned strategically along a coastal cliff edge to intercept incoming migrants. Photograph by the author.

contrast, in southern European countries and in most of France, hunting is associated with the notion of a free right of gathering and the rejection of any idea of reasoned management of the wild fauna. It follows that the taking of wild birds should be more indiscriminate in the south, where it is more loosely embedded (if at all) in structures of control and management. Simply put, in the south, most birds, and especially migratory species, are considered fair game.

I think Hell is broadly right, with three important qualifiers. First, it makes sense to think of his argument as a distinction between two ideal types, each of which tends to prevail in its respective geographical area. This leaves room for all-important exceptions, such as the now-defunct practice in Malta of encouraging, say, sparrows to multiply in order to eventually provide targets and food. (If not quite management and harvesting, this certainly was a form of enhanced gathering.) Second, it is reasonable to argue that it is particularly in the Mediterranean that the southern notion of hunting as free gathering (as opposed to harvesting) makes itself felt. It is often the case that hunters in the Mediterranean are dependent on migrating birds and are therefore alien to the reproductive processes of their quarry. The notion of free gathering of a transient resource, which is experientially and conceptually removed from the population dynamics of what is gathered, is neatly summed up in the story of the sudden influx of birds in Exodus 16:13: 'That evening quail came and covered the camp.' The story highlights the presence and availability of birds as a disconnected moment rather than as part of an ecological process. A substantial slice of what follows in this book makes more sense when located in this regional-cultural context. Third, one should not over-egg the distinction between indiscriminate hunting in the south and controlled hunting in the north. Shrubb (2013), for example, provides ample historical evidence of widespread hunting for all manner of birds in Britain well into the twentieth century. Useful though arguments for fundamental distinctions might be, they ought to be made with caution.

The second general point about the intensity of hunting in the Mediterranean is that it may be historically embedded in a specific type of economic production. Brochet et al. (2016) have drawn on a broad range of multicountry data in order to attempt to quantify and rank the reasons for the taking of wild birds in the Mediterranean. They cite sport (82–85 per cent), food (65–71 per cent) and capture for use as cage birds or decoys (29–39 per cent) as the main reasons. Most species (62 per cent) were reported to be killed for multiple reasons – for example, for food and sport together, where birds killed for sport are taken home and eaten. The relative importance of these reasons varied across the region. Taxidermy and predator control were of relatively minor importance, and predator control was listed in some European countries (for example, France, Portugal and Spain) as the primary reason for targeting birds of prey. The main drift is that although few if any people anywhere in the Mediterranean depend on hunting for their survival, most of the birds that are taken are in fact eaten. (That the taking itself is deemed enjoyable – and thus 'sport' – does nothing to the equation.) With the exceptions of finch trapping and taxidermy, Malta is a case in point. Therefore, it may be argued that hunting in Malta is embedded in a regional context in which migrating wild birds were and are routinely hunted and, in most cases, eaten.

That in itself does not make a case for Mediterranean specificity. Food production strategies that involve the exploitation of wild fauna and flora are by no means endemic to the Mediterranean. As has already been noted, Shrubb (2013) has usefully looked at the historical exploitation of wild birds in Britain and northern Europe. Although it was only in the nineteenth and early twentieth centuries that birds were systematically hunted for taxidermy collections and feathers, all manner of birds were hunted for food by country people as far back as the evidence shows. This was carried out using a bewildering range of techniques that included punt-gunning, flight nets, permanent elaborate traps, coordinated drives and so on.

Perhaps the difference lies elsewhere. Thirsk's work on what she calls 'alternative agriculture' may provide a part of the puzzle. Thirsk holds that the development of mainstream agriculture – the production of the cereals and meat that constitute the staples of Western peoples – has in the past several centuries at least been punctuated by periods in which circumstances changed radically, prompting farmers to seek alternatives. As she puts it:

> The interpretation of our agricultural history . . . stresses a sequence of movements from mainstream farming to alternatives, and then back again. Major disjunctures have occurred, obliging farmers to divert their energies from the primary pursuit of grain and meat, to investigate other activities. On each occasion, when diversification has been necessary, farmers' ingenuity has been taxed, but it has successfully produced solutions which enabled them to survive until the older one returned. (Thirsk 1997: 2–3)

Thirsk goes on to present detailed evidence for three such phases of alternative agriculture in English history, each sandwiched between periods of mainstream farming. The first occurred after the Black Death from 1350 until about 1500; the second between about 1650 and 1750; and the third from 1879 to 1939. She also contends that a path for a fourth phase was opened from the 1970s. The details need not detain us here, but we should note two things. First, the notion of alternative agriculture implies, amongst other practices, an increased exploitation of wild foods – venison, rabbits, wild birds and so on. Second, and perhaps more importantly, alternative agriculture is in Thirsk's view a response to a crisis that is destined in due course to pass: 'no phase of alternative agriculture lasts for ever' (1997: 2).

Or does it? Thirsk, I emphasize, draws on data from and argues specifically for the British and northern European context. Horden and Purcell (2000) identify a number of risk factors (in particular, climatic conditions, hydrological and soil conditions, and natural disasters) that historically have led to a 'marginal' type of food production in the Mediterranean. Whereas in northwestern Europe, shifts from mainstream to alternative types of agriculture occurred under sporadic and special circumstances (Thirsk's argument), in the Mediterranean, a number of conditions occurred that required people to combine, on an everyday and regular basis, mainstream farming with other forms of food production: 'in the Mediterranean those disjunctions are typical accidents of everyday experience, and rather than "a sequence of movements", we find a coexistence between "normal" and "alternative" agriculture' (Horden and Purcell 2000: 179). Wild foods and in particular migratory birds thus came to represent a regular food source, and their taking an essential strand in the fabric of economic production. The ready availability of salt and pickling techniques helped by making it possible for bulk catches of migratory birds to be stored seasonally.

As in the case of Hell's point about north–south hunting cultures, one should not make the mistake of overessentializing the distinction. Once more, perhaps it is useful to think in terms of ideal types. In the north, an ideal type prevailed that empirically manifested itself in the combination of mainstream with alternative food-producing strategies on a sporadic basis. In the Mediterranean, on the other hand, ecological conditions encouraged the development of different strategies that, when extrapolated analytically into a dominant ideal type, give us a relatively high and regular dependence on wild foods and especially migrating birds. This would explain the historical economic importance of foods such as the *beccafichi* and *ambelopoulia* (pickled passerines) of Italy and Cyprus respectively, which were until fairly recently exported in their millions. No one in Malta today would seriously consider wild birds to be a regular food source, but the techniques of preserving and preparing for consumption all manner of birds have only recently begun to slip into folk memory. Even apparently unpalatable types like birds of prey and herons were routinely eaten. The English painter and explorer George French Angas, who visited Malta in the autumn of 1841, observed rails, larks and wheatears – all of which are wild migratory birds – at poulterers' stalls at the Valletta market, where quail were 'very abundant in April and September' (Angas 1842: 69), and an early ornithologist like Despott could count on productive visits to the same market in Valletta where 'during the spring and the autumn . . . the poulterers' stalls are frequently stocked with many interesting species of migratory birds (Despott 1917: 285).

Tellingly, this legacy seems to be stronger on the islands – Malta, Zakynthos (Theodossopoulos 2003), Cyprus,[15] Ischia,[16] Majorca (Thirsk 1997) and doubtless many others display a particularly intense exploitation of wild migratory birds. Indeed, one of the things that first aroused my scholarly interest in hunting was the portrayal of trapping and hunting in Lampedusa in Emanuele Crialese's film *Respiro* (2002). (In 2009, I did several weeks of fieldwork with hunters in Lampedusa.) The intensity of hunting on islands would support the argument for a meaningful convergence between hunting and marginal economic production. As Braudel points out, the historical-ecological lot of the average Mediterranean island has been particularly 'precarious, restricted, and threatened' (1975: 154).[17] With respect to Malta, it is perhaps significant that the very first description of the island, written in 1536, emphasized the aridity and frugality of the terrain (d'Autun 1980).

Tentatively, then, and with a watchful eye on the pitfall of facile generalization, the 'Maltese obsession with killing birds' might partially but no less usefully be understood as the historical product – via a circuitous and uneven route – of a very particular and regionally specific type of economic production.

The Experience of Fieldwork

In his book about the conflicts over turtle conservation on the Greek island of Zakynthos, Theodossopoulos (2003) tells a story that is thematically reminiscent of the conversion narratives of certain Christian saints. He first went to Zakynthos as an 'ecologist' and activist for the protection of sea turtles and especially of the beaches where they nested. This placed him and his colleagues in direct conflict with the locals, who had other plans for the beaches. One night during a protest, things took a turn for the worse and he was hit over the head with a stick by a local. His description of the days spent recovering in bed is worth quoting in full:

> I was left alone, with plenty of time to contemplate my predicament in my beautiful Mediterranean prison. What I could not understand then was why those 'locals' were so gravely frustrated with conservationists such as myself: individuals whom I visualised as prompted solely by noble and selfless intentions. How could those 'locals' be so insensitive to the fate of such a unique reptilian species and what morality justified their lack of consideration, I wondered. (Theodossopoulos 2003: 5)

These were the questions that led him to produce his fine ethnography.

My experience is both similar to and different from that of Theodossopoulos. Like him, my first interest in hunting in Malta was as a hostile outsider. Unlike many Maltese people, I cannot find a single hunter in the family. My interest in nature goes back to butterfly collecting in childhood. Later, in my teens, I took up birdwatching and became very involved in amateur ornithology, at one point as a licensed bird ringer and editor of the scientific journal of the MOS. I was also an activist – I planted trees, kept records of shot birds, wrote angry missives to the press, took part in protests and went to great lengths to obstruct a practice I saw as primitive and completely unacceptable. A good number of the people I socialized with were activists who had similar ideas.

Unlike Theodossopoulos, I was spared the stick. My own road to Damascus was a slower and healthier one, and a direct result of a university education in anthropology. Enticed by the carrot of anthropological understanding, I found myself looking at hunters not as primitive savages, but rather as people who valued a set of motivations and practices. I started to interview hunters and later to join them in the field (though I never actually shot or trapped birds), and at the same time to view and question the tenets of bird protection activists as simply another form of appropriation of nature. I also mapped hunting territories, attended formal policy meetings, participated in field surveillance by bird protectionists and so on. Between 2014 and 2017, I chaired a government committee that advised policy-makers on hunting and conservation; this gave me direct access to the politics of conservation and to the dynamics of contestation between hunters and bird protection ENGOs. The composite nature of my field experience proved useful. I discovered, for example, that hunting felt much more acceptable when one was positioned at the right end of the gun in the company of hunters, as opposed to experiencing it through the simulated point of view of a bird, through binoculars and in the company of activists. This may sound an obvious and banal point, but it is actually one about lived experience and positionality. A few years on, I still think that birds make more sense flying about than dead or locked in cages, but I also understand why hunters think otherwise. I also hope to have built enough knowledge of hunting for me to do justice to it.

In this respect, my capital proved tremendously useful: first, because I already had extensive knowledge-by-observation when I started asking hunters about their practices; and second, and more importantly, because my own experience of birds, migration and nature generally dovetailed with what hunters told me about their motivations. Take spring hunting. Having experienced many springs in the field as a birdwatcher, I could understand why the season mattered so much to hunters. I could also see why the unpredictability of migration seduced people into jumping out of bed an hour before dawn. And so on. The point is that when my informants told me that they could relate to me because, regardless of my previous life as their opponent, I 'understood' them (*għax int tifhimna*), I knew exactly what they meant. To quote Kay Milton, an ethnographer of nature conservation and herself a conservationist: 'I think I know what they feel because I feel it myself' (2002: 56).

I have not always been so fortunate at the other end. Many of the environmentalists I knew and socialized with could not understand how something as obviously distasteful as hunting could be approached with feelings other than that of revulsion. I was accused, usually but not always tacitly, of romanticizing hunters and their practices; my 'understanding' was the result of gullibility, of having been taken in by the sanitized and deceitful stories that hunters tell outsiders. I experienced the kind of 'reductive dualism' that haunted Heatherington in her fieldwork in Sardinia – a dualism that made her informants tell her 'you cannot be an anthropologist and an environmentalist at the same time!' (2010: 4). The same was felt by Choy in the course of his work on ecopolitics in Hong

Kong: 'Would I side with the environmentalists' opposition to building a manicured landscape for elites in a country park, or would I instead advocate the cause of villagers who asserted indigenous land rights?' (2011: 3). In my case, my environmentalist friends resisted the idea that hunting might in some way be made sense of and rationalized. This was so even if the urge of understanding was rooted in anthropology. As they saw it, there were only two legitimate ways of writing about hunting: as folklore or as a primitive practice that had its roots in base urges and ignorance, and that by definition could not be rationalized. I once gave a lecture about my work that was attended by several friends who were also bird protection activists. After the lecture, one of them told me that although much of what I had said was true, the basic methodological premise was wrong: unlike what I had argued, there was no method to the hunting madness.

In other words, my attempt at establishing an analytical distance went down well with hunters, because they saw it as a rare instance of being taken seriously by a scholar and thus legitimated through location within a relatively prestigious system of knowledge. It was exactly the same reasoning that rubbed many bird protectionists up the wrong way; to them, hunting could not claim a rightful place in that system of knowledge. To cite Choy's description of his own positionality, 'the tools that I relied on for taking a step back from controversy in fact located me in it' (2011: 5).

Notes

1. Foreword to Natalino Fenech's *Fatal Flight* (Fenech 1992: vii).
2. LUCAS land-use survey, EUROSTAT, 2012.
3. One of Malta's best-known exports owes its origins to the period from 1530 to 1798, when the Order of St John (also known as the Hospitaller Knights) ruled Malta as a vassal state of the Crown of Aragon. The fictional 'Maltese falcon' of the 1930 novel and the 1941 film was a precious statue intended as a gift from the Order to the King of Spain. The story has some basis in historical fact: the status of the Order as a fiefholder was marked by an annual tribute of a falcon to the viceroy of Sicily (Freller 2010). The reputation of Malta as a source of the highly prized peregrine falcon goes back to the medieval trade in birds used in falconry (Fiorini 2001; Dalli 2006).
4. The mould was somewhat broken in the 2013 and 2017 general elections, in which the Labour Party prevailed with an advantage of over 10 per cent of the vote.
5. A total of 2.6 million in 2018, with a total expenditure of €2.1 billion (€809 per capita). The country's GDP for the same year was €12.3 billion (source: 'Tourism in Malta: Facts & Figures 2018', Malta Tourism Authority).

6. The people who were puzzled by migration patterns, or rather their apparent lack, included the Scottish naturalist Andrew Leith Adams (1827–82). The following is an excerpt from his account of Malta: 'I had a great difficulty at first in accounting for the circumstance, that whenever a large flight of quails appeared, it was often on the very opposite aspect of the island one would expect them to alight at that time of the year, and the same was noticed with certain other gregarious birds' (Adams 1870: 99).

7. In this case, another significant factor was a social and lifestyle transformation that meant that boys were less inclined to spend their free time outdoors with traps and slingshots.

8. In September 2019, there were 13,638 hunting and 4,537 trapping licences; a number of hunters and trappers held multiple licences (source: Wild Birds Regulation Unit, Government of Malta). It is not easy to quantify huntable land, but an approximate figure can be worked out by subtracting built-up areas, the airfield and protected areas from the total land mass of Malta. If anything, the figure of seventy hunters per km² of huntable land is very conservative.

9. The relentless persecution of birds in Malta had already attracted the attention of ornithologists and naturalists. Giuseppe Despott (1878–1933), a Maltese ornithologist of considerable note, wrote about the 'war waged against the feathered creatures' (1917: 283) and lamented that Maltese farmers were 'very ignorant of the real economic value of birds' (1917: 285).

10. 'When Mintoff closed the hunting season', *Malta Today*, 11 March 2015. The reference to binoculars is a mocking allusion to voyeurism.

11. Jonathan Franzen, 'Emptying the Skies', *New Yorker*, 26 July 2010.

12. S. Woldhek, 'Bird Killing in the Mediterranean', European Committee for the Prevention of Mass Destruction of Migratory Birds, ICBP, October 1979.

13. G. Magnin, 'An Assessment of Illegal Shooting and Catching of Birds in Malta', ICBP, April 1986.

14. CMS Mission Statement, 2016.

15. S. Woldhek, 'Bird Killing in the Mediterranean', European Committee for the Prevention of Mass Destruction of Migratory Birds, ICBP, October 1979.

16. See 'Italy's Fight against Illegal Bird Hunts', *BBC News Online*, 22 May 2006.

17. Braudel (1975) also documents that thousands of barrels of 'vine birds' (small passerines) pickled in vinegar were exported from Cyprus to Venice and Rome in the sixteenth century. For Braudel, such instances of abundance were a rare treat and did nothing to dent the general argument for the precarious lives of Mediterranean islanders.

CHAPTER 2

All in the Blood

The beauty and brilliance of this insect are indescribable, and none but a naturalist can understand the intense excitement I experienced when at length I captured it. On taking it out of my net and opening the glorious wings, my heart began to beat violently, the blood rushed to my head, and I felt more like fainting than I have done when in apprehension of immediate death. I had a headache the rest of the day, so great was the excitement produced by what will appear to most people a very inadequate cause.

—Alfred Russel Wallace, *The Malay Archipelago*[1]

Ħaġar Qim (Stones of Worship) is possibly the most impressive of Malta's Neolithic temples. Built around 5,000 years ago and first systematically excavated in the early nineteenth century (Trump 2002), its architecture of megaliths, altars and kidney-shaped apses lends visitors an evocative glimpse of prehistoric ritual lives. While the dreamtimes of animal sacrifice and mother-goddess cults are far removed from contemporary Catholic belief and ritual, the temples retain their sacredness in more ways than one. First, they furnish the national (and nationalist) imaginary with a claim to some of the oldest structures in the world and therefore to a measure of autochthonous uniqueness and sophistication. Second, as main attractions to the tourists who visit the country, they are not just a national patrimony, but one that sells well. Set in a dramatic landscape overlooking the sea on the western coast, Ħaġar Qim and its sister temple of Mnajdra are visited by hundreds of tourists (and one or two coach-loads of schoolchildren) every day.

Early one morning in 1991, the guides walked up to the gate for another day's work. They soon discovered that the temples had had a night visitor. Someone had painted 'Namur jew intajru' in large black letters on the path that leads to the main entrance. The smoking gun led straight to hunters, who at the time were involved in a vociferous opposition to new and restrictive legislation. The part that concerns me here is the language itself: 'Namur jew intajru' means '*namur* or we'll blow [the temples] up'.

Namur is not an easy word to translate. It is a variant of the commoner *namra*, which means a passion for something. Courting couples, for example, are called *namrati* (lit. 'in passion') and an older married couple who hold hands might be described as *qishom namrati* ('they are like lovers') to emphasize their (untypical, presumably) state of youthful courtship. In the usage that concerns me more directly, *namra* is used to describe a passion for a particular thing or practice. In this usage the word is strongly masculinized and one may have a *namra* for fishing, keeping horses or pigeons, making fireworks and especially hunting and trapping – all of which are traditionally thought to be men's practices in Malta. (When this usage of *namra* is ascribed to a woman, it is usually to emphasize a state that is not typical of her gender.) And yet, in spite of this semantic breadth, not one person in the whole of Malta thought that the ominous scrawl on the path at Ħaġar Qim was the work of a spurned lover.

In this chapter I shall first explore some of the ways in which *namra* punctuates and underwrites the practices of hunting and trapping. I then go on to look at how it is embedded in the politics of conservation, with an emphasis on representations of alterity, modernity and gender. The case can hardly be overstated because hunters consistently recognize *namra* as the passion that propels them to great lengths in their pursuit of birds. *Namra* is the semantic equivalent of the *pathos* described by hunters on the Greek island of Zakynthos (Theodossopoulos 2003), the *Jagdfieber* (lit. hunting fever) of German-speaking hunters, the *passione* of Italian hunters (Barca et al. 2016), and the bug that afflicts hunters in the United States (Hell 1996; Falzon 2008). Maltese hunters universally claim that, without *namra*, one cannot be a real hunter. Taking this foundational truth as its point of departure, the chapter aims to convey a sense of the hunting experience and why it matters so much to the people who participate in it.

Blood and Practice: The Making of *Namra*

Hunters think of *namra* as a substance that must be produced and reproduced, and that can be quantified. At the same time, it is also *fid-demm* (in the blood). The blood metaphor is well known amongst hunters in Europe. Hell describes it as the 'absolute natural demarcation between hunters and non-hunters' and holds that hunters 'do not become so by choice or by chance, their destiny is inscribed in their "black blood", the ultimate legitimation of their particular status (1996: 209). In Malta, hunting blood can mean one or both of two things.

First, the metaphor of blood, in Maltese as in many other languages, is a byword for kinship. The surest route to *namra* is heredity, especially that of the patrilineal kind. Many hunters will attribute their *namra* to direct descent from father to son, although it is also known to skip generations and manifest itself at will. Hunters and trappers believe that while *namra* can be transmitted in a state of dormancy, blood will usually out. However, if it remains dormant for successive generations, it can become extinct in that particular line. Take Joe, a trapper who I met at his small landholding where he grows crops and traps finches. The land originally belonged to his grandfather, a trapper who died before Joe was born. Joe's father was neither a trapper nor a hunter. When Joe's grandfather died, the land was inherited by Joe's father's sister, who was unmarried and who eventually lent Joe its usufruct for agriculture and general recreation (not trapping, however, since that activity had been discontinued on the site since the death of his grandfather); she also promised him he would be her heir. Meanwhile, however, an affinal uncle (mother's sister's husband) of Joe's who was an avid trapper asked if he could trap on the land. Joe's aunt let him do so and this meant that Joe, then still a young man, found himself joining his uncle at the *mansab*. The result was that the *namra*, which Joe now believes was inherited (in a state of dormancy) in the male line from his grandfather through his father to him, was rekindled. As Joe told me: 'The *namra* took root [*reggħet nibtet*] in me. It had been *bierda* (cool) because my father was not a trapper. Were it not for my uncle it may well have been lost.'

Second, the language of blood brings home the notion that *namra* is part of the person's physical constitution and can never be entirely disowned, although it can be repressed or fall into disuse, so to speak. The case is compounded in that not all sons inherit *namra* equally – some, in fact, may not inherit it at all. Further, the passion for hunting can also develop through contact, usually in childhood, with avuncular figures or older men generally who are hunters. This way, it is possible for men who are not part of hunting families to discover they have *namra*, usually after joining someone in the field. The point is that while there are many routes to *namra*, none is straightforward or mechanistic.

Thus, for example, George, with whom I spent many a morning in the field, is the third youngest of nine siblings. His five brothers are avid hunters; none of his sisters are, though two of his sisters' sons are also hunters. George's father had no interest in hunting, but he was the tenant of a stretch of salt pans on the southeast coast of Malta. Salt pans being something of a magnet for migrating waders, his brothers (some of whom were several years older than him) used to invite their friends to hunt there. That was how George's and his brothers' passion for hunting was first ignited. George, who was in his late fifties at the time of my fieldwork, has two sons, both hunters. The elder, John, has two young sons. George used the example of his grandsons to illustrate the baffling nature of *namra*: 'Look at John's boys. With one you can tell the passion is there – mention a shotgun and his eyes light up. The other has no interest in hunting whatsoever. That's *namra* for you.'

This elusive nature of *namra* is not limited to humans. Hunting dogs too may be said to have *namra*, especially if they display a keenness for birds and for the chase. While certain breeds – pointers, for example, or the Maltese flushing breed known as *kelb tal-kaċċa* ('hunting dog') – are more likely to perform in the field, breed alone is no guarantee of keenness. Like humans, dogs too are said to have a passion for hunting that is an individual and inborn character trait. On one occasion, for example, a hunter described to me a dog that had so much *namra* that it would jump into the sea whenever a gull flew by, even if its owner was out walking rather than hunting. In the field, a hunter will watch his dogs, talk to them and comment on their *namra* and hunting ability. It is also common for hunters to try out different dogs before settling on one or more; once that choice is made, dogs become close companions and partners-in-passion. Marvin (2003) has described much the same for the hounds used in foxhunting. Although they are referred to as 'working animals', it is not expected that the work of hunting should be a chore for them; rather, good hounds are spoken of as displaying not only a willingness to hunt, but also a joy. Certainly with respect to hunting passion, dogs are quasi-human.

Back to full humans, it is worth asking why this 'joy' and passion develops in some men but not in others who find themselves in much the same circumstances. It is a question that hunters often ask themselves and that lends *namra* a certain inscrutable charm. My informants tended to point me in the direction of experiences, usually in early childhood, through which they discovered they had *namra*. I was once talking to an old trapper about his attraction to birds, and to flowers and nature generally. He told me, not without a sense of poignancy and loss, about the plentiful flowers that once grew in the fields near his home in Kalkara, an area that is now entirely built up. He mentioned one purple flower in particular that, as a child, he used to trap butterflies (*nonsob għall-friefet*) with, using a system based on that used by grown-ups to trap birds. (It was a kind of miniature clap-net device with strips of cloth for nets and clumps of flowers for decoys.) He would spend whole days waiting for butterflies to make an unwise move and already felt, even at that time, that trapping was his passion. This little story shows two things. The first is how powerful and culturally rooted the appropriation of nature by means of *insib* and *kaċċa* is. It was the only form of interaction between him and his boyhood friends, and butterflies and flowers; the memory was located within this form of appropriation and scarcely existed, let alone made sense, outside of it. It was only insofar as flowers were used as decoys and butterflies were trapped that they formed part of the child's experience and eventually the old man's memory. This explains why so many of my informants described how they first experienced *namra* when, as young boys, they roamed the countryside with their robin traps. It was common practice until recently for hunters to furnish their sons with robin traps and to encourage them to 'play' at catching robins (they actually did) while they hunted. Sometimes they would also make wooden models of shotguns for their sons to 'hunt' with, usually while they were in the field together. Through this childhood play, boys developed an awareness and knowledge of, and a passion for, birds and their migration that was mediated through the practice of hunting.

Second, and perhaps more importantly, it offers a glimpse into a passion for nature that is born of an individual's interaction with and experience of the world around them. The work of Milton is crucial in this respect. Milton's point of departure is to ask why and how some people, but not others, love nature. The question is fundamental because the love of nature is what drives and underwrites the work of the conservationists and environmentalists who are the object of her study. Milton rejects models of emotion that rely exclusively on essentialist/positivist or culturalist/constructionist approaches. Essentialist models emphasize feeling, but tend to ignore meaning, while constructionist models focus on meaning at the expense of feeling. Thus, 'both kinds of approach fail to take account of the special nature of emotions, the fact that they consist of both feelings and meanings' (2002: 4). Having established this 'dual character' of emotions, Milton goes on to look at how the feelings-meanings alloy is forged. She draws on the work of theorists like Ingold, Damasio and von Uexküll to privilege individual experience and knowledge of the world – in her case, the ways in which individual conservationists and nature protectionists come to feel about, understand and act towards nature as they do. 'Paradoxically', she argues, 'this broadening of the enquiry brings a narrowing of focus, on the human being as an individual organism living in an environment and learning about that environment (and about themselves) through their engagement with it' (Milton 2002: 147).

The emphasis on the individual and their direct and subjective experience of the world is important because it effectively eschews approaches to emotions that are based exclusively on cultural contexts and processes of socialization. Simply put, such approaches cannot account for the observable fact that individuals who inhabit the same cultural and social context do not necessarily exhibit the same feelings for a given object (nature in this case). At the same time, experience does not consist only of individual interaction with the world, but rather includes the contexts within which that interaction develops (in my example, the man's childhood friends and the fields where they roamed). In this way, experience functions as a middle ground where individuality, culture, socioeconomic variables and so on converge. Methodologically, it also opens up a space for understanding, not least since experience is something that can be encountered and studied empirically in the field.

Milton's point about the primacy of experience is eminently applicable to the case at hand. Take Joe, the trapper whose experience I described earlier, and his emphasis on the role played by his uncle. For all its attributed blood-fuelled atavistic powers and resilience, *namra* can only flourish if it is coupled with practice. But this is exactly what Milton means by experience. For instance, she discusses biophilia, Wilson's well-trodden notion in which evolutionary mechanisms predispose humans as a species to exhibit emotional responses to certain objects in nature (Wilson 1984). Thus, an encounter with a snake, for example, tends to evoke a fear of snakes ingrained in generations of humans as a survival mechanism; the mechanism is a generic one for humans in the presence of snakes and can manifest itself even if the snake happens to be harmless or is merely a representation (a photograph, for example). While Milton does not entirely or necessarily jettison biophilia, she argues that the point is elsewhere: it is that 'the encounter [with the snake] still has to take place' (2002: 62). It follows that a love for, or revulsion towards, aspects of nature makes sense as part of experience – whether or not it is innate, a primordial survival mechanism and so on. Empirically, the biographies of environmentalists who love nature almost invariably refer to direct, personal experience of the object of their emotion, particularly in early childhood: 'The message of these personal histories seems quite clear. These environmentalists believed that they had come to love nature at least partly through their direct experience of natural things. Implicit in their statements is that they had come to love nature in the process of learning *about* nature, by discovering what nature is like' (2002: 64, emphasis in original). Milton goes on to posit a link with theories of self-perception, but the parts that concern me are, first, that emotions are about an object (more on this shortly) and, second, that they exist only in and of experience and knowledge of the world – in other words, that the key to understanding an emotion is by looking at its practice.

In the case of hunting in Malta, this practice is known as *delizzju*. This word literally translates as 'pastime', but in this sense it means a blend of practice, passion and knowledge that threatens to absorb the person and rob them of their free (and not so free) time. The word is not limited to hunting and it is also semantically broader than *namra*. It may refer to practices like photography or building scale models – things, in other words, that the word 'namra' would scarcely ever be linked to. In its most dilute form, *delizzju* can come close to 'hobby', in the sense that it can mean things that people (usually men – the word is also male-gendered, if to a lesser extent than *namra*) do to while away the time, with or without the implications of commitment and passion. The person who practises a *delizzju* is known as a *dilettant*. 'Dilettant' is quantifiable and it carries none of the pejorative connotations of the English word 'dilettante'. Thus, a hunter who is considered by his peers to be a master of his practice, who is totally immersed in it and who is highly knowledgeable about the techniques and lore of hunting will be described as a *dilettant ta' veru* ('a real dilettant'). Clearly, although such a type will invariably produce more *namra* than he could ever consume, it is precisely the coupling of *delizzju* and *namra* that makes the real hunter.

What this means is that while *namra* is an emotion, it cannot be understood unless its 'aboutness', to borrow a word from Gordon (1987), is taken into account. Gordon argues that emotions must have some kind of reference to the world. Thus, the fundamental question to ask of someone who is angry, for example, is 'What about?', for two reasons: first, no one is truly angry unless they are angry about something, which means that the emotion can only reasonably exist in the presence of its aboutness; and, second, not knowing what an emotion is about leaves us clueless as to how to deal with it – in practice, that is, emotions have little predictive value unless we factor in their aboutness. Any emotion must therefore have an intentionality content; in other words, it must be meaningfully directed towards an object in the world. In the case of *namra*, that object is the actual practice of hunting. In fact, the ways in which emotion and practice are linked constitute some of the more fascinating aspects of the experience of being a hunter – or, for that matter, a bird protectionist intent on putting an end to hunting.

The *Namra* That Rational Men Feel

As expected for an emotion, *namra* is primarily felt. While it is not possible for scholarly writing to replicate feelings, I shall attempt to convey some sense of the anatomy and aboutness of *namra*. The first thing that hunters say is that they alone can understand *namra*. (They often slip in a reference to some other supposedly unfathomable feeling by way of analogy.)

The hope is that, armed as we are with participant observation, anthropologists are an exception to the rule. In my case, my long experience as a birdwatcher and amateur naturalist generally meant that my own *namra* turned out to be very similar to what my informants described; the reason why will become apparent as I develop those descriptions. The other thing to add is that the power and unfathomability (to non-hunters) of *namra* has become a dominant discourse in its own right and one that has strong political moorings. This is because it is used by hunters to represent themselves as a perennially misunderstood type. For example, during my fieldwork I was often told by hunters that I was an exception and one worth cooperating with, '*għax inti ̇tifhimna*' ('because you understand us'). Tellingly, my rating in this department went up following an interview on national television in which I explained just how much *namra* meant to hunters. The idea is that a feeling of such potency deserves to be taken seriously and, to some extent, accommodated as a legitimate player – not least by the state.

This last point is important because it underlines that *namra* is also about the politics of hunting. Take the notion of *sagrifiċċju* (sacrifice), which is very often a key part of representations of *namra* by hunters. This is how Charles, a trapper, explained it:

> Trapping requires huge sacrifices [*sagrifiċċji kbar*]. You need to have the decoys, the place . . . no matter how much you have, you never have enough. You're always spending money on medicine and a million other things. It's a huge commitment – wherever you go and whatever you do, your mind is always elsewhere. When I get home after a day's work, the first thing I do is feed my birds; only then can I think of having dinner. My wife and I seldom go out during the migration season – I simply don't have the time or thought to spare from trapping.

In order to understand how this discourse is meaningfully located within the politics of hunting, it is worth looking at another practice that has a high profile in the Maltese context. The manufacture and letting off of fireworks at village and town feasts that celebrate Catholic saints is a cherished practice to many people, but it is also maligned by others on account of the noise it makes. One of the things that fireworks enthusiasts (*dilettanti tan-nar*) constantly emphasize is that the manufacture of fireworks is rooted in a strong *namra* and is a *delizzju* that demands very considerable sacrifices of those who practise it (Falzon and Cassar 2015). The implication, in both the case of fireworks enthusiasts and that of hunters, is that groups of people who go to such great lengths and who give up so much in pursuit of their practice deserve to be taken seriously. More specifically, because *dilettanti* are not just about play and frivolous enjoyment, they have a rightful place in the polity as active and productive citizens. One might add that the word *'sagrifiċċji'* itself carries much baggage. Whatever the value of its moorings in Christian theology and popular belief – and the association is probably significant in the Maltese context – *sagrifiċċji* is always used to imply a worthy cause. One may legitimately sacrifice one's free time to the benefit of family, career, love of country and so on – none of which are widely thought to be frivolous.

Further, *sagrifiċċji* are represented as one of the criteria that separate the *'true' dilettant* from a casual hunter. The former is he who has mastered the vast repertoire of technique and lore that is associated with hunting. He is also a man who single-mindedly seeks to deepen his knowledge by socializing with other *dilettanti*, experimenting with new techniques, watching documentary films on birds and maybe even buying the odd identification guide book. These are some of the characteristics of 'mature' hunters, who are knowledgeable and discriminating. Their attributes are conceptually opposed to the *bluha* (mindlessness) of immature and trigger-happy hunters, who are often described as *tfal* ('children'). Hunters are keen to point out that their bad collective reputation derives from the senselessness of 'a few fools' ('erba boloh') who have not fully developed their *namra* into a serious and temperate, and ultimately more socially acceptable, practice. They often refer to their own past and emphasize that it is just that; as one hunter told me: 'I remember when, as trigger-happy youths, we used to spend summer evenings taking potshots at bats. The one who shot the smallest number would buy *pastizzi* [a popular pastry snack] for the lot. But that was the past and I wouldn't dream of doing that now.' In the course of my fieldwork I met many hunters who told me that individuals who were indiscriminate and broke the law routinely were not 'real hunters' ('*dawk mhux veru kaċċaturi*').

There are two points to be made here. First, the coupled notions of juvenile *bluha* and faux hunters serve as a device by which hunters accommodate – even as they section them – practices that are considered dubious or downright wrongful (at law or otherwise) into a bigger picture that, all said, is legitimate. Second, *namra* functions as a qualitative indicator of rationality in the sense that, as a man matures, his passion mellows as reason and emotion converge. 'Real' *namra*, then, is more akin to an 'organized form of human existence' (Sartre 1962: 28) than to an irrational psychological force.

This articulation of *namra* thus brings out the opposition between emotion and rationality that theoretical formulations have repeatedly put forward (see, for instance, Williams 2001; Milton and Svašek 2005). Again, Milton's (2002) work is particularly valuable. She asks why, despite longstanding and sustained attempts by theorists to deconstruct it, the opposition between emotion and rationality has proved to be such a durable feature of Western culture. Her answer, which she supports with ample data from the field of nature conservation, is that the opposition can be and often is a very useful device in public discourse: 'it can be used to discredit the arguments of opponents by exposing them, depending on the context and the issues involved, as too emotional (and therefore irrational), or not emotional enough (and therefore insensitive), or as failing to strike an appropriate balance between emotion and rationality' (2002: 132).

In Malta, hunters find themselves having to defend their *delizzju* against the rising tide of bird protectionism and environmentalist notions more generally. This will be discussed in more detail in Chapter 3, but it is important to note at this stage that *namra* functions as a key political device in at least one sense. Represented as a strong and authentic emotion, it establishes hunters as the favoured opposite of bloodless environmentalists and their cerebral language of populations, sustainability and so on. However, even as it does this, it exposes hunters to the charge of a mindless emotionality that is out of touch with the rational truths of ecology. This kind of sparring is a defining feature of the encounter between hunting and conservation in Malta today, but it is more complicated than a simple hunter (emotional) versus environmentalist (rational) formula might suggest. Namra may be an emotion that defies reason and social values, but, when tamed by the 'real' hunter, it translates into rational, temperate and socially responsible practice, and retains its emotionality content in the process. As seen and represented by environmentalists, on the other hand, this alchemy is difficult if not impossible to achieve in practice, simply because emotions are the antithesis of reason. Further, it is not easy to reconcile a practice that is rooted in emotion with modern concepts of the state as a rational actor made up of rational parts.

Anatomy of an Emotion

Before I go on to discuss the conditions under which *namra* is produced, it is worth exploring some of the ways in which it is actually felt and represented. First, *namra* is described by hunters as an overpowering feeling that they do not have full (if any) control over and that threatens to rob them of their better judgement. It is *namra* that makes a hunter lose sleep, leave the house well before dawn and spend hours sitting *fuq il-ġebla* (on a cold stone), often *mid-dlam sad-dlam* (from dawn to dusk), waiting for birds to fly over. The ambivalence is intriguing. On the one hand, *namra* is a desirable and rewarding feeling that makes the hunting experience worthwhile; more broadly, it is described as something – in some cases the only thing – that makes life worth living. On the other hand, *namra* often demands *sagrifiċċji* (sacrifices) in the form of time, money and effort. Taken to the limit, it can take the reason prisoner and make a man *iffissat* (obsessed) or even *miġnun* (mad). I came across very many stories of otherwise-sane people whom *namra* had made irrational and impulsive: a commonly used expression is that *in-namra tagħmik* ('*namra* blinds you'). For example, Dione, himself a hunter, has a brother who is *iffissat* about trapping. He was once caught trapping in spring, during the closed season, and risked a heavy fine and confiscation of his birds and equipment. He told the police that he would be back on site the next morning and that if they persisted, he would bundle all his cages in a sack and plunge off a cliff into the sea. He kept his word and was back in the field the next morning, so completely obsessed was he. The police apparently figured out that he really was the type who would jump off any cliff and never bothered him again. Many hunters told me that their priorities in life were family and *namra*, in that order but only just. I listened to stories of how they had turned up late for family weddings, forgot about a child's christening or missed out on some important work commitment. This is how Fredu, a trapper and a hunter, put it: 'The first thing I told my girlfriend at the time, later my wife, was that she would have to forget me [*tinsini*] from September to November and from March to May. I built her two small huts by the sea so that we could enjoy our summers together as a family, but I've never gone back on that first condition.' There is no doubt much hyperbole and poetic licence in these stories. Nor are they context-specific: in a conversation with a club veteran in London, budding pigeon fancier and author Jon Day was told that 'pretty soon the lofts will have taken over your garden and your wife will have left you' (Day 2019: 103). The point is that they are a rhetorical device by which the power of *namra* is preached, especially to nonbelievers.

The second facet of the phenomenology of *namra* is that it has the power to transform bodies. Hell (1996) argues that hunters' discourses on 'fever' are not abstract discourses, but rather ones grounded in beliefs about the body. Hunters experience high body heat, boiling bodily humours and a sharpening of the senses. In any individual hunter, these symptoms are positively correlated to the level of concentration of 'black blood' and ultimately linked to practice. In northwestern Europe at least, those who are least affected by hunting fever tend to hunt communally and in contexts in which social control keeps passion in check; poachers and 'woodsmen' are at the other end of the fever spectrum.

There was no doubt among my hunter informants that they felt *namra* physically through their bodies. Like the migratory birds they hunt, they experience the symptoms of what ornithologists call '*Zugunruhe*', the 'seasonally occurring restlessness during migration seasons' (Helm 2006: 533). For example, they talk about a *rogħda*, a nervous tremble that afflicts them on days that hold the promise of migrant birds, and say that is especially strong if they happen not to be in the field. Further, it is the anticipation or the deficiency of practice (for whatever reason) that brings about the strongest bodily symptoms of *namra*. This is how one hunter explained it: 'There were times in the run-up to the spring hunting refer-endum when, out of despair, I would blaspheme when something went wrong at work. During confession I would try to explain my state of mind to the priest. I would tell him, "What I mean by *namra* is something that you feel in your insides, deep within your body. Namra is what comes out of your body".'

In a peculiar twist on the bodily symptoms of deficiency, the FKNK commissioned a study on the psychological effects on hunters of the ban on spring hunting as a result of EU accession. The research, which took place between June and September 2009 and involved a sample of 780 FKNK members, was conducted by the Malta Association of Psychiatric Nurses. A total of 61 per cent of the respondents said that they had sought professional psychiatric or psychological services to help them cope with the 'mental problems' brought about by the hunting ban. Of these, 30 per cent were prescribed medication, while 21 per cent were diagnosed with severe depression. Hunters whose *namra* went back to childhood expe-rienced levels of anxiety, depression or stress that were up to four times higher than average. The study also came across unconfirmed instances of hunters who had committed suicide. Finally, the lead researcher described a 'downward shift in mental wellbeing' and called on politi-cians to consider the effects of their actions on the wellbeing of minority groups, in this case hunters and trappers.[2]

Not everyone was moved to tears. Schadenfreude aside, some saw the study as a cynical *mise-en-scène* designed to win public sympathy. Others wheeled out their best sarcastic tone and said things like '*imsieken*' and '*jaħasra*' ('poor things'). This second response found considerable reso-nance among a substantial segment of the public that was accustomed to thinking of hunters as untouchable bullies rather than martyrs. The third reaction was perhaps the most ingenious. It was pointed out, notably by people who were part of or close to the bird protection ENGOs, that the study effectively confirmed what they had been saying all along – that is, that hunting was a pathology. Besides, if hunters were so prone to mental problems and neurotic withdrawal symptoms, how could they be trusted to act as rational, restrained and self-regulating people in the field?

Be that as it may, the results of the study came as no surprise to me. I had come across countless stories of hunters (and especially finch trappers, since finch trapping was completely banned from 2008 to 2014 and again from 2018) who had suffered severe depression and whose lives had become all but pointless. One Joseph, for example, told me of his brother Anġlu, a very pleasant and otherwise-balanced stonemason in his fifties whom I had joined a couple of times at his trapping site. Anġlu, it seems, had become so anxious and mentally unwell that he had been prescribed medication by a psychiatrist. More drastically, stories of men who had shot themselves in the head (*sparaw għal rashom*) were in standard circulation. As seen by hunters and trappers, and their sympathizers, these instances and stories were clear evidence, first, of the power (and, by inference, the legitimacy) of *namra*, and, second, of the heartlessness of protectionists who valued birds, and possibly their own hatred of hunters, above human wellbeing – indeed, above human life itself.

A third aspect of the way in which *namra* is experienced has to do with seasonality and the elements, and with how seasons and elements link up to the vagaries of migration. Hunters will describe how *namra* rises and ebbs as the year progresses. The first months of the year are ones of low *namra* if any. Migrating birds are almost entirely absent and the few wintering huntable species (thrushes, for example) will have wised up to the game and become *tal-post* (lit. 'of the place', meaning a bird that stays in the same place for several weeks or more and becomes very cunning and hard to catch out) and not particularly interesting as potential game. The first pangs of *namra* are felt as the days get longer and warmer in March. When the first spring migrants make an appearance, sometimes as early as late February, hunters circulate news of sightings with mounting excitement. From April, and especially between mid-April and early May, *namra* is at its strongest. What that means in practice is that even the mildest of *dilettanti* will watch the weather, be on a constant lookout – often while going about daily routines other than hunting – for signs of migration, and so on. Many of them will also be in the field as often as possible during this time. The social media, in particular Facebook pages and the FKNK hunters' forum, experience the heaviest traffic of the year. By late May, when the days get hotter and spring gradually gives way to summer, the passion again enters a period of relative stupor. With some exceptions, most of which are of not much interest to hunters, migrating birds are few and far between from June to August. Many hunters often indulge in other passions at this time, of which fishing is a main example. *Namra* sets in again from mid-August and lasts until late November, the weeks between mid-October and mid-November representing the peak as thrushes, larks and starlings migrate in considerable quantities.

Clearly, this calendar can and does vary according to individual preferences and circumstances. Thus, trappers, for example, tend to experience *namra* highs twice in the year. The first runs from mid-February to late March, when linnets migrate in their red-breasted breeding plumage. These birds are called *ġojjini ta' Marzu* ('March linnets') and are the trapper's counterpart of the hunter's *ġamiema t'April* ('spring turtle dove'). Trappers talk of the high excitement of days spent in the countryside in spring and the possibility of catching some of these beautiful birds. (They use the past tense, since spring trapping is now outlawed.) The second high *namra* period kicks off in September, when trappers begin to refurbish their sites in preparation for the autumn season. It heats up when the first chaffinches (usually the first species of finch to migrate, sometimes as early as late September) are seen. It is at its best from mid-October to early December, when the migration of all seven finch species is in full swing. However, even then, December or January influxes of finches (usually the result of cold spells on the Continent) bring about temporary spells of *namra*. Hunters who hunt ducks at sea or at strategic spots along the coast are at highest *namra* levels from mid-November to late December, and again from mid-February to late March, while those who specialize in woodcock are at their most passionate from early November to mid-December. The point is that while spring and, to a lesser extent, autumn represent the highest points of *namra* for hunters generally, the exact seasonality of the emotion will vary according to the migration period for a particular type of bird, as well as on the whims of off-season passages. This highlights two things: first, that Maltese hunters and trappers are heavily dependent on seasonal migration, as opposed to resident bird populations; and, second, that *Zugunruhe* is as much about the domain of anthropology as it is of ornithology.

An element that is closely linked to seasonality is weather. Hunters use the expression *jibda' jaqleb it-temp* to describe the changes in weather from winter to spring and from summer to autumn. In the latter case, the first clouds of any substance usually make an appearance around mid-August. These are called, and not exclusively by hunters, *l-għarajjex ta' Santa Marija* because they tend to coincide with 15 August, which is the feast of Santa Marija (the Assumption). Their arrival breaks the monotony of a cloudless summer sky and, if they happen to bring rain, of the parched and dusty appearance of the countryside in July and early August. Even if regular rain is typically several weeks away, *l-għarajjex ta' Santa Marija* mean a change in weather and the onset of the autumn passage of birds over the islands. The arrival of spring is less easy to pinpoint, but people (including and especially hunters) speak of a change in the light, lengthening days and a certain 'spring air' (*temp tar-rebbiegħa*). As expected, both the spring and autumn changes are described by hunters as conducive to *namra*.

That, however, is the general picture. In practice, it is not just spring and autumn weather generically that is linked to *namra*, but rather very specific weather types. There are two levels to this and both are a direct result of the complete dependence on migration of Maltese hunters and trappers. The first is the more general one. Migration is a highly complex phenomenon that is related to a host of variables. That is why hunters say *'fil-passa kisser il-pinnur u oħroġ kuljum'* ('during the migration period, weathervane be damned and go out hunting every day'). In other words, there is no fixed formula that can guarantee strong migration on any given day. That said, it is a well-known fact, both ornithologically and popularly among hunters, that most species of migrant birds are more likely to make landfall in their numbers in inclement weather. Large 'falls' (the sudden appearance of large numbers of migratory birds) have been linked to the overcast skies and rain produced when depressions move northeast over North Africa and meet anticyclones over southern and southeastern Europe. Under these conditions, migrants become disoriented and make for the nearest land. What was probably the biggest fall in recent history happened during heavy storms in late September 1969, when the islands were flooded with grounded birds. Similar weather conditions produced smaller falls in 1971, 1975 and 1976 (Sultana and Gauci 1982). It follows that such weather brings about bouts of *namra*, even if in practice (*delizzju*) it is wise to damn the weathervane and be in the field as often as possible. The weather that hunters consistently describe as being conducive to the strongest feelings of *namra* is overcast spring days with the wind blowing from the east. On such days, no hunter who is even remotely serious about his practice would dare stay away from the field (assuming he had a choice).

The other level at which the link between the weather and *namra* operates is more individual and localized. Each hunting location has its own bespoke relationship with the weather. Thus, although northwesterly winds are generally considered to be the least desirable, they are known to bring rich pickings to some areas in the south of Malta, to the extent that this stretch of coast is known among hunters as *kosta tal-majjistral* ('coast of northwesterlies'). Clearly, for the hunters who hunt there, this wind direction brings on *namra*. This is how Salvu, who hunts on his land at a place called Baħrija in the west, put it: 'When the weather forecast mentions a light to moderate northeasterly wind, I don't sleep at night. If I do, I wake up around midnight and sit up in bed fully awake, counting the minutes and hours.' In Salvu's case, his patch happens to be at its most desirable when the wind veers to the northeast. The point is that although certain broad rules of thumb apply, *namra* does not affect hunters equally across the islands.

The fourth way in which *namra* is experienced takes us to the heart of the symbiotic relationship between emotion and practice. On one occasion I was talking to man who, mostly due to the demands of his growing private business, had given up hunting a couple of years earlier. At one point he told me (half-jokingly) that our conversation was not a terribly good idea, simply because it was bringing back his *namra*. The point is that *namra* thrives not least on exposure to anything that brings practice to mind. For example, hunters will sometimes suffer a bout of out-of-season *namra* while watching a television documentary on birds, and one hunter told me of how, while on pilgrimage in Lourdes, he had found himself watching the sky constantly – for phenomena that were other than the supernatural.

It is here that the small size of the Maltese islands matters. The typical person, hunter or not, will in the course of an average day walk or drive past patches of countryside; even if they happen not to, the sounds of that countryside and in particular loud gunshots will still reach them. What this means is that not a single person in Malta is ever too effectively insulated from the practice of hunting – it is as if the entire population neighbours and eavesdrops on a hunting estate. The fact that hunting in Malta depends on migration and that migrating birds are not necessarily put off by the towns and villages across their path adds to this proximity. Clearly, for people who live in villages or hamlets surrounded with countryside, the cohabitation is even more intimate.

The effects on *namra* of this porosity between the practice or possibility of hunting and everyday life are profound. If *namra* is fuelled by practice, it follows that the constant presence of that practice threatens to keep *namra* permanently on a full tank. Take Pietru, a builder who happened to be laying slabs on a roof on 14 April 2007: 'It was a cloudless day with a strong northwesterly wind. The thought of migration was fairly distant from my mind, until I heard the shots and saw one, then two, then dozens of turtle doves whizzing past the rooftops. Suddenly it hit me. I downed my tools, bundled my two sons into the car, and raced off to my field.' It was on the same day that Mark, who works as an air-traffic controller, was on a short break from work having tea with a few colleagues and friends (some of whom were themselves hunters) outside a bar in urban Luqa. 'My heart stopped. We were four *dilettanti* out there, and suddenly the doves started flying over in streams and layers. I really don't know how I survived that morning. You know, I think I will never die after that.' For Fredu, who lives in the rural hamlet of Bidnija, the effect was an even nearer-death experience. Most of my informants spoke of that day and of how their routines were interrupted by the sight of migrating turtle doves and, as the day progressed, the growing cacophony of shots.

The point is that none of them was in the field to start off with; rather, they were going about their daily lives.

If heightened *namra* is linked to an intensification of practice, the obverse is also true. Men who used to hunt but no longer do so, or who hunt less and less, describe how their passion petered out. The word they use is typically *'bridt'* ('I cooled down', a direct reference to *namra* as emotion), but – and tellingly, given my argument – they might just say *'ma bqajtx dilettant'* or *'żarmajt'* ('I stopped practising' or 'I put everything away', direct references to hunting as practice). Three types of reason are given. The first is the least vertebrate: some people, it seems, simply lose the urge to hunt – they lose their *namra* and stop hunting altogether. Their peers will usually summon the benefit of hindsight to say of them that they never really had true *namra* to begin with and that their time as hunters was a flash in the pan, possibly brought about by temporary circumstances and certainly not embedded in the long-term dynamics of practice that accompany real *namra*. A young woman described to me how her father had gone through such a phase when the family moved house to a different village. He had felt isolated and hunting had been his way of trying to make new friends. 'He was never into it, he knew nothing about hunting and I doubt he ever managed to shoot a single bird. I suspect that the one or two he did bring home on rare occasions would have been given to him by his friends, out of philanthropy', she joked.

The second type of reason involves a decrease of practice and a corresponding cooling down of *namra*. In some cases, the cause is a change in the person's life (work or family pressures, for example) that has nothing to do with hunting. More relevantly, some hunters experience practical difficulties in the field and end up giving up on hunting altogether. Access to land is a perennial headache in this respect. Hunters whose access to land is too tenuous and fickle, usually because they do not have stable rights but hunt in an area at the owner's mercy, may find the experience too stressful. Andrew, for example, told me how he had always been chasing about from place to place and how difficult it had become for him to feel secure in the field. His small salary (he works as a beadle) would never have permitted him to buy his own land and he eventually gave up altogether. This reason has recently become more pressing, as hunting has become more spatially confined and dependent on sustained rights to land use.

The third reason has to do with recent changes in law-enforcement regimes. As discussed elsewhere in this volume, the last fifteen years or so have brought about a creeping sense of *sikkatura* ('tightness') among hunters. In the field, the average hunter now has to contend with an increased police presence, and with BirdLife Malta and other activists who monitor hunting areas with binoculars, telescopes, video cameras and record sheets. This is especially true during the spring season, which is in any case short and, since it involves applying a derogation from the Birds Directive, is thought of as something of a special and fragile concession. One might add that in spring, the police are joined by the army in their enforcement routines, which, as the derogation demands, are also more stringent and choreographed. Especially in spring but throughout the year more generally, there is also a heightened awareness of hunting activities among the public at large, in part as a result of appeals in the press by BirdLife Malta that urge the public to watch out for and report illegalities. Besides, there is also pressure by other hunters who have an interest in avoiding undue attention from the long list of uniformed and self-appointed law enforcers. The last is important because it represents a type of peer surveillance, with all the implications that this brings. Many of the hunters I worked with felt that a true *dilettant* should try to be *bil-għaqal* ('well behaved', as in generally observant of the law) at all times and that a failure to do so would ultimately contribute to a negative collective image. So strong is the urge to cultivate the collective image that colourful or otherwise desirable birds that are fully protected are referred to by hunters as *tal-inkwiet* ('bringers of trouble'). The idea is that the appearance of these (migrant) birds threatens to seduce hunters into breaking the law and risking a public-image disaster in the process.

It follows that this also translates directly into a kind of self-surveillance. Alfred, for example, told me about the time he last shot a honey buzzard (a protected species since 1980, but also one that was routinely shot on sight well into the 1990s), in 2008:

> I was alone in the field on a September afternoon. Suddenly a honey buzzard dived out of nowhere towards my clump of trees. Without thinking, and perfunctorily more than anything else, I shot it. I quickly retrieved it, put it away, and looked around me. I was concerned about my hunter neighbours but I swear to you that none of them saw me shoot it. I never said a word to anyone about it.

Another hunter said that it was not just a matter of being fined; even if no one saw him shoot a protected bird, he would still feel 'bad with himself' about it. As he put it, *'qisek tistħi minnek innifsek, tiddejjaq'* ('you feel ashamed, it's not an enjoyable experience at all').

The outcome is not necessarily that protected birds are never ever shot, although they are infinitely safer today than was the case some years ago. Rather, and especially in the context of the present argument, the point is that hunters can no longer look forward to the composite thrill of shooting a rare or attractive bird, adding it to their collection and cashing in on bragging rights. If they shoot such a bird at all, they almost always do so on the sly and not without a sense of shame and guilt, although it should be pointed out that the other side of that particular coin is bravado. This holds especially for the larger and rarer species – typically birds of prey, herons and so on.

With respect to *namra*, this shift has put a dent in the practice that fuels it. I met at least three people who had given up hunting precisely because of the effects of *sikkatura*. The first two told me that what had really fed their passion was the chance to shoot a *tajra*, generally speaking any huntable bird, but in this usage one that is usually large and likely to be mounted and added to a taxidermy collection. As hunters, they had not been terribly interested in small game birds like quail or thrushes. Given the new *sikkatura* and the fact that they felt they could not trust themselves to behave if they ever took to the field again, they had decided to stop hunting altogether rather than face the trouble of police chases and fines. They added that they were family men (*għandi l-familja*) and that that sort of trouble would scarcely do. This is how the third, who when I met him was a hunter on the wane, put it:

> I used to have more *namra*. It's inevitable. We've now reached a point where one can't shoot anything. More often than not I don't shoot a single bird, because how many turtle doves and quail does one see? I have to drive all the way across Malta to maybe shoot a single quail. One begins to question if it's worth the effort, and goes out hunting less and less. I've gone whole seasons without a single outing.

These experiences serve to support my argument about the close symbiosis between *namra* and practice. That said, it is not one that all hunters would accept in principle. The reason is that there is a tendency for active hunters to emphasize the intangible essence (that is, the *namra*) of hunting rather than its actual practice. For example, when I discussed the three examples I mentioned above with a very active and passionate hunter, he dismissed them as instances of people who did not really have *namra* and who therefore had not been 'real' hunters in the first place. Partly the reason for this insistence is that in a political landscape that increasingly questions the whole point of hunting and that accuses hunters of shooting anything that flies, a valuation that emphasizes deep-seated and inexorable motives rather than the actual shooting of birds becomes increasingly appealing.

What Is *Namra* for?

Having looked at some of the ways in which *namra* is experienced, I shall now go on to discuss its various 'aboutnesses', in Gordon's (1987) sense.

Not surprisingly, the first thing is the quarry itself. This might sound obvious, but what I mean here is four things specifically: the number of birds, their characteristics, the way in which they present themselves to hunters and the lore that they evoke.

First, bag size matters. In my fieldwork with hunters, they invariably described special days when large numbers of birds were migrating and when they caught more than their normal share. In a way, many of the land transformations and other field techniques are aimed primarily at attracting and possibly shooting or trapping as many birds as possible. Certainly the thrill of shooting is part of this, but it cannot be separated from the attraction of large bags. When a hunter says of a day in the field *'illum ħadt pjaċir'* ('today was a good one'), what he usually means is that there were plenty of birds to shoot at and that he shot a fair few, certainly more than average. This first factor is also why Maltese hunters increasingly travel to hunt in places that hold the promise of large bags – and, in some cases, of lax law enforcement that lets them hunt indiscriminately. Egypt, Tunisia, Romania, Hungary and Britain are popular destinations, but it is Argentina that is considered to be the top draw. The species that inflates bags in Argentina is the eared dove, a bird that achieves extraordinary densities in parts of the country where the population explosion is linked to intensive agriculture (Cocker 2013). Increasingly, groups from Malta are among the overseas hunters who flock to the destination, attracted by the prospect of shooting hundreds of doves a day per person; from time to time, images surface of Maltese hunters posing with heaps of bagged doves. The attraction is evidently a strong one for many hunters, who usually pay up to €6,000 (the average annual salary in Malta is about €16,000) for a two-week shooting trip.

The second aboutness is the characteristics of birds. The turtle dove (*gamiema*, pl. *gamiem*) is probably the one species that almost all hunters agree brings on a strong *namra*. This does not mean that the average hunter prizes a bagged turtle dove over a woodcock or a duck. But as a species, turtle doves and their migration (*il-passa tal-gamiem*) hold a special place in the collective imaginary and emotionality of Maltese hunters. Hunters talk about the beauty of the species and the magic of its purring call (onomatopoeically, *tparpir*). These characteristics are all but limited to the spring migration, which is why hunters will usually point out that their *namra* is not just for *gamiem* generally, but *il-gamiema t'April* (spring turtle dove). There are seasonal differences in the plumage of the birds. In spring, doves fly north to breed in their most attractive plumage; the word used by hunters is *imbiddlin*, which literally means doves that are dressed up in their Sunday best. Since most autumn birds are first-year juveniles or adults in worn post-breeding plumage, they simply cannot match the beauty of *il-gamiema t'April*. In autumn too, it is very rare to hear the species purr. All of this means that *namra* for autumn turtle doves is nowhere near as strong as that for spring ones. Other birds may be prized for characteristics other than plumage. Thus, quail, for example, summon *namra* through their habit (again, mostly in spring) of skulking in cornfields and calling loudly (*ifaqqa'*). The list is long and complicated, but the point is that the morphological and other qualities of birds are among the key 'aboutnesses' of *namra*.

The aesthetic valuation of birds is both palpable and consequential. Taxidermy, for example, is popular among hunters and a big bone of contention with conservationists. In the nineteenth and early twentieth centuries, collections of stuffed birds were largely the preserve of a few well-heeled people who were probably also inspired by the great interest that existed in Britain at the time. It was only in the postwar decades, and with rising standards of living, that Maltese hunters generally began to amass collections of stuffed birds in their homes. These ranged from a few trophies – usually herons, birds of prey and other large or colourful species – placed in conspicuous places about the house (and sometimes on windowsills, visible from the street) to systematic collections of hundreds of specimens. By the 1980s, which is when the interest in taxidermy peaked, the average hunter had a showcase with a few dozen stuffed and mounted birds. The occasional police raid on a taxidermist would typically produce huge chest freezers with many hundreds of all kinds of dead birds waiting to be stuffed and mounted. Although most hunters limited their collections to birds they had shot themselves, there were many collectors who readily bought specimens. An underground trade in unusual species (most of which were fully protected) developed and rare birds like eagles could fetch hundreds of Maltese liri (one lira was roughly equivalent to £2), especially if they had a good provenance that showed they had been shot in Malta. The rider was important since there was a parallel flow of specimens smuggled into the country from elsewhere; in some cases, these would be palmed off as having been shot in Malta. So strong was the attraction of a large and varied collection that, on one occasion, a man who had just been on a hunting trip to Egypt was stopped at customs and found to be carrying several dead birds strapped to his body.[3] The evidence suggests that the importation (or the smuggling) of foreign-shot birds has recently increased.

The new regime of law enforcement in Malta and stricter controls at customs have made it more difficult for hunters to add specimens to their collections. As a result, the overall extent of the actual practice of taxidermy has declined[4] considerably, and with it the attractiveness of birds that a few years ago would have qualified as fine specimens for the showcase. This aspect of *namra* is/was therefore fuelled by two things: the intrinsic characteristics of birds, and the competition that existed, and to a lesser extent still exists, among hunters to add unusual or rare birds to their collections.

The third thing about *namra* is the way in which the quarry presents itself to the hunter in the field. This aspect is well known in the literature. The attraction of foxhunting in Britain from the nineteenth century, for example, depended very much on the notion of the 'chase': 'the short, fast and furious chase . . . killing the fox in covert, without a chance of a gallop after it, was considered one of the worst things that could happen . . . ideally the hounds would stick to the same one until the death, but if they changed prey in a covert at least the field would still get their gallop' (de Belin 2013: 68–69). In the case of grouse hunting in Britain, by far the most highly prized type of encounter is that between hunters who sit concealed in shooting butts and birds that are 'driven' towards the guns by teams of beaters; grouse that are 'walked up' by hunters travelling on foot are less in demand and the land that hosts the practice is let at substantially lower rates. Further, there is a hierarchy of value of drives, with those that best bring out the birds' ability for agile flight being the most highly prized (Richards 2004). These and other examples show that success and bag size are only part of what makes a good hunt and that equally important is what might be called the aesthetics of the encounter between hunter and quarry. Clearly, attempts to set the stage for an aesthetically pleasing hunt are often linked to transformations of the landscape.

In the case of Malta, there are two aspects in particular that are important. First, the encounter between hunters and their quarry is strongly marked by the fact that all huntable (and hunted) birds are migratory. Thus, it is not just individual birds or flocks of birds that hunters interact with, but migration as a natural phenomenon. Hunters experience, and often talk about, *il-passa* (migration) as something that induces *namra* in its own right. For example, they might observe birds making for land from far out at sea, birds of prey gaining height on thermal air currents or flocks of birds flying low against strong headwinds. Migration also has a connective element about it that is especially appealing on a small island surrounded on all sides by an empty horizon. Bird migration collapses and juxtaposes space, and brings far-removed places together through the phenomenon of long-distance connective flyways. Through projection, these connections and flyways may be re-enacted by humans. That migration is unpredictable adds to the potency of the encounter. During my fieldwork, I often discussed this with hunters who had hunted abroad, in game reserves where the quarry was predictable, if not quite guaranteed. This, to them, detracted from the quality of the experience: as one informant put it, 'qisek qed tispara ġo guva' ('it's like shooting inside an aviary'). What made hunting in Malta so particular, they explained to me, was the perennial and unpredictable play between presence and absence, as well as the uncertainty of what the quarry might be, in what numbers and in which conditions. Bird protectionists often accuse hunters of undervaluing the magic of migration, of thoughtlessly killing birds that would have flown thousands of miles across sea and desert simply to meet a sorry end in Malta. To hunters, however, it is precisely the magic of migration that is encountered and appropriated through the hunt.

The second and related aspect, and one that is equally closely linked to *namra*, is the way in which birds present themselves to hunters in the field. Certainly it is not just a matter of being in range; rather, it is the way in which the bird comes within that range that really matters. Let us again take the example of turtle doves. One of the reasons why autumn birds are less prized is that they do not display the agility and direct flight patterns of spring ones. This is probably because birds in spring are themselves full of another kind of *namra* and are in a hurry to get to their breeding grounds. Spring doves also have a habit of diving into range (especially when attracted by trees and decoys) from a great height, their wings making a unique sound as they do so. They can also take to wing very low above the ground (*toħroġlok baxxa*), a quality that many hunters find desirable since it adds to the element of surprise and immediacy with the target. Besides, the first hint that a dove is around is often a particular alarm call made by sparrows (a common resident species). This sound, called (again onomatopoeically) *iżarżar*, is linked to the sparrows' breeding behaviour and is rarely heard in autumn. It is a sound that is guaranteed to set a hunter's pulse racing and is considered a significant contributor to *namra*.[5] The point is that it is one thing to bag a dove, but it is quite another to manage to shoot one that enters one's range (*tidħollok għat-tir*) in a way that is exciting, challenging and involves all manner of meaningful engagement with the landscape. Marvin (2003) makes a telling point in this vein. He draws a distinction between a farmer out culling foxes in the countryside and foxhunting. The key difference is presence: whereas the former attempts to be a nonpresence, the hunt openly and deliberately announces itself in the landscape. The hunt 'engages and connects human and animal bodies, generates excitement and emotion, both mental and visceral, and dramatically enacts a set of relationships with the natural world' (Marvin 2003: 48). The point is perfectly illustrated in a story told to me by Publius, a sixty-year-old hunter:

Once, on a very hot September afternoon, I was walking along some dense foliage with a young budding hunter, when I heard a *bufula* [Sardinian warbler, a small passerine bird] clicking constantly. I told him: 'There's something in those trees, I'm sure.' Suddenly we heard the clapping sound of a turtle dove taking to wing. '*Gamiema!*', I cried, and swung my gun to where my long experience told me the bird would be. The only thing I saw was a shadow through the trees. I fired, but we saw nothing fall, nor did we hear the thump of a dead bird hitting the ground. 'You haven't scored', my young companion told me. And then, floating towards us on a hot south wind, I saw a single feather: I hadn't missed after all. It was a moment I will never forget.

The importance of this aspect is reflected in the lexical richness of the language hunters use to talk about it. Trappers will talk about the *namra* of watching a linnet half-close its wings in a swerving and undulating flight as it enters the trapping area; this flight pattern, called *ipanni*, is highly prized. The relatively few people who trap plovers look forward to the moment at which an approaching bird droops and curves its wings as it heads for the trapping site; this time the metaphor used is *iqammar*, which means that the bird holds its wings in the shape of a crescent moon. To be in the field with hunters and trappers is to spend hours listening to richly seasoned stories of these special moments. These stories are almost invariably accompanied by gestures and sound effects that bring the choreography of the moment to life. There is a strong anthropomorphizing element by which hunters (and to a lesser extent trappers) on the one hand ascribe human-like characteristics to birds, and on the other hand use their bodies to bring avian behaviour to life. For example, it is common to see hunters stretch out their arms or make hand movements to imitate the flight of birds. Trappers often make soft whistling noises that imitate the calls of finches as they go about their daily lives in situations that often have nothing to do with trapping.

The third aboutness of *namra* is the lore that the different species of birds evoke. I mentioned above that *il-gamiema t'April* holds a special place in the collective imaginary of hunters. Morphological and behavioural characteristics apart, the reason is that the type is embedded in a rich and deep-rooted set of narratives and memories that distinguish it as the quintessential game bird and repository of *namra* aboutness. In this sense, every dove – or, often, the mere thought of it – evokes a palimpsest of narratives about hunting and trapping.

I should point out that although hunters experience a general *namra* for all or most forms of the practice, there are differences and variations. The first is the obvious one between hunting and trapping; clearly, hunters experience a stronger *namra* for hunting, and trappers for trapping. Perhaps more importantly, there are differences within each of these two practices. For example, there are many hunters for whom the experience of hunting with pointing dogs is a particularly rewarding experience. For them, the moment at which the dog freezes and 'points' (*jiffirma*) at hidden birds (usually quail or woodcock) is the sublimation of *namra*. Again, there is a range of words with which many of these *namra*-inducing behaviours are described. Frans, who keeps three dogs in his garage, told me about the thrill of this kind of hunting:

> Nothing compares to hunting with dogs. I take my dogs out every single day, even outside of the hunting season, just to watch them search and point. The rare occasions when all three pick up a scent and point at the same time are magical. I once went to Egypt on a hunting tour at a time when there were few restrictions. We shot all kinds of birds by the sackload. The day I came back to Malta I caught a single quail that was so emaciated I could feel its breast bone. Hand on heart, that one quail was more precious to me than all the birds I had shot in Egypt.

Some hunters specialize in and especially prize a kind of hunting in which woodcock are shot on the wing at dawn or dusk when the species exhibits a kind of flight known as 'roding' (*tissiefaħ*); others describe this as too mechanistic and find more passion in the skill of flushing woodcock from inaccessible places. Some feel the strongest *namra* for the practice of luring plovers within range by means of artisanally made whistles that are only effective in experienced mouths. In some cases a hunter will specialize in a very restricted field; for example, one trapper I met was mostly interested in ortolan buntings, a rare species that is now fully protected legally. The processes by which particular hunters become attached to particular forms of hunting or types of birds are many and complex. They include heredity (in some cases whole families specialize), access to land that is more attractive to one type of bird and a kind of double-cream *namra* that combines a love for dogs with that for hunting.

It is useful at this stage to discuss in some detail the making of the conceptual category *kaċċa* – the category, that is, that includes birds that hunters see as legitimate game. But first, a caveat is in order. What follows does not mean that hunters will never shoot anything that is not considered game. Indeed, and as discussed elsewhere in this volume, the killing of nonhuntable bird species was and to a lesser extent is one of the perennial bones of contention of hunting in Malta. Increasingly, however, formal and nonformal discourses by the FKNK and by hunters, respectively, disown the killing of nonhuntable birds as 'poaching'. This is especially true of public-sphere discourse, where the word first made its appearance about fifteen years ago and has since become common. The relation is as follows: hunting = *kaċċa* = game = legal, as opposed to poaching = *tajra* = nongame = illegal. The fact that there has been a considerable and consequential crystallization of the terms and of the dichotomy makes it all the more important to properly understand how a particular bird species becomes classified as game and its hunting as *kaċċa*, while another becomes classified as *tajr* and its shooting as poaching.

The term 'game' is invariably rooted in particular legal and social contexts. For example, in Britain, an impressive fifty-three hunting Acts and regulations were passed in the period from 1671 (the date of the Game Act) to 1831 (the Game Reform Act) alone. The purpose of this legislation was to render the hunting of game – defined as partridges, pheasants, grouse, bustards and hares – an exclusive privilege of the landed gentry. Two things can be noted here. First, there were anomalies even within this system. For example, while quail were not legally defined as game-birds, the Game Reform Act of 1831 made trespass in their pursuit an offence and laid down that a game licence was required to take or kill them (Shrubb 2013). Second, and perhaps more importantly, outside the category 'game' and the bounded spaces and social circles in which it was hunted, a wide range of birds continued to be shot, netted and trapped on open or common land. This suggests that 'game' has a meaning that goes beyond legislation and is embedded in much broader social notions.

In Malta, the absence of hunting estates and the paucity of resident species means that the classification of certain bird species as game (*kaċċa*) and their conceptual opposition to *tajr protett* (nonhuntable birds) has tended to take place in a more organic fashion. Outside the sharp-edged definitions of the law, it is also a work in progress. The process by which hunters construct the category *kaċċa* involves criteria such as history and lore (turtle doves and quail, for example, are embedded in deep-rooted narratives of hunting and trapping), edibility, broader geographical contexts (thrushes and skylarks, for example, are considered game in most of Europe) and morphological characteristics (a colourful species like the hoopoe is increasingly considered a pity to shoot – see Lišková and Frynta 2013).

There are several points to be made here. First, the criteria are not mutually exclusive. Thus, for example, turtle doves have a rich history of being hunted, are steeped in hunting lore, are regularly cooked and eaten as delicacies, are valued for their plumage and are hunted within a broader regional (southern European at least) context. Second, the classification is based on valuations rather than intrinsic qualities. Thus, turtle doves are not valued primarily for their aesthetic appeal, even though they happen to be colourful and are commonly described by hunters as one of the most beautiful birds that may be hunted, especially in spring. Third, the location of a species within a category is often contested. Nightjars, for example, have been fully protected for a couple of decades, but many hunters still think of them as game on account of their prized flesh.

Can *Namra* Ever Be Modern?

I have so far discussed *namra* in fairly neutral terms. However, the point is that it lies at the heart of a much-contested discursive field. To hunters themselves, the overwhelming strength of *namra* legitimates hunting as a practice that is essential to their lives and therefore one that deserves to be accommodated within society, the physical landscape and the polity. For their part, bird protectionists depart from much the same assumptions about *namra* to reach a radically different conclusion. As they see and represent it, *namra* is a pathology that has no place in a modern rational society, and that therefore should be completely or at least partially cured (i.e. eradicated or controlled). A good part of what follows in this book is about that stand-off, but we must first look at some of the explanations for *namra* and its consequences by bird protectionists. In particular, *namra* is imagined and represented as primitive, and as a symptom and display of an innate malignant masculinity. Both instances are underwritten throughout by a double exceptionalism that posits the Mediterranean as a special case and Malta as a special case in the Mediterranean. In this way, the regional intensity of hunting discussed in Chapter 1 is naturalized and ascribed to the inherent cultural qualities of a geographical region.

In order for the argument to make sense, it is necessary first to look briefly at the historical production of alterity in Malta and the Mediterranean. Prior to the nineteenth century, ornithology in Malta was concerned mainly with the procurement of specimens destined for European cabinets of curiosities, some of which were later incorporated into museums (see MacGregor 2007; Sultana and Borg 2015). It was only in the nineteenth century that travellers' accounts of Malta turned their attention to indigenous hunting and trapping. From that time onwards, the zeal with which wild birds were hunted in Malta invariably caught the eye of visitors from the north. A detailed history is beyond the scope of this book, but a few examples will suffice to illustrate the point. Writing in 1805, de Boisgelin noted the 'great perseverance' with which Maltese hunters shot and trapped all manner of migrating birds; Badger did the same in 1838; in 1839, Macgill wrote about the 'immense number of sportsmen' on the island; and in 1861, Tallack mentioned the large quantities of shot birds sold at markets (as cited in Fenech 2010). In 1870, the Scottish naturalist and traveller Andrew Leith Adams noted the 'lucklessness' of the golden orioles that attempted to rest in Malta: 'for no sooner is their attractive plumage noticed than a dozen guns are put in requisition, when, if not annihilated, they are at least expelled beyond the precincts of the island' (1870: 103). Heavy passages of yellow wagtails meant that the bird catcher was 'hard at work filling his cages with hundreds, all of which will be dead and eaten before another day' (1870: 108) and turtle doves were 'captured in numbers' by means of clap-nets and decoy birds. There is more than a hint of poignancy to Leith Adams' descriptions. Writing about the heaps of dead nightingales at markets, he added that:

> It may be a small subject on which to moralize, but I don't think anyone who can appreciate the beautiful in nature, but would feel somewhat sorry to witness such a scene, when he thinks of the hundreds of mellow throats now silenced for ever, that might in more northern climes have gladdened the heart and aroused the finer feelings of humanity; and all for what? (1870: 101-2)

The tendency to describe Malta as a place where rural people were overwhelmingly passionate about hunting gathered pace in twentieth-century accounts by observers from northern Europe. One example will suffice. Robin Bryans, the Belfast-born travel writer and author of *Gateway to the Khyber* (1959), visited Malta in the early 1960s. Having hunted and trapped with the Blackfoot and Stony people in the United States some years earlier, Bryans was no stranger to the chase.[6] And yet it appears that its ubiquity and scale in Malta still made an impression. On one occasion, he visited a Maltese home and was told that a stuffed heron standing in a corner had been shot locally by a member of the family. In Gozo, he 'seldom walked across the rocky wastelands without encountering bird catchers in their hideouts' (Bryans 1966: 232). It would appear that Bryans' visit coincided with the spring trapping season for finches. The locals he met, who included shepherds, farm boys, plasterers and the village barman and schoolmaster, 'all had one interest in common besides music. They not only talked about birds, but the London Bar closed early so that they could be up and out of doors by three o'clock the next morning to go netting. Sometimes the captured birds were brought into the bar in tiny cages' (1966: 232). Bryans was himself a birdwatcher of sorts and was not entirely at ease with what he observed. He describes how, in April, the hunters were all over the countryside with their guns. Quail, thrushes, nightjars, larks, doves, plovers and woodcock were shot for the pot; in rural areas the list included falcons and harriers. His drift throughout is that nothing was spared. His descriptions, particularly of trapping, are evocative:

Blown on the breeze from the sea came more sounds of bird song than I had heard for a long time. Then Saviour pointed and I saw that the songsters were decoys. We climbed some stone walls and approached the bird catchers and their nets. A ten-year-old boy crouched in a low stone enclosure . . . And around the nets a dozen linnets and finches sang lustily in tiny cages which had been placed on short piles of rocks. Farther out still from the nets another dozen decoy cages of trilling songsters stood about the stone walls of fields. The sport of netting invited disapproval, yet even the most outraged bird lover would have to admire the ingenuity involved. Moreover, the boys and men who indulged in netting were extremely proud and fond of their catches, which they took home to tame and keep as pets. The boys also knew and could imitate bird calls as they sat in their hideouts . . . Seagulls sailing in the void were specks of no interest to five very young netters who sat dangerously near the cliff edge, bird whistling. I wondered for how many hundreds of years boys with just those brown handsome faces, dark eyes and black hair had sat up there. (1966: 247–48)

Drawing on the work of Chambers (2008) among others, Heatherington (2010) has argued that historical discourses of alterity were not limited to European accounts of colonial outposts, the 'Orient' or the New World. Rather, they also constructed a heterogeneous cultural geography of urban and rural, east and west, and north and south differences within Europe itself. The Mediterranean in particular was ascribed a timeless marginality and was set up as a boundary object of Europe in the emerging cultural schema. For example, in his account of a journey to Sardinia in 1921, D.H. Lawrence ushered readers into an orientalist vision of cultural difference; the island was a strange, harsh and ultimately unknowable landscape inhabited by people who were trapped in a timeless past and who looked rather like 'esquimos'; Sardinia thus became evocative of the Mediterranean imaginary (Heatherington 2010).

The travellers' accounts of Malta can be both comfortably and usefully accommodated within this analytical drift. Although there are important differences – for example, the kind of montane ruggedness that nourished discourses of Sardinian backwardness does not apply to Malta – it is clear that the two islands belong to the same historical discourse of alterity. This is especially so because, like Sardinia, Malta is not just any place in the Mediterranean, but rather an island. As anyone who has watched Robert J. Flaherty's film *Man of Aran* (1934) will know, islands have routinely been accorded a privileged place in the cultural geography of regional alterity, backwardness and marginality. It is hard not to spot this in Bryans' description of the generations of dark boys and men who had sat whistling for birds on rocky cliff edges for hundreds of years. The point is not that Bryans, and other observers, made up stories to produce alterity; rather, it is that descriptions of hunting in Malta were often located within a regionalist grand narrative. Indeed, I would argue that bird catching played the same role in Malta that mountains and violence-prone islanders did in Sardinia: it served as a literary device by which to evoke a powerful discourse of Mediterranean alterity. The crucial point is that the same discourse, latterly produced in part by indigenous sources, continues to pattern the field of hunting and conservation in Malta today in striking and far-reaching ways. I shall focus here on two of them.

The location of Maltese hunters, and their passions, within a discourse of alterity hinges on two sets of representations. The first is that of timelessness, or of time that moves very slowly. Horden and Purcell (2000) have productively discussed the persistent idea that at least some areas of the Mediterranean, or some aspects of Mediterranean life, have, since Antiquity, remained virtually immune to change. They were and are, effectively, 'museums of Man'. There is a meaningful convergence between this conceptual framework and discourses and valuations of hunting in Malta. From early on, ENGOs constructed a representation of Maltese hunters and their *namra* as a relic whose practices were anachronistic and unlikely to ever change. It was not just hunting generally that was out of its time, but the Maltese hunter as a specific type. Hunters were portrayed – literally, in magazines and other indigenous literature produced by the ENGOs – as short, stocky, 'primitive' men with ample body hair and protruding lower jaws. For example, a campaign poster from the late 1980s showed just such a type dragging a bird carcass and wielding a club; the caption was *'Fil-qedem essenzjali, illum saret banali'* ('Essential in the past, pointless in the present'). According to this formula, which caught on and inspired a generation of cartoonists for the Maltese press, hunters were mired in a primordial past in which men were prone to irrational and primitive passions (hence the overpowering strength of *namra*). Further – and this is where notions of a Mediterranean alterity come in – change could only come from the outside, specifically from northern European sources that were supposedly at the cutting edge of conservation ecology. The ENGOs were and are mainly made up of Maltese people, of course, but they positioned themselves as bringers of the northern European gift of progressive and fast-moving time. Maltese hunters were, and would always be, out of their time and ruled by the kind of primordial passions that the Mediterranean generally and its islands in particular were heir to.

The second set of representations within which *namra* is politically embedded is that of gender. The bird protection lobby is keen to emphasize that hunting and its passions are strongly male-gendered and ultimately rooted in a retrograde Mediterranean masculinity that jars with modern models of gender equality. Certainly the first part seems to be

FIL-QEDEM ESSENZJALI...

...ILLUM SARET BANALI

KAMPANJA KONTRA L-KAĊĊA ŻGHAŻAGH GHALL-AMBJENT. 133, TRIQ MELITA, IL-BELT   SPONSORED BY COMMITTEE AGAINST BIRD KILLING, GERMANY

Figure 2.1. ENGO poster from the late 1980s showing hunting as a relic of a primitive past: 'Essential in the past, pointless in the present'. Published with permission.

borne out by the evidence. Earlier in the chapter, I described some of the ways in which *namra* is largely the preserve of men. Unlike in some other contexts (see, for instance, Fitzgerald (2005) for an account of the sharp increase in women hunters in the United States), there is no perceptible increase in the number of women hunters in Malta today, and they remain a rare exception. Girlfriends, wives and daughters do sometimes join men in the field, but never as hunters in their own right. If they display *namra* at all, it is seen as an accident of heredity that will not lead to actual *delizzju*: 'My mother is madder about hunting than I am. She would tell my father not to dawdle at home, that there was shooting going on and that he should be in the field. She did sometimes join me, and was always very keen. But she did not actually shoot.' To all intents and purposes, hunting in Malta is the preserve of men.

This is a fact that the anti-hunting lobby has made much of. Again, *Fatal Flight* provides a useful and sustained instance of a broad discourse. The title of an entire chapter of the book is 'Metaphors of Superiority, Masculinity, Virility and Machismo'. We are assured that 'there is something very manly about carrying a gun' (Fenech 1992: 92), and that 'one can often see men with cartridge belts on near the village bars . . . they are shooters returning from a shoot, who keep their sign of manliness on even while stopping for a chat, a boast and a coffee' (1992: 94). Two aspects in particular are pointed out. First, the author ascribes a 'Rambo mentality' to hunters. He compares hunting to warfare and describes the aggressive attitude of hunters, both towards the public and within their own circles: 'there is no respect towards other shooters and arguments leading to serious quarrels and fights frequently arise when more than one shooter shoots and kills the same bird' (1992: 94). It is worth noting that, in public commentary in Malta, 'Rambos' is often a byword for hunters, presumably on account of their penchant for violence and intimidation. Second, Fenech draws our attention to the gender of bird names. He picks a fairly contrived selection of Maltese names to argue that 'somehow, shooters always seem to "catch" a female' (1992: 93).

It is fairly standard fare to represent hunting as a formulaic display of an essentialized masculinity. Fitzgerald (2005: 86) calls it 'a sport that is infamous for being male-dominated'. Perhaps the best known explanation is the 'hunting hypothesis', which locates the practice within the evolutionary process (from apelike ancestors) and its corollaries, aggression and male dominance over women. Within this scheme, man-the-hunter serves as the model for evolution, in part because aggression and male dominance are key structural components of the hunt (Shiva 1989; see also Cartmill 1993). Ecofeminist[7] writers who have dealt with the issue of sport hunting (they tend to distinguish it from subsistence hunting) argue that these components enable hunters to affirm their masculinity and dominance over women, also because there are parallels between the practice of and weapons used in hunting, and warfare and aggression generally. Writing about hunting in Norway, Dahles (1993) describes it as staged combat in which hunters play off their masculinity against the gender (masculinity or otherwise) ascribed to game animals.

It is telling, if not surprising, that this is the drift of *Fatal Flight* and of anti-hunting discourses in contemporary Malta. Drawing on a number of sources and evidence from various parts of the world, Wilson and Peden (2014) have made the point that hunt opponents often describe hunters as motivated by violent male aggression and oppression, redirected social aggression or predatory aggressive instincts. In Malta, the connection seems to gather support by the evidence on the ground – quite literally, in the case of '*Namur jew intajru*' (see above). Over the years, there have been a number of incidents in which hunters attacked birdwatchers or their property; in some cases, the victims included journalists, countryside walkers and so on. In recent years, such incidents have tended to be filmed and posted on social media and on video-sharing internet sites, notably YouTube. And yet, the logic is facile and misleading. '*Namur jew intajru*', for example, appears to be a straightforward case of aggression.

There is, however, a different reading in which the use of the conjunction *jew* ('or') in effect represents *namra* as the alternative rather than as an accessory to violence. This warrants a second, longer look.

Empirically, the link between hunting and masculinity (and gender more broadly) takes on as many forms as there are contexts. A few examples will suffice. In medieval England and France, falconry had resonances for seigneurial men and played an important part in the construction of an elite (and particularly a courtly) masculinity. Deer hunting was more nuanced and fallow deer were seen as the appropriate quarry for aristocratic or royal women hunters, who also tended to hunt in enclosed parks according to contemporary spatial gender ideologies. Game (deer) was anthropomorphized into a complex and gendered hierarchy (Richardson 2012). In nineteenth-century India, tiger hunting emerged as an important symbol in the construction of British imperial and masculine identities: 'only by successfully vanquishing tigers would Britons prove their manliness and their fitness to rule over Indians' (Sramek 2006: 659). The rationale of British hunters was multifaceted: it emulated the traditional tiger hunts of the Mughals and other Indian rulers; it staged the defeat of Tipu Sultan (the 'Tiger of Mysore') and other indigenous rulers who stood in the way of imperial conquest; it enacted the imperial domination of the natural environment of India; and it epitomized the 'facing it like a Briton' notion of imperial masculinity. In the postwar years up to about 1975, deer hunting emerged as a key signifier of masculine working-class identities among workers in motor companies in the United States. In a Michigan motor company studied by Fine, hunting 'tied them [hunters] to their fellow workers, filled their days and minds with excitement and joy, and provided an important and enduring source of their masculine, white, working class culture and identity' (2000: 817). Finally, in contemporary Norway, elk hunting plays an important role in the shaping of masculine rural identities. Young men who live in wooded regions are 'gradually initiated into the male and generation community of the local society through participation in the elk hunting party' (Bye 2003: 145).

The contexts are many and varied. However, there are two general points to be made. First, in none is the link between hunting and masculinity straightforward or unchanging. Certainly Richardson is wary of applying facile gender dichotomies to medieval hunting practices: 'classifications of . . . gender, in hunting, are fluid, dependent on type and sex of quarry, method, and no doubt historical specificity – a point worth remembering if one is tempted similarly to categorise the hunters!' (2012: 258). In colonial India, what at first seems like a stable formula for a type of masculinity enacted by tiger hunters in fact changed around 1870, when hunting methods emerged that were associated with conceptions of passive and docile natives (Sramek 2006). In Michigan, the gender equation became less straightforward as increasing numbers of women hunters brought 'woman-the-hunter' (Fitzgerald 2005) into competition with the staple type. And in Norway, there are indications that rural masculine identities are losing ground, or at least changing in character, as new groups of people – and, increasingly, women – enter the picture (Bye 2003). Second, and perhaps more importantly, it is clear that in any specific hunting context, masculinity intersects with variables that may include class, colonial hierarchies, race and ethnicity, notions of rurality and historical context, among many others. To put it differently, a useful understanding of the link between masculinity and hunting must look, first, at the ways in which that link is embedded in broader discourses, practices and heuristic frameworks of specific contexts, and, second, at the intersection between that link and other variables. It is here that the discourse of hunting, and *namra*, as symptoms of a primordial Mediterranean masculinity begins to make sense.

It is worth noting that in anthropology, the study of masculinity has often been linked to culture areas and notably to the Mediterranean. The argument is that a set of qualities, beliefs and practices associated with masculinity are in some significant way more marked in this culture area than anywhere else in the world (Gutmann 1997). Mediterranean hunting practices could be read as a stage for masculine performances of the 'southern' type – the 'I also have a moustache' set of pan-Mediterranean values discussed (and problematized) by Horden and Purcell (2000: 485), among others. For example, writing about Zakynthos, Theodossopoulos (2003) points out that hunters are exclusively men. He describes the hunt (in particular that for migrating turtle doves) as a performative context where male identities are asserted and reinforced. This emphasis on the performance of manhood rehearses Herzfeld's key contribution to the anthropology of masculinity. Herzfeld (1985) wrote about men in rural Crete who distinguish between 'being a good man' and 'being good at being a man' – rather than being born male, it is the 'performative excellence' of manliness that really matters. In Zakynthos, hunting 'provides opportunities for the Vassilikiot hunters to articulate their claims to manhood . . . to affirm their friendship with other local men and compete with outsiders, to perform and recount their achievements. Boys are given a chance to fail, to try again and to succeed. Adult men can seize the occasion and excel by becoming more successful men' (2003: 157). This invites parallels with the descriptions in *Fatal Flight* or with Sicily and southern Italy, where, as the saying goes, a man who shoots a honey buzzard secures one year's immunity from being cuckolded by his wife.

And yet, it is Herzfeld himself who warns us against the notion of an essentialized Mediterranean culture and its equally essentialized corollaries. Ethnographers in particular have a lot to answer for in this respect, as they may have unwittingly contributed to the creation of a stereotype and a self-fulfilling prophecy (Herzfeld 1987); this is an argument 'that may be extended to critique a cultural regionalism of masculinity' (Gutmann 1997: 390). Where, then, does that leave hunting in Malta? The answer is to be found, I believe, in the two points I made earlier. First, the link between hunting and masculinity in Malta is neither straightforward nor unchanging. While there is some truth in the descriptions of men wielding 'manly' weapons and wearing cartridge belts outside village bars, they are ultimately superficial, caricatures even. My earlier analysis of 'real' *namra*, as opposed to excess and unchecked passion, suggests that it is not stereotypical manliness that hunting in Malta produces and performs. Rather, real *namra* and the restrained *delizzju* that goes with it suggest a kind of man who knows his place in nature and society. I had many occasions during my fieldwork to talk to hunters whose sons also hunted or to women whose husbands were hunters. Invariably, the emphasis was on how hunting is conducive to a respectable and family-centred moral order. The Maltese word used is *ġabra*, the meaning of which is somewhere between rectitude, self-restraint, domesticity and doing what is good for the family, in this case as a man. As Pawlu, whom I met stalking woodcock along a cliff edge told me: 'I'm happy my two sons and my nephews are hunters . . . that way they're *miġbura* [*miġbur* is the past participle of *ġabra*].' This is hardly an image of hirsute masculinity – so much so that hunters argue that it is the *absence* of hunting that would lead to unrestrained masculine passions. George, an industrious carpenter and family man who values *ġabra* highly, put it succinctly: 'These last two years have been difficult, what with the spring hunting season outlawed. You know, if someone asked me to go with him you-know-where [to a prostitute], I'd say Yes. That's what desperation does to you.' Being good at being a man, then, is about the successful management of a composite of passions of which *namra* is but one.

These renditions are reminiscent of Littlefield's important fieldwork with hunters in the United States. The ecofeminist plot of aggression, killing, violence, and domination of nature and women was not what Littlefield found. Instead, the hunters he worked with expressed a variety of masculinities that often included aspects of traditional, family-related values, mastery of technology, a deep immersion in nature, a social connections with other humans and even a connection with the animals they hunted. Littlefield's hunters 'did not stress how hunting would allow younger generations to "be men" in a stereotypically masculine way, but [would] allow them to find a respect for other lives and their place in the world' (2010: 114). Further, there is evidence that hunters in Malta in fact situationally perform more than one kind of masculinity.

Second, I earlier suggested that the link between hunting and masculinity is embedded in broader discourses, practices and heuristic frameworks of specific contexts, and that notions of masculinity typically intersect with other variables in any given context. In the case of Malta, the masculinity ascribed to hunters is located within historical and contemporary discourses of Mediterranean alterity. It also carries implications of class. The latter is a point I will take up in Chapter 3, but the argument is that *namra* is not seen as merely a man's world (and therefore also sexist and out of touch with modernity imagined as a gender-neutral space), but rather one of rural or working-class men whose lack of education and backwardness, so to speak, feeds into a primordial tendency to enact an anachronistic Mediterranean masculinity that is prone to aggression and lack of restraint. As represented by bird protectionists, it is an affliction that only a northern-inspired cache of education, legislation and cultural values can keep in check. As it happens, ENGOs see themselves – and are widely seen popularly – as the rightful holders and bringers of this gift.

Of course, the narrative of Mediterranean alterity can be stood on its head. In 2009, for example, FACE Med launched a booklet with the title *Hunting in the Mediterranean: Management and Sustainability for Future Generations*. FACE Med is a branch of FACE (the European Federation for Hunting and Conservation) that is made up of Italian, Spanish, French, Portuguese, Greek, Cypriot and Maltese hunting federations, and that 'was born with the intention to co-ordinate between them the hunting politics of the Mediterranean countries, so as to define common strategies both for the promotion of sustainable hunting as well as for the resolutions of the shared problems in view of the common historical, social and cultural roots'. The booklet, the English-language version of which was produced by the FKNK, was intended to make the point that hunting is rooted in the lives of Mediterranean people. It described the practice in the Mediterranean as 'popular heritage', 'history and tradition', 'preceding the registers of human civilization', 'management of natural habitat', 'a source of income for tens of thousands of people', 'scientific research' ('the foremost nature lovers and ornithologists of Mediterranean origin were hunters'), a 'responsible activity of volunteers', 'international cooperation' (between hunters from various countries) and, finally, 'gastronomical culture'. The booklet thus accepted the idea that there was something particular and primordial about Mediterranean hunters – only it was precisely that something that made the practice worth preserving.

By this account, not only is *namra not* the partner-in-crime of anachronistic Mediterranean characteristics; rather, it is modern precisely *because* regional culture is one of the legitimate protagonists of modernity.

In this chapter I have looked at some of the ways in which *namra* drives hunters in Malta today and at its links with practice and referents in the social and natural worlds. I have also discussed how representations of *namra* are located within broader discourses of alterity, masculinity and modernity. Throughout, the emphasis has been to de-essentialize passion as a malleable and politicized emotion, even as it plays a central role in the experience of hunting. I now turn my attention to the encounter between hunting and the rising tide of bird conservation, and to the ways in which the two are embedded in national and supranational structures of governance.

Notes

1. Wallace 2017: 365–66.
2. 'Maltese Hunters and Trappers: A Bio-psychosocial Perspective', unpublished FKNK report, 2009.
3. The newspaper report is so extraordinary that it reads like a spoof: 'A passenger who had just flown in from Cairo was either very muscular or was hiding something under his clothes, customs officials reckoned yesterday . . . They were particularly intrigued at the way he was moving and decided to investigate. They found nothing in his luggage but a body search turned up about 10 rare and protected birds strapped around different parts of his body. The species included a spoonbill, little terns, and a Senegal tickney [*sic*]'. 'Body Language Gives Bird Smuggler away', *Times of Malta*, 22 February 2005.
4. Declined, but certainly not disappeared. In August 2019, for example, hundreds of exotic birds that were waiting to be mounted were discovered in a police raid. Most had obviously been smuggled from abroad and it seems that foreign-sourced birds have to some extent replaced locally caught ones.
5. In the spring of 2015, a hunter was booked for shooting a cuckoo (a protected species). In the media fracas that followed, he gave an interview in which he said he had mistaken the bird for a turtle dove, especially since a sparrow had sounded the alarm call. His defence was that the alarm call had put him on edge and he was therefore more likely to make a mistake. To nonhunters, of course, it was a flaccid excuse.
6. 'Robin Bryans: Prolific Travel Writer with a Crisp, Anecdotal Style', obituary by Paul Clements, *The Guardian*, 23 August 2005.
7. Ecofeminism is defined by Littlefield as 'a feminist philosophy that relates oppression of nature with oppression of women, and highlights the role of men and of hegemonic masculinity it its critical discourse' (2010: 98).

CHAPTER 3

The Rising Tide of Conservation

Bird migration is implicitly connective. It is about systems of animal life that traverse continents and implicate expansive and sometimes disparate spaces in shared ecological stories. It follows that the conservation of migratory animals (birds in this case) is imagined and practised in ways that cannot be contained within local or national contexts. At the same time, conservation programmes, and especially environmental legislation and its enforcement, are often embedded within these very contexts and their historically and culturally specific power dynamics.

In this chapter I shall explore some of the key intersections between conservation and hunting in Malta today. I first trace the origins and rise of ENGOs, in particular those that have to do with the study and conservation of birds; the ways in which ENGOs embedded themselves in discourses and cartographies of progress and privileged knowledge and practices are emphasized. I then move on to look at how, as a result of the work of ENGOs, hunting was sectioned as a practice and hunters were ascribed a morality within a Manichean universe. In the third section, I discuss the politics of hunting and conservation, and the national and supranational structures of power they invoke. Finally, I take up the case study of a 2015 national referendum on spring hunting to bring the many strands of the chapter together.

Histories, Geographies, Lineages

In her seminal work on conservation in the rainforests of Indonesia, Tsing identifies what she calls a 'capital-N Nature' – a 'singular global system uniting all life' (2005: 91) – as the 'touchstone of biodiversity discourse' and a 'resource for environmental politics' (2005: 95). The defining characteristic of capital-N Nature (and the one that lends it its potency) is universality – put simply, it allows the biological and ecological sciences, as well as conservation projects, to locate themselves within a universalizing schema of global biodiversity and its protection. Of course, the idea of a universal Nature did not just come about spontaneously. Rather, it had to be made over the course of centuries, and originally in association with ideas about the universality of God, Themself imagined as the singular, universal author of the 'Book of Nature'. In Tsing's words: 'to "think globally" is no easy task. To recognize the globe as the relevant unit for our imaginations requires work. Moreover, establishing Nature has never been simple' (2005: 88–89). One might cite the example of cabinets of curiosity and collections in the seventeenth and eighteenth centuries to understand the ways in which art, God, the Book of Nature, and animal and plant species came to be imagined as interrelated and overlapping universals (see, for instance, MacGregor 2007; van de Roemer 2018). Applying Tsing's thinking, these cabinets were one way in which disparate particular facts were brought together in a space of compatibility, which in turn enabled generalization to the universal. They showed how 'tentative and contingent collaborations among disparate knowledge seekers and their disparate forms of knowledge can turn incompatible facts and observations into compatible ones' (Tsing 2005: 89).

Tsing's argument has been taken up, and in some cases developed, by a number of scholars. Keller (2015), for example, uses it to discuss connections between twinned conservation projects in Switzerland and Madagascar. In her work on conservation in Sardinia, Heatherington borrows on Australian aboriginal beliefs to posit universal (and universalizing) 'global dreamtimes of environmentalism', which she defines as 'a supple dimension of cultural imagination which overlays regional geographies with stories evoking the presence of a universal, sacred, transcendent, timeless, and global Nature – a Nature now increasingly at risk, apparently demanding new forms of reverence' (2010: 23). Crucially, Heatherington goes on to expose these dreamtimes, and the models of environmental governance they spawn, as a form of global power and hegemony, in this sense a hegemony that is 'produced in the unreflective appeal to "the environment" as a universal value, and in the unstable equation of indigeneity with primitive nature' (2010: 38). Power, then, is a key variable in this scheme. In fact, one of the strengths of Tsing's model is that it signals alternatives to reductive 'clash of cultures' ideas. Her antidote is what she calls 'friction' – the 'awkward, unequal, unstable, and creative qualities of interconnections across difference' (2005: 4) that continually coproduce cultures. Thus, for example, the culture of 'nature loving' in Indonesia lies at the 'confluence of a number of cultural lineages that, taken together, give popular force to both its cosmopolitan yearnings and its locally distinctive features' (2005: 124).

In what follows, I bring the notions of capital-N Nature, collaborations that bring disparate facts together, environmentalism as a form of global power and hegemony, and cultural lineages, to an understanding of the relations between ENGOs and hunters in Malta. I argue that, since their inception, and originally through their proximity to British organizations, Maltese ENGOs were grafted onto a cultural lineage that enabled them to position themselves as the local stewards of Nature – in the case of bird protectionists, of Nature as represented by migrant birds. They have also systematically drawn upon their bearings in global environmentalism – upon their dreamtimes, so to speak – to construct a cast of local laggards (of whom hunters are the paragon) guilty of a brutish incomprehension of universal environmentalist values. These bearings continue to be relevant, for example, to our understanding of the different ways in which ENGOs and the hunting lobby engage with the EU.

Although BirdLife Malta is the organization that concerns hunters directly, it would be a mistake to consider it in isolation. Rather, it forms part of a much broader environmentalist movement that originated in the 1960s and that has since gathered considerable social, cultural and political momentum. An early significant moment came in 1962, when a small group of people, some of whom were also involved that same year in the founding of what eventually became BirdLife Malta, set up the Natural History Society of Malta (NHSM). Tellingly in light of the cultural lineages argument, the founding meeting was held at the British Council premises in Valletta. The Maltese rock-centaury, an endemic species of plant that was eventually declared Malta's national plant in 1973, was chosen as the NHSM's emblem. The society's early work consisted mainly of talks, exhibitions, field outings and participation in radio and television programmes. There were also a number of regular publications, mostly of a scientific bent. In 1979, it was renamed the Society for the Study and Conservation of Nature (SSCN), partly due to a 1978 law that prohibited the nongovernmental official use of the word 'Malta', but also in order to better reflect its twin aims. Initially the SSCN was a fairly minor player that tended to focus on specific causes, such as the protection of the rare freshwater crab and the French daffodil. Successive campaigns meant that these and other species of plants and animals became iconic as the local incarnations of a global narrative of conservation. Subsequent work included technical reports on sites of potential protection; very often these reports, as well as other work, were carried out jointly by a number of ENGOs. The SSCN became Nature Trust (Malta) in 1999, and in 2017 it was renamed Nature Trust-FEE Malta as the Malta coordinator of the international ENGO Foundation for Environmental Education (FEE). Among its many international connections, Nature

Trust-FEE Malta is a 'privileged partner' of the World Wildlife Fund (WWF).

Due in part to a building spree that took off in the 1960s and to date shows no signs of slowing down, swathes of countryside were swallowed up under housing, industrial, commercial and infrastructural development, to the extent that many villages merged into a more or less continuous conurbation that covers a substantial chunk of the eastern half of Malta. Substantial lengths of the coast too were given over to tourism and recreational development. There was a growing sense that the countryside and its contents were under threat, which in turn converged with and was nourished by the rise of global environmentalist groups and movements that followed the publication of Rachel Carson's *Silent Spring* in 1962. In Malta, ENGOs multiplied and amassed considerable clout, particularly from the mid-1980s. When the SSCN changed its name to Nature Trust (Malta) in 1999, it was because of a merger with three other organizations: Arbor, founded in 1989, Verde, founded in 1997, and the Marine Life Care Group. These were among the many ENGOs active at the time. For instance, Żgħażagħ għall-Ambjent ('Youth for the Environment') was formed as an umbrella organization for activists in the mid-1980s. It eventually became the Moviment għall-Ambjent ('Movement for the Environment') and the stock for two further organizations: Friends of the Earth (Malta), which is part of Friends of the Earth International; and a political party, Alternattiva Demokratika ('Democratic Alternative'), founded in 1989 and later a member of the European Green Party. In 2006, a further ENGO called Flimkien Għal Ambjent Aħjar ('Together for a Better Environment') was set up. There have been one-off issue-specific environmentalist coalitions, notably the Front Kontra l-Golf Kors ('Front Against the Golf Course') set up in 2004 to oppose the building of a golf course on arable land, and the Front Ħarsien ODZ ('Front for the Protection of ODZ' – ODZ means greenbelt land that is classified as being outside the development zone) formed in 2015. In addition, formal groups such as the Ramblers' Association of Malta and the Bicycle Advocacy Group often effectively function as ENGOs. It is beyond the scope of the present work to present a detailed history and analysis of these many groups. The point is that they represent a cross-cutting – in terms of aims, activism practices and especially human resources (many individuals are active in more than one organization) – matrix of environmentalist thought and action in contemporary Malta. They are popularly and generically called *ambjentalisti* ('environmentalists') and are a major force for hunters, among others, to contend with. Crucially, and in spite of their complex genealogy, they are all offshoots of a common cultural lineage.

In the context of this book, BirdLife Malta is by far the most relevant ENGO, in that it introduced, formalized and stewarded the systematic study and conservation of birds, as well as the requisite opposition to hunting. There had been, to be sure, earlier sporadic voices in that direction – in 1908, for example, there was a suggestion to set up a society for the protection of birds.[1] This had to wait until 1961, when an Oxfordshire woman called Elizabeth Coxon visited an expatriate British friend living in Gozo and was introduced to, among other people, a local historian at a village cultural centre. It was at that meeting that the subject of a society for the protection of birds was first brought up. Upon her return to England, Coxon found out that the Royal Society for the Protection of Birds (RSPB) already had one Maltese person on its list of members; through her lobbying, the RSPB encouraged him to go ahead with the plan. A meeting was held in Malta on 25 January 1962 and the Malta Ornithological Society (MOS) was officially set up; later that year, a Gozo branch was added. The first seven members of the MOS included Guido Lanfranco, a science teacher who had published (and went on to publish) solid and empirically researched books on the flora and fauna of Malta. The other members were well-educated urbanites with interests in art, history and natural history.

Coxon visited Malta again three years later to propose the setting up of a bird-ringing scheme.[2] This time she drew on her connections at the Banbury Ornithological Society and harnessed the approval and support of the Ringing and Migration section of the British Trust for Ornithology (BTO), which sent British ringers to Malta to train locals and set up a ringing scheme. The first bird, a migratory icterine warbler, was trapped and ringed in Gozo in 1965. Unusually for such a tightly regulated practice, the BTO eventually issued ringing licences to MOS-trained ringers and allowed them to use BTO rings (see Sultana and Borg 2015).

The umbilical link between the early MOS and prestigious British institutions like the RSPB and the BTO was to prove extremely consequential for at least two reasons. First, by direct association with an 'advanced' industrial society that was seen by many as the apex of progress (Malta was still a Crown Colony in 1962), it baptized the study and conservation of birds in Malta as a forward-looking practice. Most of the books, newsletters and other materials published by the MOS were in English, the 'high' language of Malta since the 1930s (see Brincat 2011). Since its inception, the MOS was therefore associated with writing, education and progressive understandings and appropriations of nature. This also meant that the organization could build a strong presence in the English-language press (notably in the *Times of Malta*), with all the class connotations that came with this. All of this was very significant, because it played an important part in constructing, from the 1960s onwards, hunting and trapping as retrograde and anachronistic practices that were dissonant with modern, Western and enlightened ways of appropriating nature.

Second, the early association with the RSPB and the BTO effectively located the MOS within an international cartography of ornithology and conservation. The name of the organization is significant in this respect. In 1992, the global ENGO BirdLife International was set up to replace the International Council for Bird Preservation (ICBP). In 1995, the MOS changed its name to 'BirdLife Malta MOS' to reflect its partnership with BirdLife International; in 1996, 'MOS' was dropped altogether and the local ENGO became 'BirdLife Malta'. The new name simultaneously indigenizes a global organization and globalizes an indigenous one. Although the links with British institutions remained strong, in time the MOS also cultivated close collaborations with ENGOs such as the Deutscher Bund für Vogelschutz (DBV) in Germany and the Lega Italiana Protezione Uccelli (LIPU) in Italy. This cartography is significant in a number of ways. Conceptually, it involves a global and canonical set of ideas about species conservation, protected areas and reserves, the threats posed by hunting and so on. In practice, it is enacted in the form of conferences, visits, youth camps, circulation of published material and funding for campaigns. Some of the more prominent people in BirdLife Malta, and especially those who have carried out ornithological research, have multicountry connections of friends and acquaintances developed over the course of years of travel and correspondence. Their biographies are characterized by what Salazar (2018) calls 'momentous mobilities'. The model works equally well for BirdLife Malta collectively. At the time of writing, it describes its 'environmental network' as being made up of three types of organizations: first, ENGOs – BirdLife International, the RSPB, the Sociedade Portuguesa para o Estudo das Aves (SPEA) in Portugal, the Nature and Biodiversity Conservation Union (NABU) in Germany and the League Against Cruel Sports in Britain; second, EU programmes – Life, Erasmus+ and Natura 2000; and, third, two Government of Malta entities – the Ministry for Education and Employment, and the Ministry for Sustainable Development, the Environment and Climate Change.

BirdLife Malta's long-term embeddedness in global and multicountry conservation networks is evident in other ways that are equally relevant in the context of this work. First, many of the organization's activities have always had a non-Maltese presence in the form of funding, expertise or some other kind of support. This tendency gained considerable traction when the organization became increasingly professionalized and started employing full-time and part-time staff in the 1990s. The people employed were drawn partly from BirdLife Malta's domestic pool of members and associates, but they also included many non-Maltese who got the job on the merits of their background in environmental activism or ornithology elsewhere. At one point, the administrative-strategic and the ornithological sections were run by a Turkish ex-Greenpeace activist (as Executive Director) and a British professional ornithologist (as Conservation Manager). Second, BirdLife Malta's connections and activism routes were a major force that set the tone for the coverage of hunting in Malta in the international press. A cursory online search using the keywords 'BBC', 'hunting' and 'Malta', for example, produces scores of results. Hunting in Malta is a topic that has generated a mini-industry of international press reports and commentary. The point is that BirdLife Malta put its cartography to good use and successfully positioned Malta as a 'black spot' for migrating birds and a site of urgent concern for international conservation, especially since the birds killed or trapped were often the same kinds that BBC audiences and readers of British or German newspapers were familiar with in their gardens and countryside.

There is a third and closely related way in which BirdLife Malta's long-term embeddedness in global and multicountry conservation networks matters. Over the years, a stream of high-profile visitors and observers have had their say on hunting in Malta. In the spring of 2014, for example, they included two well-known British faces: ornithologist, comedian and television presenter Bill Oddie and Queen guitarist Brian May. Oddie spent a few days in Malta in April and joined local birdwatchers and conservationists in their anti-hunting crusade. On his part, May urged his audience at a concert held in the capital to take a stand against spring hunting (his visit coincided with the campaign for the national referendum on spring hunting). He told a crowd of rockers that 'real men' were not cruel to wildlife. The following spring, the star visitor was British naturalist, television presenter and author Chris Packham.

The fourth way in which the spatial promiscuity of BirdLife Malta has proved relevant concerns CABS, Springwatch and the other surveillance initiatives that in recent years have significantly altered the relationship between hunters and the landscape. They are described in detail elsewhere in this volume; in the context of this section, the point is that all of these initiatives involve activists from various countries. In other words, the work of BirdLife Malta is premised on mobilities.

To revisit Tsing's point on the active manufacture of a universal capital-N Nature, migrating birds lend themselves particularly well to this. Classification and naming serve up a useful illustration of some of the processes involved. As early as the nineteenth century, the ornithological literature encountered the birds of Malta as part of two larger wholes: birds as a biological class and a universal nature more broadly. The kinds of birds that bred in or migrated over Malta were thus classified and named according to the taxonomic knowledge of the time, which was itself located within a schema governed by Linnaean classification and binomial nomenclature. This, however, was not necessarily how birds were classified by hunters. According to (often fuzzy and idiosyncratic) indigenous classifications, a number of separate species might be classified under a single rubric underwritten by some kind of perceived morphological or behavioural similarity. Thus, for example, many hunters referred to small passerines they had no particular interest in as *tal-maltemp* (lit. 'of storms', probably referring to the kind of weather that made their appearance in Malta more likely). The term is still in fairly common use among hunters today and few draw distinctions between the many different species of, say, warblers. At first glance, therefore, there appears to be a clear disjuncture (friction) between global-ornithological and indigenous systems of classification.

Yet this is a facile reading. First, ornithology in Malta has sought to indigenize its knowledge by digging out and attaching a Maltese name to every individual species. In the many cases where such names could not be found, they were invented. The process of invention is still going on and is evident in cases of newly recorded species. Thus, for example, when BirdLife Malta bird-ringers trapped Malta's first Pallas's leaf warbler in 1987, they formally christened it 'Vjolin ta' Pallas' (*vjolin* being the generic Maltese name for leaf warblers, used in the ornithological literature, but never in everyday birdwatching circles and certainly not by hunters; 'Pallas' is a direct loan from the English name). Second, and especially for birds of a certain size that are deemed to be desirable taxidermy trophies, hunters themselves have increasingly and independently acquainted themselves with the classification and naming canons of ornithology. Hunters almost always use the English names found in international guide books rather than the Maltese ones given in ornithological accounts of the birds of Malta. This, then, is another instance of the simultaneous globalization of the indigenous and indigenization of the global.

That said, the cultural lineages of bird protectionists and those of hunters could not be more disparate and friction-prone. The rising tide of environmentalism in Malta was the main reason why, in 1973, hunters and trappers set up the Għaqda Nazzjonali Kaċċaturi u Nassaba (National Association of Hunters and Trappers). Bird protection activism had had a head start of eleven years, and it was increasingly clear that the laws on hunting and trapping were about to become much more restrictive. At a big public protest held in 1977, members of the Association were told that the changes to the laws had been shelved (Azzopardi 1985). They were – but only for three years, because in 1980 comprehensive legislation was introduced that established closed seasons and made it illegal to shoot or trap most kinds of birds (prior to 1980, only twenty-two species had been protected). In 1982, the association was revamped and became the Għaqda Kaċċaturi u Nassaba (Association of Hunters and Trappers); in 1984, its name was changed to Għaqda Kaċċaturi Nassaba Konservazzjonisti (Association of Hunters, Trappers and Conservationists) and, a few years later, to Federazzjoni Kaċċaturi Nassaba Konservazzjonisti (FKNK). The FKNK is a member of FACE (the European Federation for Hunting and Conservation established in 1977) and thus to some extent is also aligned with interests that go beyond Malta. There are, however, two key differences. The first is one of direction: while BirdLife Malta can claim direct descent from global ornithology and environmentalism, the relationship between the FKNK and FACE is one of affiliation in the opposite direction, that is, a homegrown organization that eventually affiliated itself with a broader one. Second, because it represents highly divergent hunting traditions, it is much harder for FACE to claim a universalizing project or for the FKNK to claim to be part of one. Simply put, while it is relatively easy to claim continuities for the observation and conservation of migratory birds, it is more difficult to subsume under a single set of ideas practices as different as, say, hunting migratory birds in Malta and stalking deer on an estate in Scotland.

These divergent cultural lineages, and the fact that BirdLife Malta cannot neatly be compartmentalized as a domestic ENGO, are among the most hotly contested issues with hunters. The FKNK, and hunters and trappers popularly, repeatedly point out that the bird conservation lobby is overrun by *barranin* (foreigners). As they see and represent it (especially in the media), this characteristic fails the test on at least three counts. First, the notion of *indħil barrani* (foreign interference) has deep cultural roots in Malta. It was even formalized at law in the Foreign Interference Act, which was enacted to 'regulate the limitations on the political activities of aliens'.[3] More popularly, the notion is often invoked in political discourse and rhetoric as an affront to national sovereignty and autonomy. In the case at hand, BirdLife Malta is seen as doubly guilty since it does not merely passively accept *indħil barrani*, but rather actively invites and courts it. The hunting lobby seeks to delegitimize the discourses and actions of the organization by exposing them as a foreign intrusion. Second, BirdLife Malta is accused by hunters of damaging Malta's reputation internationally (*iħammġu isem Malta*, lit. 'they sully the good name of Malta'). This damage supposedly shames the country and harms its tourist industry, among other effects, and in theory comes with economic consequences. There is a fascinating twist here, because the bird protection lobby often accuses hunters of doing exactly the same thing, in that indiscriminate hunting, and the killing of 'European' birds, is a national embarrassment that gives Malta a bad name. Third, the interfering *barranin* are accused of systematic hypocrisy – they turn a blind eye to bird killing in their own countries, even as they write about Malta as a bird conservation disaster.

The accusation of hypocrisy can go further. In my activist days, I once told off a hunter who was shooting swallows. For some reason, probably because I spoke English and was with a fair-complexioned person, he thought I was British. It was the time of the invasion of Iraq and his retort was: 'But you kill people!' More commonly, *barranin* have often been accused by hunters of protecting birds even as they condone the killing of 'babies' (abortion is illegal in Malta). Given this context, it is not surprising that the non-Maltese people who do 'interfere' are often attacked, in the press and elsewhere. Bill Oddie's 2014 visit, for example, prompted the FKNK to issue a press release calling him a 'madman and BBC renegade' (the former referred to his well-known bipolar condition). As for Brian May, the requisite press release called him a 'hypocrite' for having once allowed hunters to shoot 'Bambi' (deer) on his estate. Nor were hunters amused by his comment that 'real men' do not kill birds. They replied in kind by fishing out a music video from his Queen days ('I Want to Break Free') in which he wore hair rollers and a dress.

Never the Twain Shall Meet

In the course of my teaching at university, I sometimes talk about hunting. On occasion, a student will come up to me after a lecture to tell me that their father is a hunter, but that they do not like to say so in front of other students. Shyness has nothing to do with it. Rather, the reason is that hunting in Malta today carries a rather heavy baggage in certain circles and one that is often at odds with contemporary values and aspirations. In this section I shall explore how, over the course of a few decades, hunting was sectioned and corralled as a distinct practice and ascribed a number of moral and social attributes. In particular, I foreground the reductive dualism that characterizes understandings of hunting and conservation on either side.

Just as the *caganer*, a figure of a defecating man, is a standard humorous fixture of nativity scenes in Catalan culture, the *kaċċatur* was traditionally the standard equivalent in nativity scenes in Malta – folkloristic trivia perhaps, but telling in the present context. Until the late twentieth century, hunting was not considered a particularly specialized or differentiated practice; rather, it simply inhabited society and the landscape as one of a cast of characters. As early as the mid-nineteenth century (see Cassar 2018), guns were in common circulation and most men especially in rural areas hunted more or less regularly in a manner that was tied in with everyday routines. The practice was not assigned a specific morality, nor was it ritualized in any significant way. With the exception of the gentry, who to some extent mimicked the shooting etiquette of British elites, men hunted in their everyday clothes (as opposed to today's camouflage). Old photographs of Maltese villages regularly turn up images of men with shotguns slung over their backs, on the way to or coming from hunting grounds that were equally undifferentiated and often in close proximity to built-up areas.

Partly as a result of the work of ENGOs, all of that changed in the last decades of the twentieth century. Increasingly, *kaċċaturi* and *nassaba* came to be seen as a distinct type with equally distinct attributes. Three in particular are worth discussing: class, morality and anachronism. It is well known that class associations and class politics characterize hunting and conservation discourses and action in many contexts (see Cartmill (1993) for an extended discussion). Thus, for example, even if the debate over hunting with dogs in Britain in the late 1990s to the early 2000s largely centred around arguments of animal welfare, there was a strong undercurrent among those who upheld the ban that hunting was essentially the preserve of 'toffs' who used it to parade and uphold their class status. Many of the same arguments are made by opponents of grouse shooting today: 'Driven grouse shooting involves a line of relatively poor people, the beaters, walking across a stretch of moorland with flags and whistles and, by so doing, pushing the Red Grouse that live there towards a line of relatively rich people' (Avery 2015: 49).

Arguments from class are equally prevalent in Malta, except they operate in the opposite direction. For various reasons, urban elites and the landowning gentry largely gave up hunting altogether in the last few decades of the twentieth century. With some exceptions that do nothing to the rule, hunters today tend to come from rural and/or working-class social backgrounds. Most of my informants were tradesmen or low-level employees by occupation and very few had a postsecondary or higher level of education. Still, and especially in the absence of statistically representative quantitative data, socioeconomic profiles are not the point here. I am more interested in how class tropes have been used to categorize hunters in environmentalist discourses. It is significant, for example, that hunting has generally got a bad press in the English-language media. In middle-class social circles, hunting is typically seen as an uncouth and plebeian practice, and hunters as uneducated people who at best do not know better. I have often heard people describe hunters as *slavaġ* ('savages'). The practice is also thought to be antithetical to social aspiration and progress, sometimes by hunters themselves.

A second way in which hunting is sectioned by environmentalists has to do with morality. Key to this is animal welfare. In principle, BirdLife Malta is opposed to hunting on the grounds of conservation of species and habitats rather than a concern for the welfare of individual birds. In practice, however, activists are often motivated by empathy for hunted birds. The activists I worked with had strong feelings about what they described as the suffering caused by hunters. As they saw it, it was entirely gratuitous: even if hunted birds were consumed, humans no longer had any real need to hunt in order to procure meat. The fact that hunting in Malta targets migrant birds adds to the poignancy. The image of a tired bird that crosses sea and desert against the odds, only to be shot for pleasure by a Maltese hunter, is a key trope of bird protectionist discourses, as is that of a decoy bird locked inside a cramped cage that is used by trappers to deceive more of its kind into terminating their own migratory journeys. In other words, if migrant journeys invite projection, so do interrupted ones.

Significantly, these feelings and discourses readily overspill the boundaries of ENGOs. Thus, there are groups of animal lovers in Malta who are not necessarily associated with BirdLife Malta – indeed, they may even resent the organization's ideas on roaming pet cats or feral ducks, for example – but who share its strong feelings on the suffering caused by hunting. A detailed discussion is beyond the scope of the present work, but suffice it to say that hunting is considered by many people as fundamentally immoral on account of the cruelty it involves. What this means is that, in different ways and to different extents, swathes of Maltese society oppose hunting in principle, not least since, as Barca et al. (2016) demonstrate in the Italian context, arguments against hunting from an animal welfare perspective effectively collapse the distinction, so crucial to hunters' own discourses and representations, between legal and illegal ('poaching') practices.

However, the immorality and cruelty attributed to hunting does not stop there. Certainly in environmentalist circles, and to some extent popularly, hunters are seen as viscerally prone to violence and lawlessness. As mentioned earlier, the image of a gun-wielding, cartridge-belt-festooned, hairy, loud man in an undervest is clearly a caricature, but one that has regularly made its way into newspaper cartoons and other popular representations, and carries considerable weight. There are many videos on the internet of hunters hurling abuse, and sometimes blows, at activists, and in some cases at members of the public who knowingly or not trespass on their land or otherwise get in their way. There have been incidents in which press photographers were attacked at hunters' protest marches or birdwatchers' cars were vandalized. On one occasion, cars belonging to bird-ringers were set on fire and destroyed at a bird sanctuary. The point is not that these things happened, or whether or not all hunters are violent, but rather that these incidents are generally perceived to be emblematic of a type that is implicitly and generally violent. Further, as activists and substantial sections of the population see it, such a lawless type can never be trusted to truthfully report the number of birds shot, for example, or to refrain from shooting at protected birds. Notions like 'self-regulation', which are sometimes put forward by hunters and hunting organizations as an alternative to heavy-handed and intrusive law enforcement, are widely perceived and represented as a contradiction in terms. So entrenched, essentialist and dualistic is the model that hunters who display some kind of law-abiding behaviour are thought to be out of character and probably adopting a public face to cover a deeper and uglier reality.

The third characteristic that is attributed to hunting is that it is not of its time. Elsewhere in this volume, I discuss the notion of subalternity in the context of Mediterranean history. Tangibly, and popularly, this often translates into a discourse in which hunting is an anachronism, an unwelcome survival that does not belong in present-day progressive Malta. ENGOs routinely portray hunting as a retrograde relationship with birds and nature that is out of touch with modern practices like birdwatching, photography and conservation generally. These modern practices are thought to come from a progressive and enlightened north – as opposed to hunting, which survives in a backward south (Mediterranean). In this sense, it is significant that hunters in Malta are men; to opponents, this is a predictable characteristic that confirms that hunting belongs to a past that was also tainted by gender inequality.

Bird conservation in Malta has generally been couched in terms of progress. In his Foreword to a book on the birds of Malta published in 1976, then-Prime Minister Dom Mintoff looked forward to a 'new age' in which 'the majority of the Maltese people discard their obscurantist tradition and embrace new ways of manifesting their affection' (Bannerman and Vella-Gaffiero 1976: v). Within this value system, hunting is fundamentally and irredeemably incompatible with forward-looking and positive valuations of birds specifically, and nature and the environment generally. As Barca et al. (2016: 191) put it:

> Much of the discourse about migratory bird protection that comes from
> conservation organizations assumes or suggests that hunters do not value
> the environment, do not value conservation, and have hunting practices

that are expressions of negative valuations of (e.g. contempt for, lack of respect for) the environment, animals, and conservation. This framing implies that only one set of practices (here, bird conservation practices) lead to positive valuations of the environment, birds, and their conservation. Conservation organizations' discourses thus present a tacit hypothesis that value alignment (being pro-conservation) requires changes in practice, in this case abandoning hunting practices in favor of bird protectionist practices.

This is why, when the hunters' association added 'conservationists' to its official name, the move was interpreted by many as both risible and cynical. As many see it, hunting and conservation are two value systems that can never meet – the only way in which hunters can become conservationists is for them to stop hunting. These dualistic attributions clearly intersect, and they also structure the thought and work of bird protection ENGOs and a part of the public sphere more broadly. Thus, someone might write a letter to a newspaper editor asking for better enforcement of the hunting laws, in the process reminding readers that hunters are Mediterranean men prone to violence and lawlessness who are in need of a proper education in modern forms of appropriation of nature that include a concern for wildlife. Press releases about hunters planting trees or otherwise 'doing their bit' for nature are often met with an online barrage of sarcasm, especially in the English-language press.

This does not mean that hunters themselves passively accept these attributes; on the contrary, they actively and vigorously oppose them, in at least two ways. The first is through the production of counternarratives. For example, in August 2016 a homemade video surfaced on the internet of a group of boaters rescuing a sea turtle that had become entangled in a length of fishing line. As one of the men carefully cut the line off the animal, another was heard repeating *'ara kemm huma qalbhom tajba l-kaċċaturi!'* ('see, that's how kind-hearted hunters really are!'). The video, which 'went viral' and even made it on to *Sky News*, soon earned itself a title: 'Hunter Saves Suffocating Turtle in Delimara'. The following day, the FKNK issued a beaming press release that identified the boater as a hunter and one of its members. It added that an internal appeal had been made that urged members to monitor a beach in the north of Malta where a turtle had nested a few days before and that the FKNK was 'a firm believer that biodiversity's conservation aspect should always be safeguarded nationwide'.[4] However, counternarratives can in turn be countered and the story did not end there. As the video did the online rounds, someone pointed out that it also showed that the rescuer had discarded the fishing line back into the sea after he cut it off the turtle. More damningly, a turtle with fishing-line cut marks and damage to one fin had been picked up in the area on the same day and taken to a rehab centre; that turtle looked suspiciously like the one in the video.

My hunter informants consistently emphasized that they were people who loved nature and animals (not surprisingly, dogs were often singled out), and who wanted nothing better than to be left in peace. They often drew comparisons with recreational fishing, which also involved killing wild animals, to make the point that there was nothing about hunting in particular that made it cruel or immoral. Formal and informal self-representations by hunters centre on the practice as essentially about bringing men and families together in a healthy and wholesome environment that in turn fosters a broader individual and social wellbeing. '*Aħjar delizzju milli vizzju*' ('better a pastime than a [bad] habit') is a popular rhyming slogan at hunting demonstrations, and my informants invariably told me that hunting was a means by which young men stayed away from *vizzji koroħ* (bad habits) and, in particular, drug use. As one woman whose husband and two sons hunt put it to me: 'My sons never stay out late at night, because they want to be able to get up early in the morning . . . I'm secure in the knowledge that they're out hunting with their father and uncles, rather than heaven-knows-where drinking or keeping bad company.' Hunting, then, is thought to be and is represented by hunters as conducive to moral and social order. Nor is it one that is restricted to a specific class. Indeed, hunters are keen to purge their public image of its associations with uneducated and working-class categories of society. During my fieldwork, I was told about lawyers and doctors who were avid hunters and about university graduates who managed companies, but found the time to hunt. Throughout, in both formal and informal discourse and representations, hunters resist the sectioning and allocation of essentialist attributes by ENGOs and insist that they rightfully belong in society as an undifferentiated group of people who happen to hunt. In these discourses, hunting is often projected onto a horizontal plane of value and morality where it cohabits with a number of other (legitimate) pastimes and sports.

For reasons that will become clear later on in this chapter, the contestation by hunters of a Manichean value system that allocates them negative attributes and distances them from conservation has greatly increased in recent years. Hunting in Malta, one might say, has experienced a degree of gentrification. Over the last couple of decades, and especially in the years following Malta's accession as a member of the EU, hunting discourses and practices have displayed a consistent attempt to rehabilitate the practice into the mainstream. Many of my informants described to me how, far from being violent lawbreakers who shot at protected birds and threatened anyone who trespassed on their land, they were in fact inclined to enjoy observing migrating protected birds and to be friendly to the people with whom they shared the countryside. I was told stories of ramblers, tourists and even birdwatchers who had been invited to share food and coffee. Increasingly, hunters take part in public clean-ups in which litter and junk are removed from the countryside in choreographed and publicized displays of civil responsibility. In at least one way, the process of gentrification has been formalized. In 1996, a small group of hunters set up an association known as Kaċċaturi San Ubertu (St Hubert Hunters, KSU). The prime mover was a hunter and the author of the 1985 *The Maltese Shooter's Handbook* (Azzopardi 1985). The idea was to bring together a core of people motivated by high ethical standards and respect for the law. The code of conduct of the KSU includes: strict adherence to the hunting laws and a duty to serve as an example to other hunters; the use of double-barrel as opposed to semi-automatic shotguns; the conservation of hunting territories and bird habitats; the use of naturally occurring materials in the building of hunting hides; and 'proper gentlemanly conduct'. The KSU, whose stock has risen in recent years, has also sought to introduce an element of ritual into hunting. Hunters who are members of the KSU tend to wear 'sporting' clothes in the field, for example, and they often gather for communal game roasts. They also make it a point to hear Mass on 3 November, the feast of St Hubert. The KSU, then, aligns itself with and represents the model of the 'gentleman hunter' (see Cartmill 1993).

As mentioned in passing earlier, the twin processes of corralling and negative attributions were the result of years of work by ENGOs that often incorporated older renditions of subalternity. In particular, two areas of activism are worth briefly discussing. (A third, the production of scientific knowledge and numbers, is dealt with in detail in Chapter 6.) The first is the production of images, perhaps the most powerful of which have been those of injured or dead birds. Even as large or colourful birds are ('were', increasingly) desirable to hunters as trophies, photographs that show them bloodied and shot-shattered are desirable to BirdLife Malta as part of its activism. Dead or injured birds that are found by birdwatchers in the field or passed on by members of the public are systematically photographed to this end; there have also been photographs of groups of BirdLife Malta activists standing around small piles of dead birds or each holding an injured one. *Malta – Massacre on Migration*, a 2014 documentary by BBC presenter Chris Packham, includes several sequences of dead or injured birds filmed where they were found or at a veterinary clinic.

Hunters react to these images in two ways: first, and usually privately, they describe them as a mawkish and sensationalist ploy by BirdLife Malta to manipulate public emotion; and, second, they condemn them as fake. For example, in December 2016, BirdLife Malta used a photograph of a golden plover in a small cage to make a point about trapping. The following day, the FKNK issued a strongly worded press release that pointed out that plovers were normally kept in much bigger cages and that no trapper would ever 'allow such cruelty'. The ENGO was accused of deception and, by implication, of cruelty to animals in the making of the image. The FKNK's statement went on to say that BirdLife Malta was 'at the end of its line' in its efforts to abolish trapping and called on the authorities to take action against the organization.[5] My informants often told me that they rarely if ever came across injured birds in the field and that they found it odd that other people seemed to do so regularly. They told me that they could tell, just by looking at the photographs, that the dead birds had been defrosted for the occasion; they also made frequent reference to the 'BirdLife freezer' in which dead birds were kept indefinitely, to be wheeled out at added value at the right time. The argument is that activists recycle the few birds they have stowed away over and over again, usually as the hunting season approaches, for reasons of publicity. The FKNK has even produced this story formally in press releases. The argument is of course dismissed by BirdLife Malta as fanciful denial. The point is that the images, which are powerful and tend to resonate with the public, find themselves embedded in a fabric of contested credibility and morality.

The second important area of activism is education. It is perhaps telling that some of BirdLife Malta's most active and prominent activists have been teachers. The organization has focused a great deal of its energies on schools, the guiding principle being that it is only education that can effect a long-term cultural change towards the 'right' forms of appreciation and appropriation of birds and nature. While practising hunters and trappers are thought to be too set in their ways to educate (for them, the only effective remedies are laws and their enforcement), children are seen as an opportunity to mould minds and hearts according to universal and progressive principles of conservation. It would require a separate book to detail the various initiatives by BirdLife Malta in this field throughout the years. They have included a vast number of booklets, leaflets, stickers, posters, field visits, school nature reserve competitions, quizzes and so on.[6] In contrast to BirdLife Malta's ornithological and (to a lesser extent) campaigning publications, its educational materials tend to be in Maltese. One campaign in particular ran for several years and was aimed at eradicating the practice, ubiquitous among boys into the late 1980s, of robin trapping using cage-traps and live decoys. It is nowadays extremely rare to come across, and BirdLife Malta has unofficially declared victory and discontinued the campaign.

As a result of the many years of focused educational campaigning, BirdLife Malta enjoys a very strong presence in schools and even employs full-time staff to oversee the various initiatives. They include Dinja Waħda ('One World'), described by the ENGO as its 'major educational initiative in its commitment to protect wildlife and its habitats [and that] taps young people's innate fascination with nature and seeks to develop it into a sense of responsibility towards the natural world'.[7] The project involves giving all primary school teachers an 'Action Guide' and a set of educational posters; teachers are also encouraged to take pupils on outings to nature reserves and in particular to Għadira and Simar (see Chapter 5). In addition to Dinja Waħda, BirdLife Malta also runs, at the time of writing, a project called 'Lifelong Learning through Nature'. This project, which involves the collaborative partnership of the Ministry of Education and Employment, the RSPB, Birdwatch Ireland and the Polish Society for the Protection of Birds, is funded by the European Commission and is 'designed to develop an environmental and sustainability education programme which engages young people aged 5–21 in Malta, through formal education, vocational training courses, non-formal and informal education'.[8]

BirdLife Malta's educational efforts, and especially its presence in schools, have long been a bone of contention with the FKNK formally and with hunters in general informally. The ENGO has regularly been accused of 'infiltrating' schools and 'brainwashing' children against hunting and trapping. Many hunters I spoke to, and especially those who had young children or grandchildren, complained to me that teachers only presented one side of the argument. Worse, they sowed family discord by turning children against their fathers. In recent years, the FKNK has responded by setting up its own formal educational initiatives and taking them to schools. Two of the organization's branches deal specifically with education. The Public Relations and Educational Commission and the CUBS children's club are aimed primarily at the children of hunters and trappers, but there have also been initiatives intended for schoolchildren in general. In 2015, for example, the FKNK launched a 'Bird Feeder Campaign' and distributed FKNK logo-embossed feeders in schools. True to the dualistic model, the idea was not without its detractors: as one newspaper columnist put it, it was a case of 'buy your FKNK bird feeder now and shoot them when they land'.[9]

BirdLife Malta's more recent, better-funded and more sophisticated educational campaigns have also met with stiff resistance from the FKNK. The education matter went to court in 2009, when the FKNK issued a press release complaining about a reading pack that BirdLife Malta had distributed in schools as part of Dinja Waħda. The press release, entitled

'BirdLife Malta Infiltrate Education Department', argued that 'BirdLife is renowned for its anti-hunting lobby and more so for its gradual brainwashing of children through the supply of misinterpreted and misrepresented facts, depriving them of a fair and unbiased platform about what the environment and conservation should be all about'. By way of a redress, the Education Department agreed that the FKNK be allowed to distribute its own 'teachers' pack' that explained the part played by hunters and trappers in conservation. However, the then-President and Secretary of BirdLife Malta sued for libel, arguing that it had not infiltrated anything and that it had been defamed. In 2016, the court dismissed the libel suit, arguing that BirdLife Malta's booklet had not contemplated legal hunting and therefore 'failed to strike a balance'.[10] The FKNK hailed the decision as 'yet another victory over BirdLife Malta' and pointed out that: 'BLM's true identity and intentions have finally been revealed, since they could not stomach the relative Sentence handed down by the Court. In not so many words, BLM admitted that their only objective is to abolish Maltese hunting and trapping passions, because they do not, and can never come to accept such traditions.'[11]

Contexts of Politics and Governance

I have so far established the following: first, that conservation and hunting in Malta draw on different cultural lineages that in turn embed them in different cartographies; second, that the interconnections across difference are often characterized by friction (see Tsing 2005); and, third, that bird protectionists have sought – with considerable success – to section, corral and pathologize hunting in Malta as an immoral, lawless and retrograde practice. I shall now discuss some of the ways in which these dynamics translate into a political process, of which the key transformation was Malta's accession as an EU Member State in 2004.

This book is not intended as a history of hunting in Malta; for a longer-term understanding of the relations between hunting and the state, the reader is referred to sources such as Fenech (2010) and Cassar (2018). Closer to the present, the first sustained political involvement goes back to the 1970s, when the pressure, campaigns and political lobbying piled up by ENGOs resulted in the bird conservation legislation of 1980 (Legal Notice 68 of 1980). On paper, it rewrote the books. The list of species that could be legally hunted shrank as dramatically as that of protected areas and other restrictions grew. In practice, however, very little changed. Law enforcement on the ground was sparse and lethargic at best, and hunters who remember that time recall that they could carry on largely as they pleased – *sikkatura* (tightness) was still in the future. There were, of course, trenchant contestations over media images of dead birds, campaigns, incidents involving clashes between hunters and activists and so on. Yet, on the ground, all manner of birds continued to be shot fairly indiscriminately and most protected areas were routinely transgressed.

The broad understanding among activists and the public at large was that there was a looming reason why, in spite of all the activism and the rising tide of public opinion, the hunting laws were a paper tiger: politics. The narrow margin that separated the two main parties, and that manifested itself in seesaw politics, was seen as the main motive why domestic governance was so ineffectual at enforcing its own laws. Hunters were numerically a powerful lobby and in any case, the conservation of birds and nature was not on the list of priorities of political actors. Certainly hunters themselves capitalized on the equation and cultivated their own image as a vote bank that charged a high rate of interest. At street protests held by the FKNK in the late 1980s and early 1990s, one of the key battle cries was that hunters were a force to be reckoned with. Photographs of these events show slogans that said things like '15,000 hunters + wives + family = Votes', and indeed '15,000' became a recurring number in the political debates on hunting at the time. This was seen by many as political blackmail, or at best as a form of individual and collective patronage: individual, because stories were circulated of hunters whose weapons had been confiscated in protected areas, but who had got them back following the intervention of powerful political patrons, of cronies of government ministers who hunted with impunity in protected places like Buskett and so on; and collective, because the hunting lobby set itself up as a corporate client of political powers. This resonated well with notions of hunters as aboriginal Mediterranean men prone to patronage and forms of political action that were antithetical to the modern state (see, for instance, Horden and Purcell 2000). Of course, the equation was not straightforward. Individually, hunters were also political actors in many other ways, and the limits, faultlines and outcomes of multiple loyalties were not easy to establish. Still, a fickle vote bank is in many ways a more effective species than a predictable one, and the fluidity certainly worked in favour of the hunting lobby, which actively cultivated its own image as a high-risk category. As many people saw it, politicians were not prepared to take risks with a group that professed its *namra* above all else.

Therefore, as far as the state and hunting laws are concerned, the production of indifference (to paraphrase Herzfeld (1992)) had its roots primarily in the political risk posed by '15,000' voters whose loyalties could, in principle at least, be sold to the highest bidder. However, there were other reasons why the state appeared comatose in the face of blatant

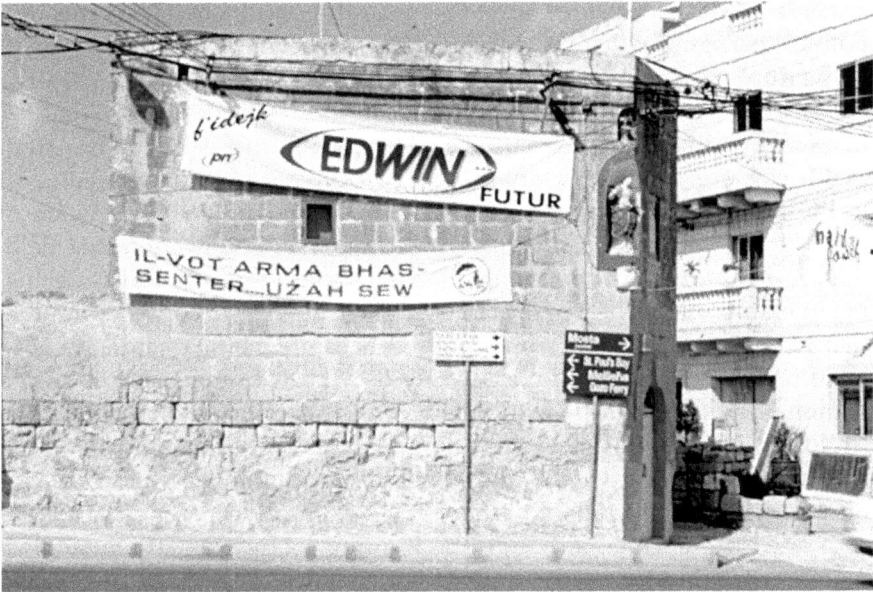

Figure 3.1. 'Just like your gun, your vote is a weapon . . . put it to good use.' Election campaign banner, 2004. Photograph by the author.

lawbreaking. Once again, the attributed characteristics of hunters discussed in the previous section are relevant. Because they were seen as largely lawless and prone to violence, hunters were also considered by the state to be a difficult group to square up to. There are parallels with other groups with which the Maltese state tacitly bargained for peace, especially in the 1990s – dockyard workers (see Falzon 2001) and 'boathouse' people who squatted on public land are cases in point. Clearly, successive governments were in no mood to risk violent street protests or worse ('*Namur jew intajru*' comes to mind), for the sake of bird conservation. Be that as it may, bird protection activists had to deal with decades of feet-dragging and back-pedalling on both legislation and enforcement. In 1993, for example, new laws were enacted that severely limited hunting and trapping in spring, only to be largely eased several months later under severe pressure from the hunting lobby. The pressure was also party-political, as the FKNK made a deal with the Labour opposition and actually directed its members to vote Labour in the 1996 elections (Briguglio 2015). In sum, while it would be extremely inaccurate to say that nothing changed (fenced reserves were set up, for example, robin trapping was all but eradicated and herons were given full protection by law), the situation on the ground as late as the end of the 1990s was not too different from what it had been thirty years earlier. It would take a major political transformation to shake the patronage structures and political bargaining that had hindered the enforcement and development of the hunting laws.

On 1 May 2004, Malta joined the EU. In the 2003 referendum that led to membership, hunting had been a fairly high-profile issue, to the extent that it was one of a number of key concessions supposedly agreed upon in the pre-accession negotiations between Malta and the EU. Aware of the risk posed by thousands of voters in such a fiercely contested field, the pro-EU Nationalist government (the Labour Opposition was against membership) did its best in the referendum campaign to convince hunters that EU membership would not adversely affect them.[12] Again, divided loyalties played a part. Take Raymond, a keen hunter who is also a Nationalist. He told me he had voted for membership, reasoning that his 'children's future' was more important than his wish to be able to hunt as he pleased. During my fieldwork, I met many hunters who had voted for membership on grounds of partisan loyalty, perceived economic advantage and so on. Thus, although the hunting lobby was largely against membership, individual aspirations and political allegiances prevented any semblance of a neat compartmentalization.

For their part, bird protection activists were strongly in favour of membership. They saw it as a hope that power would be siphoned away from national politics towards a more environmentally inclined EU. This had been one of the main thrusts of ENGOs for many years. BirdLife Malta, for example, had campaigned for many years for Malta to sign the Bern Convention on the Conservation of European Wildlife and Natural Habitats, a binding international legal instrument. It was finally ratified by the Maltese government in 1993, even if the new legislation remained largely ineffectual on the ground. For bird protectionists and for that part of the public that was sympathetic, EU membership promised that Maltese politicians would finally be held accountable, in ways that were legally and politically binding, to a system that was foreign to the domestic deadlock of patronage and vote catching.

The fears of many hunters, and the hopes of environmentalists, broadly turned out to be well founded. EU membership did three things. First, it ushered in new and more restrictive legislation, as Malta brought its hunting laws into line with the Birds Directive (79/409/EEC, amended as 2009/147/EC) of the European Parliament and of the Council. Second, it considerably altered the relationship between the Maltese state, hunters and protectionists – politicians in Malta could now pin responsibility, or at least some of it, according to circumstance and perceived dividend, on the EU, thus partially or entirely absolving themselves of direct involvement. Third, it reterritorialized the structures of legislation and enforcement within a developing framework of multilevel governance. It is telling in this last respect that the concept of multilevel governance originated precisely within analyses of the EU and 'Europeanization'. It looks at ways in which policy-making authority is shared among many different actors across subnational, national, and supranational levels, and focuses on how European politics and policy-making are linked (or not) within and across governance scales (Selin and VanDeveer 2015). One of the emphases is on 'new modes of influence of non-state actors resulting in the decreasing power of the nation-state' (Weber and Christophersen 2002: 2). All three changes benefited the opposition more than they did hunters. The discussion is taken up in more detail in Chapter 6, but the basics are worth outlining here.

When Malta joined the EU, both hunters and ENGOs sought to engage with the new circumstances. In 2004, in the first ever European Parliament elections held in Malta, one of the independent candidates was in fact the Secretary of the FKNK. Despite a campaign that urged hunters to cherish Maltese culture and traditions, and that reminded them that they ought to vote in their best interests, he only secured 3,119 first-count votes. The surprise to many was not so much that he was not elected (as expected, the two main parties carved up the field), but that the number of votes was less than a third of even the FKNK's own paid-up membership. The first foray by the hunting lobby into supranational politics had misfired. The key point is that EU membership left hunters and ENGOs located differently with respect to the new realities of multilevel governance and supranational decision-making. Partly this was because the hunting lobby had very little infrastructure to rely on that was embedded in broad cartographies. Capital-N Nature and its conservation implications and outcomes were not soil it was accustomed to tilling. This is not unique to Malta. Compared to their counterparts in the United States, for example, European hunting associations engage only weakly with conservation practice and science (Barca et al. 2016).

In contrast, and to further the point made earlier in this chapter, BirdLife Malta and other ENGOs had from their inception actively embedded themselves in cartographies of knowledge and environmentalist thought and practice that went well beyond the nation-state. Thus, when Malta joined the EU, these groups found themselves advantageously located in terms of key ideas, structures of activism and lobbying, and connections. Further, the deep-rooted and widely visible imagery of Malta as a black spot for migrating birds, and of Maltese hunters as a lawless and retrograde type, proved consequential. In his ten-year retrospective assessment of the impact of EU membership on social and economic actors in Malta, Harwood (2014) focuses on how it may have increased the resources of groups and provided new possibilities for lobbying. He argues that the impact of membership must also take into account the national level: 'if the group has experienced no tangible change in its domestic position and it remains focused on domestic policy largely under the control of government, then membership can be considered as having had only minimal impact' (2014: 218). Membership, then, primarily rewarded groups that cultivated European networks to change their fortunes in Malta. Harwood singles out BirdLife Malta as the Maltese NGO that experienced the most conspicuous change as a result of membership: 'few groups have seen their relative power increase as substantially as BirdLife Malta' (2014: 221). The tangible effects included the enforcement of EU legislation by government, as well as tremendously increased opportunities for funding.

The upshot was that hunting emerged as a perennial area of concern in the relations between Malta and the EU. In the years following accession, the European Commission opened a number of infringement cases against Malta, most of which were resolved without the need to be referred to the European Court of Justice. Hunting and trapping were among the topics. Besides, between 2004 and 2013, hunting was one of the principal topics covered by Malta-related questions put forward in the European Parliament; out of a total of 644 Malta-related questions, ninety-eight were about hunting (Harwood 2014). A government official I spoke to who had been privy to many hunting-related meetings in Brussels told me that representatives of the Commission generally showed 'complete mistrust' of their counterparts from the government of Malta. As he put it: 'you mention the *namra* of hunters, but these people from the Commission have an equally strong passion. I've seen them deal with other infringements to do with the environment. With hunting, they're different. I don't know what it is with hunting'.

The high visibility of hunting in the context of EU politics and the zeal ('passion') displayed by the Commission in the enforcement of the Birds Directive in Malta are of profound significance. The point was made earlier that the hunting laws of 1980 (and subsequently) had rarely reached the field in ways that were anything other than patchy and perfunctory. Things changed following EU accession, because bird protection activists could now appeal – and did so – directly to Brussels. In particular, the matter of derogations by the Maltese government became a highly complex and contested field, as ENGOs like BirdLife Malta opposed derogations on the basis of technical conservation arguments. In addition, enforcement increasingly became a reality on the ground, as the Maltese government found itself under severe pressure from the Commission to translate the law into tangible action. The government was now obliged to show, to a much broadened range of assessors, that it was serious about regulating hunting. This it did in various ways, which included what one might call performances of intent. A case in point was the suspension of the hunting season in 2014. On 20 September, and following the shooting of a number of migrating storks, the government announced that the hunting season would be suspended with immediate effect until 10 October. The news took everyone by surprise and somewhat eclipsed the Duke of Cambridge's visit to the island as part of the celebrations for the fiftieth anniversary of the country's independence on 21 September. It was made clear that the decision came directly from the Prime Minister[13] and that there would be no bargaining of any sort.

Shrunken Imaginings

On 11 April 2015, 253,157 Maltese people cast their votes in a national referendum. The voter turnout represented 74.8 per cent of the electorate, which was more than 3 per cent higher than that for a 2011 referendum on the introduction of divorce in Malta. The high turnout was especially striking given the sectorial nature of the question: 'Do you agree that the provisions of the "Framework for Allowing a Derogation Opening a Spring Hunting Season for Turtle Dove and Quail Regulations" (Subsidiary Legislation 504.94) should continue in force?' In other words, this was a referendum about spring hunting: a 'No' vote meant one was against and a 'Yes' that one was in favour that spring hunting be allowed. In the event, 50.44 per cent voted Yes, as opposed to 49.56 per cent who voted No. A narrow majority of just over 2,000 votes it may have been, but hunters had won the day. The politics that led up to the referendum, and the outcome of the result, add much to the arguments made in this chapter.

In July 2013, the Coalition to Abolish Spring Hunting was set up between the Green Party, BirdLife Malta, the National Trust of Malta, the Ramblers Association and a number of other ENGOs. The mission was to collect enough signatures to have a referendum called on whether or not to abolish spring hunting outright by putting an end to derogations from EU law. Maltese law (the Referenda Act) makes it possible for citizens to demand an abrogative referendum, provided at least 10 per cent of registered voters sign in support. The Coalition was well organized and over 40,000 signatures (considerably more than the required 10 per cent) were presented to the Electoral Commission in March 2014, effectively obliging the government to hold a referendum within a few months.

The background was a curious composite involving different levels of governance and their perceived functionality. The derogation in question concerned the Birds Directive and therefore the EU, but the decision whether or not to derogate was ultimately down to the Maltese government. Repeatedly, government had decided to derogate. It is clear that bird protection activists felt cheated of the full benefits of membership by Maltese politicians who persisted in pandering to the hunting lobby. As they saw it, successive governments had played, to use Barca et al.'s (2016: 190) term, 'derogation games' that had ultimately defeated the point of multilevel governance. The Ornis Committee, which had been set up as a technical part of the multilevel structure of governance of the Birds Directive, was (and is) seen as a rubber stamp at best, more likely a puppet committee that dressed politically expedient decisions by the government in the borrowed robes of ecological science. This is why, for example, the Chair of the Green Party hailed the referendum as a 'historic moment, an end to backroom dealings and the empowerment of people to set right what politicians had consistently done wrong'. It was not just Maltese politicians who were to blame; as one activist put it in a television interview, 'EU politicians and leaders do not have the guts – the balls, in plain language – to stop spring hunting'. This perceived systemic failure led the ENGO coalition to momentarily turn its back on what, in spite of spring hunting and other derogations, had been its best asset: multilevel governance and the involvement of the EU in hunting legislation and enforcement in Malta. The decision to call for a national referendum was, to paraphrase Benedict Anderson (1991: 7), a kind of 'shrunken imagining' in which, for the first time in over a decade, the hunting question was to be entirely in the hands of the Maltese electorate. The move was intriguing, not least because one of the perennial arguments of the bird protection lobby had been that the conservation of migratory birds was a concern that went beyond the confines of any nation-state.

The Coalition activists had considerable reason to feel encouraged. Successive opinion polls had suggested that the overwhelming majority of Maltese people were against spring hunting and wanted it abolished. This was also why the hunting lobby initially strongly opposed the referendum. In December 2013, the FKNK launched its own signature-collecting exercise in a bid to petition government to abolish the Referenda Act and thus the very possibility of a referendum. The FKNK argued that a referendum would constitute an attack on minority rights and cited the 'socio-cultural tradition of hunting' as one of these rights; in other words, that a referendum would set a dangerous precedent for majorities to trample on minority rights. In June 2014, hunters marched down Valletta's main street to present the 104,293 signatures they had collected to Parliament.

It was fascinating to watch the two sides play the numbers game. The Coalition's argument was that the reason why it had been so easy to collect 40,000 signatures was that the majority of Maltese people had had enough of spring hunting. The FKNK's strategy was more complex, because it claimed that its 104,293 signatures protected minority rights. On the one hand, this was a departure from the vote-bank slogans of the 1980s and 1990s, in that the argument now was that hunters were a vulnerable minority (as opposed to a powerful and high-risk block of voters). At the same time, the minority argument was lent strength precisely by the large number of signatures collected, which effectively suggested that it was in fact a majority argument. This, the FKNK claimed, meant that other minorities had aligned themselves with the cause. The list of ostensible recruits included a cast of *dilettanti*: spearfishers, fireworks-makers, racing-pigeon fanciers, offroaders and even brass-band club members – all groups that, for various reasons, were said to be under threat from the kind of meddling supposedly represented by the Coalition Against Spring Hunting.

The difficulty faced by the hunting lobby was that Maltese law made no provision for such petitions, and in January 2015 the Prime Minister announced that the referendum would be held in full respect of the law. The stage was set for various domestic interests in Malta to align themselves. The Prime Minister, who was also the leader of the party (Labour) that had won the elections by a landslide two years earlier, was one of the first to state his position. At the press conference announcing the referendum, he declared that he would be voting in favour of spring hunting on account of his electoral mandate. (The Labour Party manifesto of 2013 had specifically mentioned hunting.) A few days later, the Leader of the Opposition said that he too would be voting in favour, because he was 'a man of his word' – ten years earlier, he had been directly and prominently involved in the accession negotiations that had promised hunters that spring hunting would continue. While neither the Prime Minister nor the Leader of the Opposition committed their parties to toe the line, their positions effectively meant that hunters had the backing of a massive cross-party political consensus.

The campaign was fought between two sharply defined camps. The Coalition called its campaign 'SHout' (Spring Hunting Out) and premised it on the conservation argument that it did not make ecological sense for Maltese hunters to shoot migrating birds on their return journey from Africa and just before they were ready to breed in Europe. For its part, the hunting lobby pushed the sociological-political point that minorities ought to be able to enjoy their legitimate pastimes, especially when these involved deep-rooted aspects of Maltese tradition and culture.

It is beyond the scope of this book to present a detailed description and discussion of the campaign. However, some key points are worth noting. SHout had the declared support of the English-language newspapers and of a number of other (largely middle-class) groups. Thus, for example, an informal group of well-known lawyers openly supported the No campaign and even gave a press conference to explain the flaws in the minority arguments of the hunting lobby; hunting, they said, could not be described as a right, but rather a privilege. Another high-profile supporter was the Archbishop of Malta, who, however, emphasized that he spoke in his name alone (rather than in his official role, that is).

As expected, the campaign spawned a deluge of slogans, images and online memes. Those produced by the No camp tended to concentrate on images of dead birds, calls for access to the countryside, portrayals of hunters as uncivilized destroyers of migrating birds about to breed and the added value to tourism of a hunting-free countryside in spring. The Yes camp invested its energies in self-representations of hunting as a practice that was both steeped in tradition and had a rightful place in modernity. For example, the various images showed people in white-collar occupations who said they supported the rights of minorities; they also showed women hunters, 'gentlemen' hunters in flat caps and tweed waistcoats, and so on. It is telling that the FKNK chose a young woman lawyer who was not publicly known or associated with hunting to front the campaign. On various occasions, groups of hunters were shown cleaning up public places, donating blood at the blood bank and even on the way to missionary work in Africa. This led to the hunting lobby being accused of a cynical whitewash, an attempt to convince the public – in the face of years of evidence to the contrary – that hunting was all about law-abiding and socially responsible men and women.

The way in which the No lobby haemorrhaged support may seem remarkable at first glance. In an opinion poll held in July 2013, 60 per cent of respondents said they were against spring hunting; by the time the referendum was announced, the figure had gone down to 38 per cent.[14] The swing was probably largely down to the stance in favour of spring hunting taken by the two party leaders, but it was also clear that the No camp had underestimated the resilience of the cultural roots of hunting in Malta. When the result of the referendum was announced, thousands of hunters and supporters took to the streets to celebrate. They had won the right to continue the cherished spring hunt, no doubt the biggest bone of contention since Malta joined the EU.

Or so they thought. The spring hunting season for turtle dove and quail for 2015 opened on 14 April, barely two days after the result.

However, two weeks later – and two days before the season was due to end according to the parameters of the derogation – a protected kestrel landed badly injured in a school playground. Images of the bird, bleeding heavily and with one eye shot out of its socket, made the headlines within minutes. This was not a particularly unheard-of event, but a few hours later, a tweet by the Prime Minister – who happened to be in Azerbaijan on government business – unilaterally closed the hunting season. It said simply: 'Despite sharp decline in illegalities, today's hunting incident is inexcusable. I have decided to immediately close down the season – JM.'

The outcome of the referendum defies any semblance of a straightforward assessment. Since 2015, the Commission has not relented in its pressure on the Maltese government, which, for its part, has continued to play the 'derogation game'. Both BirdLife Malta and the FKNK have resumed their lobbying. In 2016, a moratorium was announced on turtle dove hunting in spring following a reassessment of the species' conservation status by the International Union for Conservation of Nature (IUCN) (see the detailed discussion on this in Chapter 6). It is clear that, irrespective of the result of the referendum, neither the hunting lobby nor the Maltese government are out of the reach of the supranational and international conservation matrix established through forty years of ENGO activism and eventual EU membership. At the same time, Maltese politicians have asserted their power in at least two ways: first, by strongly influencing (in the mildest of readings) the result of the referendum itself; and, second, by displaying a fairly arbitrary control over the parameters of hunting seasons (the unilateral decision by the Prime Minister to close the 2015 season being a case in point).

In this chapter, I have outlined the making, with reference to bird conservation in Malta, of 'that amateur-professional-activist synthesis that still invigorates environmentalism today' (Tsing 2005: 97). I have argued that, originally in the context of links with British organizations, ENGOs grafted themselves onto a cultural lineage that established them as the purveyors of a capital-N Nature, and its associated universalizing conservation project, to the local context. This led to a number of frictions with hunters, whose lineage was entirely a different species. It also patterned, in significant and consequential ways, the politics of hunting and conservation in Malta in the wake of EU membership and other profound transformations. In the following two chapters, I shall seek to understand these frictions with respect to the actual places where hunting is carried out.

Notes

1. A letter with the sibyllic title 'Bird Life in Malta' appeared in the *Daily Malta Chronicle* of 18 December 1908 (Sultana and Borg 2015).
2. The history of bird ringing in Malta goes back longer than that of BirdLife Malta itself. At the 1961 Gozo meeting, a local historian (Joseph Attard-Tabone) had proposed that 'instead of trapping birds and keeping them prisoners for the rest of their lives in small cages', a scientific bird-ringing scheme modelled on those in other countries should be set up (Sultana and Borg 2015: 288). The language used is significant, first, in that scientific ornithology was constructed from the very beginning as an alternative to hunting and practice, and, second, in the mention of 'other countries' as a model for Malta to emulate.
3. Act XI of 1982 of the Laws of Malta, as amended by Acts XVII of 1982, XIII of 1983 and I of 1987, as well as Legal Notice 423 of 2007. The context was the fraught political landscape of the early 1980s, in which then-Prime Minister Dom Mintoff suspected the opposition of soliciting the influence of foreign politicians to help destabilize the government (Dominic Fenech, personal communication). In the longer term, the anxiety of foreign interference is understandable in the context of the nationalist imaginary of a small island nation – especially since the dominant nationalist narrative includes as one of its central themes a long history of foreign domination.
4. 'Hunter Saves Loggerhead Turtle', FKNK press release, 20 August 2016.
5. 'BirdLife Malta and CABS at the End of Their Line', FKNK press release, 19 December 2016.
6. The published materials have tended to be of high standard, thanks to the tireless work of a gifted illustrator (Victor Falzon, himself a teacher) and foreign funding by the ENGO's many associates.
7. Retrieved 10 February 2016 from www.BirdLifemalta.org.
8. Retrieved 10 February 2016 from www.BirdLifemalta.org.
9. Daphne Caruana Galizia, 'Buy Your FKNK Bird Feeder Now and Shoot Them When They Land'. Retrieved 12 December2019 from https://daph necaruanagalizia.com/2015/03/buy-your-fknk-bird-feeder-now-and-sho ot-them-when-they-land.
10. 'FKNK's Comments on BirdLife Booklet "Not Libelous"', *Times of Malta*, 1 February 2016.
11. 'Yet Another FKNK Victory over BirdLife Malta', FKNK press release, 6 February 2016.
12. Hunters and trappers were promised, in writing, that 'Maltese hunters will continue to be able to hunt in spring . . . After membership, Maltese trappers will continue to be able to practice trapping for a number of songbird species' (Malta-EU Information Centre, MIC, information leaflet, 2003).
13. 'Prime Ministerial Intervention Leads to Closure of Autumn Hunting Season', *Malta Today*, 20 September 2014.
14. *Malta Today* polls, January 2015.

CHAPTER 4

Making Place for Hunting

I kill where I please because it is all mine.
—Ted Hughes, 'Hawk Roosting'[1]

In my diary of a single winter I have tried to preserve a unity, binding
together the bird, the watcher, and the place that holds them both.
—J.A. Baker, *The Peregrine, the Hill of Summer & Diaries*[2]

It is not always the case that arguments about hunting refer to the landscape. In Britain, for example, the reams of reports written in the runup to
the hunting ban of the early 2000s all but overlooked that aspect and were
centred instead on animal welfare. This was a glaring omission since,
certainly in the case of fox hunting, the encounters between the hunter
and the hunted are given meaning through references to the places where
they are enacted or performed. As Marvin puts it: 'the landscapes of the
countryside are not merely a stage or a setting for the event, but rather
they are essentially constitutive of fox hunting'. Encounters between
hunter and hunted thus create a 'social geography' of the countryside
that 'overlies, transgresses, and textures other more familiar spatial geographies such as farms, parishes, and counties' (2003: 51).

In this chapter I look at the physical places where hunting takes place
and at how they overlie, transgress and texture other geographies. First, I
explore some of the many and complex relations between Maltese hunters
and their environment, focusing in particular on hunting as a spatial
experience (what I call 'being-there'), the forms of access to 'pulling' land
that attracts migrating birds, and its making and transformation. I then
go on to discuss some of the ways in which transformations of land by
hunters are opposed, often vigorously, by conservationists.

Being-There: Hunting as Experience of Place

It has been said of the hunting scenes of Gustave Courbet (1819–77) that they bring together valuations of hunting and the landscape into coherent and unitary images (see Tseng 2008). It is a theme most hunters would recognize because hunting is very much about a hyphenated being-there. In other words, hunters experience and talk about their passion and practice as being fundamentally about place. For example, responding to a survey questionnaire in 2006–7, Danish hunters mentioned 'experiencing nature' (followed by 'good fellowship') as their prime motive for hunting (Lundhede et al. 2009, as cited in Primdahl et al. 2012). The case at hand is no different. Throughout my fieldwork, hunters emphasized that one of the main, if not *the* main, attractions of hunting was that it brought them into contact with the landscape and its contents – as they put it, *'jien basta qiegħed hemm'* ('what matters is that I'm in the field'). 'In contact' here is a deceptively simple term for what is in effect a complex, elemental and multisensory experience.

Spring hunting, which Maltese hunters are so loath to give up, presents a useful starting point. The opposition, and it is both numerous and vociferous, tells of the short-sightedness of killing birds on their return passage, just when they are ready to breed and a relatively short distance from their breeding grounds. Be that as it may, to hunters the ecological argument is entirely peripheral to the foundational point, which is that spring hunting takes place in spring. To them, hunting is the best (and possibly the only) way of experiencing the season. They talk of *difa*, an early-morning stillness and powdery mist that descends on the countryside at that time of year, and that contains the promise of birds. Likewise, there is a type of overcast weather and drizzle that hunters, and people generally, call *'temp tar-rebbiegħa'* ('spring weather'). The Maltese countryside is at its verdant best from mid-March to late April, and that is also the time to pick and nibble *ful* (fava beans) on the way to the hunting ground. To hunters, then, hunting is a means of inhabiting spring.

Being-there is an intense sensory *Gesamtkunstwerk*. For example, the Maltese hunter inhabits a soundscape made up of the sounds and noises of human and other presences, the calls of birds and the artificial calls produced by his own and other people's recorded decoy calls and whistles. (Traditional calling devices have in most cases been replaced with pre-recorded calls on mobile phones and high-spec bird callers – technically illegal, but in widespread use nonetheless.) It can be hard to figure out how hunters manage to distinguish the call of a migrating bird from all the cacophony. The verb trappers in particular use is *'tħoss'* ('to feel') rather than *'tisma''* ('to hear'); it is as though they 'feel' slight changes in

Figure 4.1. A hunter immersed in the spring landscape. Photograph by the author.

the soundscape; the soundscape is not so much heard as experienced, as part of a synaesthetic symphony of perceptions of the landscape.

The landscape itself is made up of two components: land and sky. The first affords what ecologists call 'micro-habitats'. A hunter will associate, based on experience and practice, the features and micro-habitats in his patch with specific kinds of bird. A useful parallel is Maurice Bloch's description of Malagasy shifting cultivators surveying the forest for promising patches of swidden. Bloch argues that when a Malagasy farmer tells his friend 'Look over there at that bit of forest, that would make a good swidden', he draws on a cognitive schema that is partly visual, partly analytical (though not necessarily in a sequential logical way) and partly welded to a series of procedures about what one should do to make and maintain a swidden (Bloch 1991). In Malta, one of the marks of a good hunter is precisely the possession of such a cognitive field, by which the countryside is schematized as a complex architecture of hunting possibilities.

The model extends to the sky, which may be compartmentalized and often imagined as a stack of layers (*saffi*) through which birds fly. Hunters talk of birds flying *fil-kewkba* (with the stars) or, more poetically, through *is-seba saff* or *is-seba sema* – literally the 'seventh heaven' of cosmological tradition. The link with the religious imaginary is also present in expressions like *'għand Kristu'* or *'m'għola Alla'* ('as high as Christ/God'), used for very high-flying birds that appear to fly through God's own layer of sky. With respect to birds themselves, they are seen to inhabit the landscape – and therefore the hunter's field – in a variety of distinct ways. The opposite of birds that fly in seventh heaven are those that fly *żaqqhom ma' l-art* (skimming the ground). Birds may fly *għat-tul* (away from the hunter) or *għad-dritt* (towards the hunter). Those that are present in an area for any length of time become *tal-post* (lit. of the place). In a fascinating inversion of roles, they wise up to the characteristics of a place and especially to its dangers, including hunters. Such birds are known as *'ħazin'* ('cunning') or *'bid-diploma'* ('graduates') and are thought to be hard to attract using decoys or to outwit in any other way. The obverse is *'tal-passa'* (migratory) birds, which are seen as spatially unschooled and relatively easy to attract and shoot, unless weather and other conditions contrive to render them *vleġeġ* (arrows), *maħrubin* (in a hurry) or *gass malpjanċa* (pedal to the metal), and therefore unlikely to settle or otherwise to present a shot.

The juxtaposition of birds and place goes further. The infinity of possible configurations of birds, weather and other variables means that even the most familiar of landscapes never gets monotonous. Franklin (2001) argues that hunting and fishing distinguish themselves from other outdoor activities in that they involve a more 'fully-sensed engagement' that resolves itself (in success or failure, or a combination of both) in a space that may be repeatedly hunted or fished, but where the excitement never diminishes. While I do not subscribe to the argument that hunting and fishing are privileged (birdwatching or rock climbing, for example, offer equally 'fully-sensed engagements' to practitioners), Franklin's point about the capacity of hunting to render a familiar place perennially novel is a useful one. With respect specifically to Malta and similar contexts, the (sometimes sudden and in any case not fully understood) arrival of migrant birds is a particularly significant factor. This is why hunters emphasize that no two days in the field are ever quite the same, no matter how familiar a place is and how frequently it is visited.

There is a parallel argument to be made for spaces of migration and their appropriation. Especially on islands like Malta and Lampedusa, the migrant bird becomes a biannual herald of connection with the unseen world beyond the horizon. In this way, migrating birds serve a connective purpose – through their appropriation, hunters as well as birdwatchers inhabit the expansive and fluid spaces across which migration takes place. This also partly explains why 'vagrant' occurrences of birds that stray far from their normal migration routes are so highly prized among hunters and birdwatchers alike (see, for instance, Liep 2001).

Being-there, then, spills beyond the actual places where hunting takes place. There are more mundane ways in which this happens. Cars, for example, may be imprinted by hanging cartridges on a rear-view mirror, fitting camouflage-pattern seat covers and even spray-painting pictures of desirable species on the body panels. Homes, too, are marked in various ways. It is common practice in Malta for even the humblest house to be given a name, which is usually displayed on a small ceramic plaque on the façade. Naming is typically inspired by local patron saints, places visited by the owners and so on, but also by bird names in the case of hunters' homes. 'Turtle Dove', 'Honey Buzzard' and 'Skylark' are not uncommon house names, and in some cases the plaque on the façade is further decorated with a small image of the bird. (Tellingly, some bird-watchers also follow this practice.) With respect to home interiors, taxidermy specimens can be very prominent indeed, especially in rooms that are used to welcome visitors.[3] In one case, and it was exceptional only in terms of extent, a hunter's home I visited contained stuffed birds in every corner; they included a flamingo and five gannets, which took up much of the space in the small parlour on account of their great size. Outside the home, this kind of place-making can include workplaces, as well as bars and restaurants. For example, a hunter who worked as a receptionist at a public institution hung the inner sides of the reception cubicle with photographs and drawings of birds. Given the rich material history of antler trophies, hunting still-lifes, moth-eaten tigers in Indian palaces and taxidermy trophies in the homes of wealthy big-game hunters, none of this will be particularly surprising. However, the point is that being-there is not necessarily limited to the actual field; on the contrary, hunters will often transform the many physical places they inhabit into ones where the experience of the hunt can be evoked, mentally re-enacted and sometimes displayed.

So far, I have discussed the inhabiting of landscape in terms of individual experience. However, while the relationship between the individual and their environment is crucial, the landscape is also inhabited socially. Hunters are acutely aware that they inhabit peopled landscapes and that successful hunting is also about locating themselves within them. Jerolmack's work provides a useful bearing. Focusing primarily on New York, Berlin and South Africa, it is a fine-grained ethnography of pigeon fanciers and pigeon–human relationships in urban contexts. The object is telling, since pigeon flying seems at first glance to be a means by which urbanites individually transcend the city and urban society to reconnect

Figure 4.2. House name in the village of Siggiewi. Photograph by the author.

and communicate with nature. In fact, it turns out that keeping pigeons is instead a way for the fanciers to embed themselves in a social world and compete for status. Thus, even though Turkish fanciers in Berlin say that pigeons anchor them to nature, Jerolmack's data show that they also anchor them to their ethnicity and notions of homeland. Crucially, these encounters are neither antithetical to nor less authentic than those that foster an individually felt connection to nature. Jerolmack draws comparisons with Durkheim's and Lévi-Strauss' thought on totemism to argue that 'social categories have *always* structured our relations with animals' (2013: 14, emphasis in original).

At the most immediate level, the presence of other hunters in the field is described by the expressions *'ta' warajja'* and *'ta' quddiemi'* ('the ones behind/in front') or, in the case of terraced slopes, *'ta' fuqi'* and *'ta' taħti'* ('the ones above/below'). These neighbours would be known to the hunter and may even be kin or friends. While in the field, the hunter is constantly in touch with other hunters in the area on two-way radio or direct voice contact. Thus, for example, if a bird happens to fly past a hunter, he will radio or turn round and shout *'ilqa' fuqek!'* ('birds forward!') to the one behind him, or *'ilqa' warajk!'* ('birds behind') to the one in front. Mobile phones have made it possible for hunters to greatly extend their real-time knowledge of exactly what happens to be migrating and where. My field sessions were typically punctuated with frequent calls to and from hunters (kin or friends) in the field elsewhere, following which the hunter would turn to me and say things like *'in-naħa l-oħra għandhom il-ġamiem'* ('there is a passage of doves on the other side [of the country]'). It is also common practice for hunters to exchange small gifts of fruit or vegetables. My informants would often get visits from other hunters, usually but not necessarily neighbours, especially when there were few birds around. They would talk over coffee, sometimes for hours, and the visitor might part with a warm and reciprocal *'ejja aqta' basket ful'* – an invitation to go pick a bag of beans. What I encountered was effectively a rural gift economy in which information about migrating birds or trees or agriculture, bags of fruit and vegetables, and shared meals were circulated between the hunters of a particular area – even as they competed for a common and limited resource (migrating birds). In some cases, this in-the-field reciprocity develops into rich and long-lasting relations of friendship and camaraderie that often spill over into areas of life other than hunting – family, work and so on. Since many hunters are tradesmen (builders, carpenters, car mechanics and so on), they often find themselves drawing on the services of the men they effectively share the landscape with, and with whom they share long-term relations of trust.

There are other aspects to the peopling of the landscape. Most hunters who hunt on their own land – and even, at times, those who do not – manage in some way or other to weave their way round the planning regime and cobble together a small field room or two. Typically, these rooms contain a few pieces of recycled furniture as well as hunting paraphernalia, tools, irrigation tubing and such. Exceptionally, hunters actually live in these rooms for the duration of the season. More commonly, they spend their hunting days there cooking, napping, tidying up, tending to trees and so on; in many ways, these places function as sites of male domesticity.[4] Hunters may also prepare large communal meals in purpose-built open-air wood ovens or portable barbecues. It is also common practice for hunters to spend time – usually on Sundays or holidays, and always when active hunting is not taking place – cooking and socializing with kin and friends. At these times, the places that are normally exclusively male-gendered and used for hunting are transformed. A related practice is that of end-of-season roasts at which hunted game is pooled, prepared and consumed communally by groups of hunters, and sometimes their families and guests. (The last can include local farmers, men who hunt in the area, work colleagues and the occasional anthropologist.)

It is, of course, crucial to note that the argument for reciprocity effectively encompasses its contrary. Relations between neighbours, and sometimes between hunters who share the same land, also involve competition, a studied lack of cooperation and sometimes outright bad blood and conflict. The reasons are various. Breaches of hunting etiquette – shooting low or when a bird is out of range, poaching a neighbour's airspace and trespassing – are taken seriously. A man who is routinely trigger-happy and who transgresses the informal morality of the hunting landscape by showing no restraint is known as a *lupu* (wolf). The word is usually used in jest and in the context of banter, but it is a classic case of humour serving to uphold, rather than subvert, norms. Trappers often complain that hunters make their lives difficult, directly by shooting birds before they can be trapped or indirectly by making birds nervous and hard to attract; these birds are sometime described as flying *fuq it-tiri* (above the shots). Not surprisingly given the notion of a limited resource, acts of sabotage are not uncommon between neighbours and they occasionally escalate into serious confrontation.

Pietru, for example, described to me the fraught relations he had had with Dione, one of his neighbours. At one point, and allegedly egged on by third parties intent on stirring up trouble ('a long story'), Dione planted a stand of reeds just across a boundary wall, seriously obstructing Pietru's field of vision; he also built a hide a few paces away in front of Pietru's, reducing his chances of getting in a fair shot at incoming birds. Nonconfrontational by nature but at the same time not one to be outwitted, Pietru said nothing. Instead, he installed a huge flag and a long string of shiny CDs along the party wall. The scarecrow effect hurt Dione more than it did Pietru, who had a second hide some distance away. To drive the point home, Pietru proceeded one morning to pluck a dove he had shot in such a way as to encourage the feathers to drift across the wall towards the fuming Dione. War had been declared without any words being exchanged. The following morning, Dione's father, who was an old and respected friend of Pietru's, showed up and asked what had happened. He immediately ordered his son, who Pietru described as a *'tifel'* (a 'boy', as in a young and immature person), to dismantle the hide and trim the reeds. Order was restored, and Pietru and Dione have been cordial neighbours ever since. Throughout my fieldwork, I listened to many stories of how hides had mysteriously collapsed, trees were vandalized and dogs were poisoned. The many, sometimes fuzzy and usually cross-cutting, types of access to land described later in this chapter do nothing to help the situation. In some cases it takes years of subtle acts of goodwill for hunters to establish some sort of functional coexistence with neighbours. Hunting, then, effectively transforms the Maltese countryside into a tissue of intersecting relations of cooperation and competition, and reciprocity and conflict.

Remembered Landscapes

Tim Ingold has written productively about the environment as the embodiment of past activity. It is, as he puts it, 'an enduring record of – and testimony to – the lives and works of past generations who have dwelt within it, and in so doing, have left there something of themselves' (2000: 189). It is also in this sense that the environment is not, as a facile cultural constructionism would have it, a blank slate onto which meanings are inscribed by conceptually detached processes of human perception and thought: 'To perceive the landscape is therefore to carry out an act of remembrance, and remembering is not so much a matter of calling up an internal image, stored in the mind, as of engaging perpetually with an environment that is itself pregnant with the past' (Ingold 2000: 189). With respect specifically to hunters, Ingold holds that they learn through an 'education of attention'. The making of a hunter involves mentoring by seniors who point out features of the country and their significance, as well as a multisensory process of self-discovery. The 'experienced hunter is the knowledgeable hunter' (2000: 190), the one who can recognize and value subtle and nuanced cues that may be insignificant to the untrained eye. That knowledge is ever a work in progress and is often expressed or explicated in the form of myths or stories.

Ingold's argument is applicable to the case at hand in a number of ways. For example, it helps us understand why hunters who are *bla post* (placeless – see the discussion later on in this chapter) feel, and are seen as, doubly deficient. If it were simply a matter of atemporal construction of landscapes, any hunter could relate to any environment at will. In fact, to be *bla post* means that one is not able to engage with and grow into a familiar and known place: in this way, and because it lacks a vital part of the human–environment interaction, the experience of the hunt is devalued. It is also relevant in this vein that hunters who also hunt abroad will invariably say that '*aħjar taqbad gamiema waħda Malta milli elf l-Eġittu*' ('one turtle dove bagged in Malta is worth a thousand shot in Egypt'). Hunting abroad (unless one hunts regularly in the same place for a long period of time) simply cannot offer the dwelling experience that hunting in one's familiar patch can. This does not stop hunters from paying several thousand euros to spend two weeks in Argentina, but then there are other aspects to hunting than the relationship between a hunter and his environment.

A second aspect of the relationship between hunting, time and landscape is that being-there often contains an elegiac element. In contemporary Malta, understandings of and relations with the countryside are shot through with a deep-felt anxiety. At the risk of overgeneralization, one might say that many feel that Malta's coming of age as a modern nation has entailed a loss of spatial innocence – a disruption of a moral order rooted in a landscape that is rapidly dwindling. Invariably, renditions of the landscape foreground a notion of relentless loss. It is in this context that hunters reminisce about the real or imagined landscapes they or their fathers inhabited in the past, when good hunting grounds were to be found within walking distance of villages. They also cultivate mental and narrative images of the even more rural world in which their generic forebears hunted. These images and narratives may take the form of nostalgia for an idyllic time when open land was plentiful and built-up areas were few and far between, and when hunting was a treasured part of a rural moral order steeped in tradition, timeless certainties and solid families and local communities. Even though most of them had no living memory of it, my informants commonly reminisced about a time when Mass was said at 4 a.m. at country chapels especially for hunters, who would then spend a couple of hours among the sulla and carobs and shoot as many birds as they needed for the day's meal. Turtle doves migrated in such colossal numbers that they filled the sky in layers. In these renditions, some species have a stronger mnemonic potency than others. Two species that are considered particularly reminiscent of a lost landscape are the carob tree (*ħarruba*) and the sulla (*silla*). The latter can grow wild, but was widely cultivated as a fodder plant. It carpeted vast areas of the countryside well into the second half of the twentieth century (see Bowen-Jones et al. 1961). Both species are still part of the landscape inhabited by hunters today, but they have declined sharply. For the hunter, to experience the remnants is also to emotionally re-enact a golden age when plentiful migrating birds were in perfect harmony with their environment. This is how an old hunter put it:

> In those days Fgura [now a small town with no open space to speak of] was all fields and carob trees. It was an excellent place for hunting and especially so for turtle doves . . . the best area was called Tal-Krozz or Tal-Qasam and carob and almond trees grew there in thick clumps. The place and trees no longer exist because in 1969 the fields were bulldozed to make way for factories . . . old people who say that turtle doves migrated in huge flocks, layer upon layer, are right. They used to fly in from the direction of Ħal Għaxaq towards Tal-Qasam, which today is Bulebel Industrial Estate.[5]

In contrast, hunting today is thought about in terms of a dwindling countryside, greatly reduced migration, fierce competition between hunters and the perennial headache of surveillance by the police and anti-hunting activists. The irony is that environmentalist movements are predicated on the same sense of loss and anxiety. While for these movements hunting is one of the threats to the countryside, for hunters it is the exact opposite – a form of enduring relationship and stewardship. If hunters reminisce about vanished landscapes, hunting itself often becomes a way of re-inhabiting those landscapes by evocation, as it were. The sight of a turtle dove winging its way across a field conjures up collective, social and sometimes individual (if the hunter is old enough) memories of great flocks of turtle doves and the landscapes that hosted them. This is one of the key attractions of game species like the turtle dove: because of their baggage of narrative and memory, they can conjure up the lost past much more effectively than other species. It is also why *il-gamiema t'April* holds such power over the imagination of hunters and why hunting it is so valued.

The third point is about transformations and the pitfalls of essentialization. Hunting in Malta today may re-enact the landscapes of a valued past, but it is not necessarily a faithful re-enactment of past valuations of the landscape. Until well into the twentieth century, hunting was for most a largely undifferentiated practice that took place in undifferentiated places. Unlike, say, fox hunting, it was neither ritualized nor practised as a specialized 'country pursuit'. Thus, a man might hunt in a place that was a short walk away from the village house where he lived, or he might keep his shotgun in his car just in case he came across a bird on the way to work. This also explains why land generally was not transformed into a *post* (place) that was specially intended for hunting. The few exceptions included the gentry, who hunted in a landscape they did not normally inhabit, who earmarked certain places as 'reserved' for hunting and who occasionally even transformed them by building hunting lodges, for example. However, as hunting became differentiated, so did

valuations of the places in which it took place. My informants' insistence
that hunting was all about being-there and inhabiting the countryside
may in fact reflect a relatively recent phenomenon. This coincides with
the new valuations of the countryside originally peddled by ENGOs. In
the last quarter of the twentieth century, *l-ambjent* ('the environment')
became differentiated – and politicized – as a set of places that were not
those of everyday life, that were inhabited by nature and aestheticized as
'countryside', and that in turn invited inhabiting by a cast of types that
included birdwatchers, ramblers, the public and, not least, hunters themselves. The argument is not that hunters in the past did not experience
place or that being-there is a recent development; rather, it is that the
meanings of both place and 'there' have changed – to value being-there
is also to latch on to, and locate oneself as a legitimate presence within,
politically ascendent notions of place.

Before I move on to look at some of the ways in which place is made, I
wish to raise a question that is often asked by nonhunters and that underwrites a considerable part of the hunting and conservation dynamic in
Malta: if hunting is all about the landscape, why do hunters have to hunt?
Why can they not just be in and enjoy the landscape? The earlier ethnographic points on *difa*, the seasons and the landscape, would be variously
described by bird protectionists as romanticized idylls, an anthropologist's naivety or – in the worst case – apologetic of a practice that claims
to value the nature it destroys. At face value, my work with hunters in
Malta upholds this ambivalence. My informants' assurances that what
matters is being-there (*'jien basta qiegħed hemm'*) would suggest that the
practice of hunting – indeed, the very presence of birds – is peripheral to
presence in the field. And yet it is clear, not least in the lengths that hunters go to retain that practice, that it is not peripheral at all.

The key to resolving this apparent contradiction is that hunting and
being-there are mutually constitutive. Being-there is a matter of meaningfully inhabiting rather than simply being physically in a place.
Heidegger's distinction between space and place, where spaces gain
authority (and, implicitly, value) not from space appreciated mathemat-
ically, but rather place appreciated through human experience (Sharr
2007), is crucial in this respect. The emphasis is on the notions of meaningful inhabiting and human experience that, if they are to be rescued
from the blind alley of platitude, need to be explained. The multisensory
and other aspects of being-there described earlier are obviously human
experience, but there are two missing links. The first is the bird. Hunters,
and birdwatchers for that matter, experience the landscape differently,
because they see and hear differently; they are attuned to and inhabit a
'deep' landscape by virtue of seeing and hearing birds. In *The Peregrine*

(widely regarded as a masterclass of nature writing), J.A. Baker makes the memorable point that 'the hardest thing of all to see is what is really there' (2015: 33). Throughout the book, the author contrasts two ways of inhabiting the landscape: the first, a deep one mediated by the presence of birds, the second more superficial. For example: 'At three o'clock, a man walked along the sea wall, flapping with maps. Five thousand dunlin flew low inland, twenty feet above his head. He did not see them. They poured a waterfall of shadow on to his indifferent face' (2015: 52). So powerful is the inhabiting turn mediated by birds that, as Preston and Gower (2017: 3) put it, 'you can never really stop seeing birds once you've been a birdwatcher . . . You will wake up early in strange houses and hear the reckless joy of the dawn chorus building in the air'. To both birdwatchers and hunters, the 'there' in being-there is mediated through the presence of birds (or its possibility).

And yet, birdwatchers and hunters are different. The second missing link is in fact the gun (or trap). A vacant being-there is just that – it is being-there-with-a-gun that matters, so much so that the complete version is in fact '*jien basta qieghed hemm bis-senter*' ('what matters is to be there with a gun'). The gun effectively serves as the device that connects the hunter to the landscape and its sensations and possibilities. It represents the ability to meaningfully inhabit that landscape by doing something of value in it, and hopefully by producing a valued object, namely a bagged bird. The hunter therefore relates to his environment not as an abstract being, but rather as a particular and technologized self (a hunter with a gun). Birdwatching, too, is also very much about the multisensory experience of landscape, and indeed it is quite possible to see and identify some birds without the help of binoculars. But put a birdwatcher in the field without binoculars and you have a lost soul – more prosaically, one who is potentially unable to confirm a sighting and convert it into a valued object, namely a bird record. Field optics may have their limitations, but they combine with the birdwatcher's passion and skills to produce a complete and technologized self who is able to meaningfully inhabit the landscape. The same could be said of the many practices – surfing, open-water swimming, riding and so on – that involve doing something in the landscape. It is ultimately this complete self to which human experience and meaningful inhabiting belong.

Localizing Strategies

While it is generally true that, for hunters, land is the key resource, there are certain context-bound differences. Primdahl et al. (2012) draw a distinction between northern and southern European countries. In the former, the right to hunt tends to be linked to the ownership of land. In Denmark, for example, every rural landowner has the right to hunt on their land provided it is larger than 1 ha; that right may be shared with, given to or leased to other persons for a limited time if the property is larger than 5 ha. With the exception of coastal waters and beaches, the right to hunt is linked to property and cannot be exercised separately. In southern European countries, on the other hand, the right to hunt tends to be based on the *res nullius* principle by which game belongs to no one in particular and the hunting right is not directly linked to private property. That is the case as far as rights are concerned, but access to land in which to hunt is crucial across these situations. In Malta, while the right to hunt does operate on the *res nullius* principle and thus is not in any way linked to land ownership, actual practice depends on access to land, of which there are four distinct and hierarchized types: first, through individual or joint actual ownership (full title, that is); second, by short-term or long-term lease; third, through some form of informal but enduring relationship with the owner/leaseholder; and, fourth, by means of an unregulated presence on site.

Actual ownership of the land is by far the most desirable type, in part because of the deep-rooted prestige of landowning in general. It is beyond the scope of the present work to present a thoroughly researched and detailed historical account of landowning; rather, the following is intended as a basic outline. Historically, the landowning gentry, as well as smaller landowners, hunted on their own land. This does not necessarily mean that land was specially designated or managed as hunting land, or that a private piece of land would be shot over exclusively by its owners. In most cases, landholdings that were used for agriculture or grazing would double as hunting places during the migration seasons, and especially in spring. It was not unknown for landowners to retain hunting rights even in cases where the land was leased to farmers for cultivation. Landowners could invite others to join them and often did – usually some combination of peers and local subordinates (the farmers who worked the land, for example). Sometimes, hunters who were known to the landowner and/ or local farmers would be allowed limited access to private landholdings when these were not being used by the owners themselves; thus, a landowner and his guests might shoot exclusively for the first couple of hours of the day, and then vacate the field to any locals who wished to hunt there. (In the past, hunters were rarely in the field for entire days, unless birds happened to be migrating in unusually strong numbers.)

It is also common for hunting and agriculture to coexist in a kind of bricolage. In the past and to a lesser extent still today, agricultural land

Figure 4.3. This field is used to grow crops as well as to trap finches. At the bottom right is a ploughed area and at the centre left the netting site. The flat stones along the walls are used to place caged decoy birds on. Photograph by the author.

was seasonally hunted on by the farmers themselves, as well as by guests or hunters who would buy the right to exclusive access for a few hours a day. The main logic was the production of crops with hunting as a side-benefit, and land was cultivated accordingly. More recently, as tracts of agricultural land came to be valued primarily in recreational terms, this logic has often been reversed. Many hunters who have regular access to tillable land combine hunting with some sort of small-scale agricultural production.

The system of hunting privilege held largely by a landowning gentry, and of limited access embedded in a tightly woven fabric of social obligation, gradually declined in the second half of the twentieth century. One of the reasons was that, as discussed earlier in this book, hunting in Malta lost any associations it may have had with the landowning gentry – itself a long-declining species anyway – around that time, with the result that many hunters from socially privileged circles stopped hunting altogether. Another reason was changing patterns and intensity of farming and grazing, which brought about ruptures in the localized fabric of social obligation. By the late twentieth century, rising standards of living and a growing availability of cash meant that more and more people could afford to buy their own land. Nowadays, it is not uncommon for real estate companies to describe land as 'ideal for hunting'.

With some exceptions, there are two kinds of hunters who hunt on their own land today: first, people mostly from rural backgrounds with some history of local smallholding; and, second, people from working-class backgrounds who have bought land in recent years. Among the latter are self-employed tradesmen whose substantial incomes, typically from construction and its corollary trades,[6] make it possible for them to buy land to which they often have no historical connection. As a result, parts of the countryside have been colonized by smallholding hunters who own parcels of land separately or jointly (usually kin) and who use them primarily for that purpose. These landholdings tend to be small – a few tumoli[7] typically – and increasingly inward-looking, in the sense that access for hunting or otherwise is strictly limited to the owner. In this context of burgeoning smallholding, a key practical and conceptual distinction has emerged among hunters between *tkun f'tan-nies* ('to be in other people's property') and *tkun fi ħwejġek* ('to be in your own property'). The former implies being at the mercy of others, as well as a lack of attachment, in terms of both knowledge and affect, to a given patch of land – itself such an important facet of hunting. Hunters who hunt *f'tan-nies* are also unable to transform land by planting trees and so on. The urge to be *fi ħwejġek*, to have unhindered and unregulated access to your own land, has become more pressing as hunters have gained a foothold on this version of the property ladder.

The second type of access is through lease, of which there are various arrangements. The surest involves land that is leased by landlords to tenants for what are effectively peppercorn rents over the very long term. This type of lease is characterized by historically embedded rituals that bind together generations of tenants and landlords (*is-sinjuri*) in an enduring and strongly hierarchized set of relations.[8] Unless otherwise specified in the lease contract, which does sometimes happen, land that is leased for agriculture may also be used for hunting. The second type of lease is less long-term and usually involves small to medium-sized parcels of land that are formally leased out for periods of several years by landlords who might share a social background with tenants, but who have no interest in hunting and/or agriculture. The third consists of the informal seasonal lease or sublease of very small holdings, sometimes simply a spot where to sit and wait for migrating birds. This last is essentially the purchase of the right to hunt in a particular place for a few weeks during the spring or autumn migration period. It is a means by which landlords or tenants on a long lease earn some cash on the side by allowing hunters access to their patch. Although it is renewable, it does not normally imply formal long-term rights and obligations.

The more durable and substantial kinds of lease were known as *riżervat* ('reserved'). In the past, but less commonly today, they often involved syndicates of hunters, sometimes but not necessarily from urban

backgrounds, who would lease stretches of land for hunting for the duration of the migration season or, in some cases, the whole year round. One
such example I came across had been made up mostly of doctors, lawyers
and civil servants. Every year they would renew their seasonal lease of
a stretch of garrigue that enjoyed a reputation as one of the best places
anywhere for migrating quail. The members had drawn up a set of rules
that benefited them collectively.[9] They would also place announcements
in the newspapers at the start of the season that the place was reserved
and that trespassers would be fined. While they were in the field, members would hire the services of a police officer who would make sure that
no other hunters entered the area. The daughter of one of the members
told me how, as a child, she would join her father to daub white paint
on stones placed strategically around the perimeter of the reserved area.
These, together with large 'RTO' (short for *riservato*, 'reserved') signs, and
in some places markers that consisted of three stones placed on top of
each other with a wad of grass between the topmost two, served as signs
that the place was reserved (see also Azzopardi 1985). Despite these elaborate measures, trespassing was not uncommon and it was also understood that local hunters who were not members of the syndicate would
hunt there if and when no members happened to be in the field. These
kinds of arrangements have declined in recent years, as more hunters
hunt on their own privately owned patches. As a consequence, the 'RTO'
signs that used to be a common feature of the Maltese countryside have
all but faded or been replaced with 'Private' ones.

The third way in which hunters gain access to land is through informal relationships with landowners and/or leaseholders who in many
cases would themselves be hunters. Kinship, both consanguineal and
affinal, is crucial in this respect, but friendships are also significant. This
kind of arrangement, which is common, involves complex networks of
reciprocity and obligation. It is also vulnerable to changes. For example,
Sandro had for many years been allowed to hunt on land that belonged
to a friend. Relations were good until his friend's daughter married a
man who was a hunter and who had no land of his own. Sandro could
still hunt there, but he now had to compete for choice shooting spots
with the son-in-law who, as an affinal member of the landowning family,
had a stronger claim to the place than him. When I met him, Sandro was
looking to buy a place he could call his own, where he would not be
vulnerable to such shifting circumstances.

The fourth type of access is the least reliable in the longer term and
the most vulnerable to changes in local circumstances. Many hunters
have no fixed place where to hunt. The options open to them include the
woodland estates owned by the government and administered by the

FKNK. Alternatively, they can look for unoccupied places, usually on public land or private land that is used by the owners during peak times. This last kind of access is often characterized by an anxiety to *tilħaq il-post* ('to be there first'). The open stretches of garrigue in the north and west of Malta, as well as places around the coast, are often used by hunters in this way. Individual hunters may become associated with particular places through regular use, in which case they may over time gain a kind of moral claim to place that may also be socially sanctioned through sustained interaction with locals. These informal arrangements are prone to intense competition and, at times, conflict.

There are some general points to make about the different kinds of access to land. First, these distinctions are intended as an analytical typology. It is certainly not the case that individual hunters can be slotted exclusively within particular types. In fact, it is fairly common for any one hunter to have different forms of access to different patches of land that may be spread out across the islands. Many hunters – and this includes those with rooted and secure access to land – will often also roam (*immur indur dawra*) or hunt from hides on unoccupied land at certain times of year. This applies especially to low-lying coastal areas, which, albeit not normally considered choice hunting locations, may become very desirable as top spots for migrating duck, quail and other birds. It is thus not uncommon to come across hunters – many of whom would have secure access to land elsewhere – in makeshift hides along the coast in December, past the peak autumn season, but probably the best time of the year for migrating duck. Especially considering the vagaries of weather, season and migration patterns, such arrangements are considered advantageous. Besides, they also embed, to different extents and in different ways that can be rewarding, individual hunters in a range of localized dynamics of landscape and social networks. These various and shifting intersections between land, family and social fabric make-up a substantial part of hunting biographies in Malta.

The case of Frank, an 88-year-old doctor who was a hunter for over sixty years, will serve to illustrate the point. His first childhood hunting experience was with his father who, together with his brothers (Frank's uncles), leased a piece of land for hunting every year in spring. In 1947, they moved to another, more stable and better lease arrangement elsewhere. In 1953, they joined a syndicate of hunters who collectively leased the right to hunt on agricultural land in spring and autumn. They held this right until the 1980s, a period that Frank now fondly remembers as having been his happiest hunting days. However, in addition to these arrangements, he regularly joined other hunters in various places in Malta and Gozo: 'I was a general practitioner and had scores of patients whom I got to know well. I used to make it a point to get myself invited at the slightest mention of hunting. For example, one of my patients was a landowner who asked his tenants to set aside a corner for me – I was his doctor, he respected me.' Finally, Frank would occasionally roam the fields close to his home, when migration was good and local hunters were not around.

Another example that illustrates the complex processes by which hunters gain access to land is that of Anthony, a 56-year-old who considers his *namra* an inheritance from his father. His father's main interest was trapping turtle doves. He did not have any land of his own and his first form of access was as a guest of a trapper, Toni, who himself was a guest of the landowner and who was allowed to trap in return for a share (roughly half) of the birds he caught. At one point, Toni's eyesight began to wane and Anthony's father took over *fuq il-ġebla* ('on the stone', literally the strategic spot where trappers sit and wait, but here meaning the trapper in charge). The two men grew closer over the years ('it took a long time, because they would only meet for one month every year') and when Anthony's father acquired access to land elsewhere, he invited his old host Toni to join him. When Anthony was born, his father asked Toni to be the *parrinu* (godfather). The land where Anthony regularly hunts and traps is not his, but he is allowed access *bir-rispett* ('out of respect'), based on friendship and later godparenthood ties that go back more than sixty years. A number of other hunters who in their own right enjoy ties of friendship with the owners also use the land. They count on their 'man's word' not to get in each other's way. Anthony told me that this kind of arrangement is common in agricultural areas that are used seasonally for hunting.

The second point is that hunters often draw moralizing distinctions based on these different forms of access to land. Hunters who have no fixed site and who roam may find themselves disparaged by settled locals as being prone to lawlessness. As one hunter put it, 'they spell trouble, they are here today gone tomorrow, and they have nothing to lose . . . *jisparaw u jitilqu 'l hemm* [they shoot and leave]'. Roaming hunters are not embedded in the local networks of reciprocity and obligation that are in turn rooted in kinship or long-term friendship, and tend to be seen as outsiders who are not privy to and do not participate in local codes of conduct. Further, because they are situated outside locally rooted social control and therefore are more likely to misbehave by, for example, shooting protected species, they are thought to invite trouble in the form of surveillance and police attention. The figure of the faceless roaming hunter has emerged as a trope in hunters' discourses of good behaviour and observance of the law. This way, hunters project the image of the lawless hunter peddled by anti-hunting activists and present in the popular imagination generally, onto the figure of the shadowy, faceless outsider. One informant told me how, one afternoon in September, a hunter had turned up who was unknown to locals and who proceeded to shoot at protected harriers. By the time the police (who had probably been alerted by birdwatchers) arrived, he had driven off, which left local hunters to face some difficult questions: 'these people give us all a bad name . . . we would never shoot harriers, but here we were trying to explain to the police why harriers had been shot in our area'.

Clearly, each of these types calls into play a particular kind and extent of attachment to the land. The more localized and less mobile the hunter, the more complex, enduring and affective his localizing strategies. The model is discussed by Marvin (2003), among others, who privileges the case of fox hunters who tend not to travel to different parts of the country to hunt. Rather, they become members or supporters of the Hunt in their local area – an association that may endure in families for generations. The result is that they become intensely committed to their Hunt and develop a deep sense of belonging to a particular Hunt 'country', which in this sense means a local patch and countryside configuration of which they have a close and intimate knowledge that is nourished by hunting experience.

Making Place

The various kinds of access are only part of the land and hunting equation. I once asked Carmelo, a keen hunter and one of my key informants, what the characteristics of a location that was good for hunting were. '*Post taghmlu trid*', he replied, meaning that a (productive) hunting place did not just exist – rather, it had to be 'made'. True to his word, Carmelo has spent much time and money making the place where he hunts with his sons and other members of the family. The land, around 1 ha, was little more than an abandoned field when he bought it some years ago. He has since planted more than 100 trees (mostly eucalyptus, acacia and pines) and installed hunting hides at strategic points around the holding. Every Sunday morning during summer, when it rarely if ever rains, Carmelo spends three hours watering the trees with water brought in by bowser and fed through irrigation tubes that criss-cross the land. The task is as expensive as it is time-consuming, since each bowser consignment costs more than what an average household spends on mains water in a week. Carmelo, however, cherishes these Sunday mornings. As he watches the water seep into the parched soil, he inspects each sapling and tree for growth and signs of disease. He also reflects on its observed and potential attractiveness to birds, and on the long-term prospects of the land he bought, and where he hopes his grandsons will one day hunt. Carmelo knows and feels he is making place – his own place – for hunting.

I shall now discuss some of the ways in which hunters transform land to, as Carmelo put it, make a *post* – literally 'a place', but in this sense one that is conducive to productive hunting. However, before I do so, it is essential to build some understanding of the various ways in which different landscapes attract migrating birds. Hunting in Malta, it is worth emphasizing, is entirely dependent on migration. A valuation of hunting land as a kind that supports healthy populations of game simply does not make sense; rather, what makes a place good is its location on a migration flight path, as well as its ability to entice migrating birds into shooting range.

It is well known in the ornithological literature that day-flying migrant birds may respond to geomorphological features. They are often and obviously seen to follow coastlines or ranges of hills, and to fly along valleys or the edges of forests and deserts. The phenomenon is technically known as 'leading line' (a kind of 'guided broad-front') migration. The canalization of broad fronts by leading lines may lead to mass migration; where this occurs regularly, ornithologists speak of 'migration corridors' or 'flyways' (Berthold 2001). This tendency to follow specific routes offers a number of advantages. The ability to scan the visual landscape allows birds to maintain their migration direction, possibly by point-to-point navigation of a succession of landmarks, and it also enables them to monitor and perhaps correct and compensate for any tendency to be drifted off-course by cross-winds. Topographical features may also generate favourable air currents that reduce the energy cost of migration. The ecological disadvantage is that the higher the volume of birds that follow a particular leading line, the greater the competition for any staging sites (places where birds stop to rest and/or feed) along that route (Baker 1984). Intensive leading lines also make migrating birds more vulnerable to habitat loss and other forms of disturbance at key staging sites. The ornithological literature has documented two main flyways for the Maltese islands. The first concerns the autumn migration of raptors over the hill ranges in the west of Malta (e.g. Thake 1985), the second the migration of ducks through the north and south Comino channels (Falzon 1994). That, however, is only part of the story.

Even in a small place like Malta, there are, in fact, many hundreds of minor leading lines (which do not add up to flyways). Indeed, one might say that every place has its favoured routes, along which migrating birds tend to fly. These routes are too localized and changeable to figure in migration atlases, and in any case each of them concerns an infinitesimally small part of a migrating population. Even so, they are an essential aspect of informal local knowledge of bird migration – the kind of knowledge, that is, that is evident in conversations with both hunters and birdwatchers. To focus on the former, hunters pay zealous attention to these flight paths. The reason is that a sighting matters little to a hunter unless it carries the promise of a bird in the hand. By exploiting the relationship between leading lines and the local topography, hunters are able to bring themselves within shooting range of their quarry. They use the term '*jaqbduni*' (an intriguing inversion of roles, since '*jaqbduni*' literally means 'they catch me') for birds that make the grade. Short distances can make all the difference, as John told me: 'I sometimes hunt at a friend's place at Tal-Għolja which is close to a ridge. In spring it's not bad. In autumn, however, it's hopeless. Turtle doves hug the ridge and pass me by just out of range. I end up sitting there all day watching them fly past without firing a single shot.' Another hunter explained to me how birds were attracted differently to different parts of an apparently featureless and small (about 1 km²) stretch of garrigue; in particular, one corner was the favoured resting place for migrating short-eared owls. (Some time later, another local hunter independently told me the same thing.) I once asked a trapper why a mutual acquaintance persisted in trapping plovers in a field that had become surrounded by busy main roads. I was told that the place had in fact lost little of its potential and that a man was lucky who had access to such a *mamma tal-pluvieri* (plover-sweet spot, loosely translated). An expression that is often used in this sense is *hemmhekk jinħoloq għasfur* ('that place creates birds'): certain spots seem to hold such an attraction to migrating birds that even lean days will 'create' birds (out of nothing, as it were). Hunters, then, spend a considerable amount of their time in the field observing, discussing and theorizing about the ways in which migrating birds relate to the local topography.

That, of course, is the principle. The usefulness or otherwise of these leading lines – indeed, often their very occurrence – is an inexact science that must juggle a number of variables. The first is the lie of the land itself. Probably the most desirable formation is that of hill ridges and edges of cliffs, known in Maltese as *xfarijiet*. The sides of *widien* (valleys) are equally good, especially if they happen to be tall and steep. Another thing that matters considerably on a small island is the ways in which migrating birds *jaqbdu l-art* (make landfall). Distinct geomorphological elements such as headlands tend to attract more than their fair share of migrants, especially around the coast, but there are many exceptions to the rule. Be that as it may, hunters try to position their hides along these natural formations and to wait for leading-line theory to do the rest. That

Figure 4.4. What at first glance looks like a mindless scrawl turns out to be a hunter's rendition (improvised on a boundary wall during fieldwork) of the different ways in which migrant birds approach the islands and his place, according to wind direction and season. Photograph by the author.

it does not always oblige also has to do with a second variable: weather. I mentioned earlier that two reasons why birds follow topographical features are to compensate for cross-winds and to utilize favourable air currents. This also means that leading lines are directly affected by weather conditions and especially wind strength and direction, both of which are subject to tremendous and rapid variations. To improve his chances of getting within range of migrating birds, a hunter must somehow factor in all of these variables and learn the different configurations of his patch.

To further complicate matters, these configurations are in most cases seasonal as well as species-specific. For example, it is well known among hunters that while migrating turtle doves commonly disperse *go l-art* (inland) in spring, they tend to stick to coastal areas on their autumn migration. The stretch of high ground along the west coast is considered to be particularly good for autumn doves and it sometimes happens that hunters who have access to it enjoy abnormally high bags. Some places in the west are good for quail when northeasterly winds blow in autumn, but useless when the same winds blow in spring. A seasoned hunter will know which birds to hope for in which place, in which season and in which weather – which is why access to different sites around the islands is considered highly desirable. There are places that are better than others generally, but there is no single place that is good for all birds at all times.

The dependence of Maltese hunters on leading lines has led to a surprisingly high-profile and formal twist. In 2008, the European Commission instituted a case against the government of Malta for having allowed, by special derogation, the spring hunting of turtle doves and quail between 2004 and 2007. The case was heard by the Luxembourg-based European Court of Justice (ECJ) and a final judgement was given in 2009.[10] This is discussed elsewhere in this volume, but one aspect in particular concerns us here. The Maltese government built its case on what it called a 'lack of other satisfactory solution' to the spring hunting season. The argument was based on two premises: first, that Malta lay at least 300 km away from the main migratory routes and that the numbers migrating were small in any case, but especially so in autumn (so hunting did not significantly affect bird populations); and, second, that while spring migrants tended to fly over the islands in a dispersed way, the autumn migration was almost exclusively concentrated along the west coast. It followed that since 'more than 80 per cent' of hunters hunted on their own land, and that only a small part of that land was on the west coast, limiting hunting to autumn would effectively mean that hunters who had no access to that coast would have no real chance of bagging any birds – in other words, that for those hunters, there was no other satisfactory solution to spring. In the event, the Court seemed in two minds, partly because it argued that the island was too small and the west coast too easily accessible to draw such territorial distinctions. However, the point is that the popular wisdom of seasonal and local leading lines was in this instance formalized in hundreds of pages of 'scientific evidence' and presented before the EU's highest legal body.

Leading lines, geomorphology and weather variables may seem like givens, and therefore not to lend themselves to Carmelo's wisdom of making places. Hunters, however, do not just passively accept the lie of the land and the whims of weather and season. Those who own land or have regular access to a particular place often seek ways to improve their patch and to make it more attractive to migrating birds. If the place already happens to coincide with a leading line, they work at maintaining the system; if it does not, they attempt to create a leading line or to tap into one by siphoning birds off the main route. The ideal is for a place to serve as both favoured route and staging post; that way, one's chances of a catch are improved in terms both of distance and of time available (the longer a bird lingers, the better the chances of shooting it). Trappers are especially limited in this sense, as success for them means birds that are lured directly into the few square metres between the clap nets. Therefore, it is not surprising that the trapping register includes words and expressions that represent this dynamic; thus, migrating birds that appear hurried and reluctant to fly close are called *ħorox* (in this sense 'untamed'), while those that are more pliable are *ituk* (lit. 'they give you'). Throughout, one of the key variables is place – some places are more likely than others to produce birds that *ituk* and that are not *vleġeġ*, and it is to some extent possible to make these places, according to the kind of hunt. Trees are usually a good means of making place, but they are not universally so. While desirable quarry birds like turtle doves and thrushes are woodland species and are therefore attracted to trees, other – and equally desirable to some – kinds are not. Quail and plover, for example, are open-country species and are often found on garrigue or open agricultural land on migration. Trapping, too, is subject to variation. For example, trees may attract hawfinches and greenfinches, but will do nothing to improve one's chances of securing linnets. Broadly speaking, while it is true that on migration, birds tend to be more catholic with respect to habitat, it is still the case that different species favour different environments.

Be that as it may, *cherchez l'oiseau* is the best advice that can be given to those who wish to understand the Maltese countryside. The landscape is systematically transformed into *art ġebbieda* (lit. land that pulls) that has

Figure 4.5. *Cherchez l'oiseau*: in the north of Gozo, a patch of land that is reserved for hunting is both naturally on a leading line (a cliff edge close to the coast) and a 'made' place through the planting of eucalyptus trees. Photograph by the author.

the potential to 'pull' migrating birds. I shall shortly describe some of the ways in which this is done, but there are two general points to be made. First, the underlying principle by which Maltese hunters transform the landscape is distinctly different from, say, that of shooting estates in Britain. In that context, gamekeepers transform the land to best 'keep' the game – that is, to propagate (or help it do so) and contain it.[11] They might do so in ways that improve the chances of a shot and that create a landscape that looks and feels wild, unchanged and natural. Similar processes have been described in Denmark, among other places, where farmers modify their land for the purposes of hunting by planting hedgerows and trees, digging ponds and establishing other kinds of 'uncultivated' landscape elements (Primdahl et al. 2012).

By contrast, gamekeeping and the kind of land transformation processes it entails are unknown in Malta. Dependent as they are on migration, Maltese hunters think solely in terms of attracting a wild and untended resource to their patch, and just long enough to take a shot or spring a net. Second, there have been important shifts in this respect and these are linked to the transformations in access to land described earlier in this chapter. The rise of small, inward-looking landholdings owned and shot over exclusively by private individuals or families has intensified the urge to transform land into what might be called hunting micro-estates. As more and more land is parcelled up and bought by people who previously hunted on public land, there is a corresponding investment into making hunting places. (The case of Carmelo is a good example of this.) The shift is physically tangible in the Maltese countryside in ways that include clumps of trees on small pockets of land that are sometimes enclosed within chest-high walls.

Made Places, but for Who?

I shall now look at what the making of hunting places in Malta actually entails and at the value hierarchies, contestations and politics in which it is embedded. Specificities of place notwithstanding, what follows is far from unique to Malta. Similar points have in fact been made in a number of different contexts and they are worth examining. Upland grouse moors in Britain (mostly Scotland and the north of England) present us with a well-documented example. Richards (2004) shows how the management of moorland for grouse shooting involves a wide range of activities that affect and transform the landscape, often in ways that are not immediately apparent to the casual observer (who might notice little evidence of human activity other than the differently coloured vegetation and the odd vehicle track). There are two main ways in which to hunt grouse. The first is to walk up the quarry and shoot it over dogs, and it is usually practised in places where the density of game is low. The second and by far the more highly prized[12] is limited to places with a relatively high density of game, typically starting at about sixty grouse per km².[13] Grouse, usually in loose groups called 'coveys', are 'driven' towards the waiting 'guns' (shooters) by 'beaters' who walk across the moor in long lines waving white plastic flags and making noise generally. The driven-grouse landscape, which could be seen as a kind of elaborate trap, requires constant management and maintenance by gamekeepers. Their tasks include burning patches of heather in a controlled way so as to provide shorter growth as a food source and longer growth as shelter, reducing losses of grouse stock to predators like stoats, crows and foxes (and, controversially, birds of prey), keeping disease in check and building the 'butts' where the guns sit and wait. The last are 'an integral part of the shooting landscape, their ideal position being determined by the morphology of the land and the related concern of the way grouse are likely to approach them' (Richards 2004: 12).

This set of management practices does not please everyone. Critics – and they are numerous and loud – view the driven-grouse moor as an aberration, ecologically unsustainable and a departure from and a displacement of 'natural' land. Chris Packham, who is well known to hunters in Malta (see elsewhere in this volume), has produced a series of documentaries called *The Real Price of Grouse* in which he argues that driven-grouse moors suffer from poor drainage, indiscriminate burning and above all persecution of predators by gamekeepers intent on keeping the grouse population unrealistically high. With respect to the last point, the hen harrier (a rare and fully protected breeding bird in Britain) functions as an emblematic species used by conservationists to signify the effects on biodiversity of driven-grouse shooting. Packham has described driven-grouse moors as 'black holes' for hen harriers, and a recent polemical book by Avery (2015) on the environmental costs of driven-grouse moors includes a chapter with the title 'The Harrier Harried'. These arguments are rejected and resisted by the cast of people involved in shooting, who hold that the only reason why moorland exists at all is management by gamekeepers. Without controlled burning and other practices, they aver, the landscape would revert to 'scrub' and 'rank growth', and a large variety of bird, animal and plant species would be lost. Further, shooting is the main (and in many cases the only) source of income for vulnerable rural communities. In other words, shooting entails and encourages ecological, aesthetic (because moorland is enjoyed by walkers, among others) and social stewardship.

In his assessment of the situation, Richards (2004) draws a distinction between the practices and evaluations involved in grouse shooting and those that pertain to fox hunting. In the latter case, the hunt and the landscape are, in the minds of objectors, separable. It is the hunt for the fox itself rather than the landscape in which it takes place that critics object to (on animal welfare grounds, largely) and practitioners defend. A different and apparently more effective line of argument is open to those who practise grouse shooting. If the hunt and the moor are inseparable, then rather than being forced to conjure up some utilitarian benefit in the activity of killing the quarry (arguments from vermin control and so on), shooters can cite the characteristics of the grouse habitat itself in support of the shooting that creates and maintains it. As I outlined earlier, this benefit is contested by those who would have driven-grouse shooting banned. The results of such a ban might include tree growth, but even the value of that is contested. Thus, for example, Stott (as cited in Richards 2004) sees the cessation of moor management as offering the prospect of the regeneration of native pine woods. Hudson (as cited in Richards 2004), on the other hand, argues that a ban on shooting would effectively open up the moors to commercial planting of alien tree species as an alternative form of land use. (Shooting estates are also there to turn a profit, after all.) Thus, while both authors think that shooting management would likely be replaced by tree growth, they disagree over the kind and value of growth that would likely replace the moor. Forests here are portrayed as 'more than simply a landscape, with different purposes and extents of human involvement being cited to imply an evaluation – negative in one case and positive in the other – in relation to the grouse moor against which they appear as an alternative' (Richards 2004: 15). Finally, the negative evaluations of grouse moor management are often linked to apparent evaluations of the people involved – shooters, gamekeepers, estate owners and managers and so on: 'those who find cause to object to the landscape of the grouse moor . . . do so because its management practices, the identity of the people directing them and their purpose are all bound together in the evaluation of the landscape – just as they are . . . in the minds of its apologists' (Richards 2004: 13). Certainly Richards is right to point out that opposition to driven-grouse shooting and evaluations of the people involved are entangled. Packham, for example, ascribes the urge to shoot grouse to 'money and psychosis', and describes shooting circles as a 'tiny, selfish, destructive minority who measure their pleasure in the number of things they can kill' (as cited in Avery 2015: 7).

Avery describes driven-grouse shooting as a 'rather parochial and peculiarly British affair, of little interest to most of the world'. He assures us that, in conservation terms, grouse shooting is an oddity and that 'nowhere else in the world do the same issues arise, and nowhere else are the same arguments made in quite the same way, or with the same venom' (2015: 9). My work in Malta suggests otherwise. Even if the context is different – dependent on migration rather than the keeping of game, apart from other obvious differences – the notions of stewardship, evaluation of the people involved and above all afforestation all turn out to be essential to our understanding of land transformations and the kind of valuations that go with them in Malta. Afforestation and trees serve as a good illustration of the homology and are worth looking at in detail.

Trees have not, in recent history at least, been a defining feature of the Maltese landscape. Nineteenth- and early twentieth-century photographs, and earlier landscape paintings, show a treeless countryside marked by intensive agriculture and grazing, and travellers' accounts by British and other visitors often remark on the 'barren' aspect of the countryside. The exceptions included the maquis-type vegetation of valleys, the clumps of carob trees (also known as 'St John's Bread') that dotted agricultural areas and were used as a food source (the pods were used as animal fodder, to make carob syrup or simply eaten as a snack), a few scattered citrus and other orchards, and a wooded area known as Buskett (from the Italian *boschetto*, 'little wood') that was originally planted as a hunting park by a succession of grandmasters of the Order of St John.[14]

Foreign travellers aside, it was only in the twentieth century that 'treelessness' and lack of 'greenery' came to be seen as things that ought to be fixed. The first 'Arbor Day' was held in 1928 on the initiative of the Director of Education at the time. The valuation of trees as desirable objects picked up pace in the second half of the century, at a time when ENGOs – two of which, Men of the Trees (Malta) and Arbor, were concerned directly with trees[15] – were being set up. The landscape came to be valued in aesthetic, ecological and leisure-related terms rather than exclusively agricultural ones rooted in a language of productivity. Trees – often in their incarnation as 'lungs' – emerged as symbols of a healthy, pleasant and ecologically sound environment, and afforestation came on to the agenda. In the 1950s, pine, olive and other types of trees were planted by the government in various areas thought to be advantageous due to their water-catchment qualities (Bowen-Jones et al. 1961), and thousands of trees donated by the Israeli government were planted in the north of Malta. The story is long and complex, but suffice it to say that by the 1980s, places like Aħrax and Miżieb had been radically transformed from 'barren' (mostly garrigue, that is, as well as some abandoned fields) rocky ridges to ones covered in young trees. Besides, trees and afforestation came to feature prominently in a string of national environmental strategies. For example, the 1990 Structure Plan for the Maltese Islands made a number of recommendations for an active forestry strategy; significantly, they included the idea that afforestation projects in nonurban areas should only make use of indigenous or archaeophytic[16] tree species. Successive 'local plans' and 'biodiversity strategies' made similar points.[17] There are many reasons why afforestation is especially relevant within the context of this chapter generally and the present argument specifically.

The planting of trees was by no means exclusively a state enterprise. On the contrary, both ENGOs and hunters were actively and to some extent independently involved. With respect to ENGOs, trees were (and are) considered an integral part of a landscape valued for its aesthetic and ecological assets. They were planted and tended to in a number of ways: individually, by environmentalists looking to add value to public land they were familiar with as birdwatchers and such; in an informal but coordinated way, especially in or around bird reserves; and in choreographed and widely publicized 'tree planting activities'. The kind of trees that were valued the highest were those classified as 'indigenous' to Malta specifically and the Mediterranean more broadly – these included oak, pine, carob[18] and tamarisk, as well as a host of other species that bore fruit that could be eaten by birds.

For their part, hunters value trees in terms of their place-making qualities – because they serve to attract migratory birds, that is. Carob trees are particularly highly prized since they are known to attract turtle doves. However, it was only since the early 1980s or so that hunters took to planting trees as part of their place-making projects. The trickle soon became a deluge and can be seen as a corollary to the process of the privatization of hunting land discussed earlier. In many parts of Malta, substantial patches were transformed from 'bare' fields under cultivation, or rocky areas, into a patchwork of dense groves, mostly of eucalyptus and acacia. The results are dramatic in parts of south and southwest Malta, and especially in Gozo. In the latter case, water-retentive clay soils lend themselves to dense and tall eucalyptus growth. Many hunters hold that the new groves changed the configurations of the leading lines discussed earlier. If this was the point of tree planting all along, it both made and unmade leading lines. I was often told by informants that *'illum il-gamiem tferrex'* ('nowadays the turtle doves have dispersed'). What they meant is that the classic leading lines of ridges and valleys have somewhat lost their accent as migrating birds break up into small groups and head for the trees instead. Whether or not that is indeed the case, the point is that hunters perceive the landscape, and their presence in it, as fluid and competitive. Newly planted trees are thought to have the power to siphon off at least their fair share of migrating birds and, as

Figure 4.6. Extensive eucalyptus planting by hunters in Gozo. At least three elevated shooting hides are visible; also of note is how close the hunting place is to village houses. Photograph by the author.

the leading lines change, so do one's chances of taking a shot. It is a zero-sum game, the winners and losers of which keep changing as some make place to better effect than others. The result is partly a perennial urge of any individual hunter to constantly improve his patch by planting more and faster-growing trees. In this sense, Carmelo's Sunday mornings represent a continuing investment.

Both environmentalists and hunters, then, value and plant trees. And yet, rather than marking a rare instance of convergence, trees represent in fact a key site of contestation. The different approaches to trees and tree planting are exemplified on Comino, a 3.5 km² island and bird sanctuary that lies between Malta and Gozo. Comino is largely garrigue, but there are remnants of agricultural land that was once extensive. (The island supported a small community of farmers in the mid-twentieth century.) Two contrasting sites concern us here. The first is a group of semi-abandoned fields occupied by Salvu and Anġlu, two of the three remaining inhabitants of the island. Although they seldom shoot nowadays, both Salvu and his brother are keen hunters and remember a time when Comino was as intensively shot over as was the rest of Malta. Starting from the 1990s, they transformed the area into what they hoped would be a magnet for migrating turtle doves. They extended an extant olive grove by planting dozens of eucalyptus saplings and using drip irrigation to water them regularly. Extensive parts of the fields are now under dense eucalyptus growth that is about four metres high on average.

The grove is quietly frowned upon as alien and damaging to the landscape by the occupiers of another patch of formerly abandoned fields a few hundred metres away. In the late 1980s, BirdLife Malta ringers took to using the area, which is public land, as a seasonal ringing station. They eventually managed to secure its tenure and to set up a bird observatory that consists of two small field rooms where Maltese and foreign ringers can lodge during the migration seasons. Tree planting followed, and the area around the station now contains a substantial number of trees – pines, oaks, carob and specialities like the Sandarac gum tree, a locally endangered Mediterranean species and Malta's national tree. The trees are valued primarily in terms of their attractiveness to migrant birds,[19] but also as an ecological service to a landscape that was in need of indigenous tree cover. Salvu and Anġlu's, and BirdLife Malta's groves are almost literally a stone's throw apart, but they represent a disjuncture that is at the heart of land transformations by hunters and their evaluation and contestation by conservationists.

The point is that while trees and tree planting are equally valued by both sides, they are not valued generically. Rather, they are embedded in a contested hierarchy of value that in turn latches on to moral evaluations of hunting by conservationists and vice versa. Key to this hierarchy is the notion of alien species. Afforestation is one thing; afforestation made up of eucalyptus and acacia trees quite another. Environmentalists complain that these species are aliens that poison the soil, deplete water sources and use up space that would otherwise be occupied by indigenous and beneficial trees – pines, olives, carobs and so on.

It is essential at this point to briefly discuss this hierarchy of value in terms of what Subramaniam (2001) calls the 'rhetoric of biological invasions'. In recent decades, there has been a growing worldwide concern about alien species of plants and animals that, by direct or indirect anthropogenic means, invade native habitats and compete with, or displace outright, indigenous species. ('Alien', 'invade', 'native' and 'indigenous' are the standard vocabulary of this rhetoric.) Originally the preserve of specialists in ecology and conservation, this biological nativism has caught the public imagination in a number of contexts – aggressive squirrels that unseat their daintier cousins and giant snails that can gnaw the plaster off walls make for rather edible stories. Subramaniam describes it as 'one of the ironies in the world today, that in this era of globalization, there is a renewed call for the importance of the "local" and the protection of the indigenous' (2001: 26). She also notes the homology between biological nativism, 'germ panics' and xenophobic anxieties about (human) immigration. A similar point is made by Tsing (1995), who looks at how, in the United States, renditions of the invading non-European human outsider infect and infuse stories about 'killer' Africanized bees. Partly because they are so intertwined with social and cultural categories, aliens and natives raise a host of taxonomic issues. Broadly, and as Helmreich (2005) argues, questions of classification – and in particular the classification of nature – have been at the heart of anthropology. In this case, and far from being a straightforward matter of biological classification, the categorization of aliens is organized around the presence or absence of the agency of humans. It is a metataxonomic categorization that transcends the classificatory grid of biological nomenclature – as Helmreich (2005: 110) puts it, 'biogeographic status is not a Linnaean category'. The fact that alien invasions are therefore an instance of what Haraway (2008) calls 'naturecultures' and involve human agency and cultural variables means that 'not all invasions are created equal' (Carlton 2000: 42, as cited in Helmreich 2005: 111). The point is that alien invasions are located within the parameters of 'time, agency, and the politics of nature and culture in particular places' (Helmreich 2005: 125).

The *Red Data Book for the Maltese Islands*, published in 1989, was an early example of the rhetoric of biological invasions in Malta. As the authors put it, 'the indigenous flora and fauna is also under threat of being outcompeted and displaced by a variety of alien species which have been introduced into the islands over the years, sometimes by natural processes, but more often through human agency' (Schembri and Sultana 1989: 2). They also made the opposite and symmetrical case for endemics, which they described as being of 'exceptional importance' – scientifically and also because they were 'uniquely Maltese . . . should they become extinct from our islands, they will have disappeared from the face of the Earth and there is nothing anybody can do to bring them back' (Schembri and Sultana 1989: 1). The *Red Data Book* exemplified an emerging hierarchy of value that set species up in an 'alien' versus 'local' opposition; within 'local', 'indigenous' came second to 'endemic' – all endemic species are indigenous, but the former's uniqueness to Malta makes them a rarefied type indeed. This hierarchy is now so culturally embedded that it has seeped into the popular imagination. For example, the press regularly carries pieces on some alien species (marine or terrestrial, plant or animal) that threatens to displace indigenous, and in some cases endemic, nature. Each case is linked to a human activity, be it ballast water, the aquarium trade, exotic pets or garden centres. With respect to trees, the distinction was formalized in Legal Notice 200 of 2011, which outlawed the planting of aliens and especially acacia and eucalyptus. The Notice included three schedules: the first and second, lists of protected and strictly protected natives respectively; the third, of 'invasive, alien, or environmentally incompatible species'.

It is within these emerging parameters of time, agency and the politics of nature and culture in Malta that the trees 'put in place by nature', those planted by hunters and those planted by environmentalists are located. Eucalyptus and acacia trees, and in particular the former, are singled out by environmentalists as aliens that harm indigenous Maltese nature. Further, since these species are planted by hunters, it follows that hunters are agents of biological invasion. It also follows that, like the trees they plant, hunters do not really belong in the Maltese landscape. The language of 'inappropriate' trees thus serves to construct hunters as not merely a threat to the Maltese countryside, but one rooted in ignorance, egoism or both – ignorance because hunters do not understand the value of indigenous species and their rightful place in nature, and egoism because the reason why hunters plant eucalyptus is that it grows quickly.

As expected, hunters do not just accept these classifications; on the contrary, they resist and contest them. An FKNK report on the draft of the 2011 bill makes for useful reading in this respect. It described the bill, and the outlawing of eucalyptus in particular, as results of 'armchair thinking with little basis in reality' and argued that it would short-circuit what had been the 'environment miracle' of afforestation:

> This environment 'miracle' did not happen overnight. It took much time and patience, and was mainly brought about by the hunters and trappers of Malta and Gozo who did their utmost to transform their mini-acres from semi-desert into miniature oases. They did this by investing their time, labour, energy and money in planting thousands of trees and nursing them to full growth. The trees they planted were varied, and apart from the so-called 'indigenous' ones such as the carob, olive, and Aleppo pine, they also planted a host of fast-growing trees the majority of which are acacia and eucalyptus. As a result of their efforts, the Maltese and Gozitan countryside looks a great deal better than it did a generation ago. Now, however, a monster is rearing its head![20]

The monster in question was the bill itself, which made provisions for the clearing of non-indigenous species generally and eucalyptus and acacia in particular. The FKNK went on to argue that acacia trees were beautiful, made good fodder trees, provided a source of nectar for bees to make excellent honey, fixed nitrogen, were a food plant for many insects, provided birds with shelter and had various medicinal uses. For their part, eucalyptus trees were beautiful, produced a timber that lent itself to woodturning, were invaluable to beekeepers as a source of nectar and provided birds with shelter. Given the 'rocky terrain' of Malta, there was no way in which acacia and eucalyptus could ever naturally regenerate and become 'invasive'. Finally, and very significantly, the FKNK document pointed out that the bill would likely lead to 'discrimination'. ENGOs, but not hunters, would probably get away with their nonindigenous trees: 'The "Israeli" grove at Għajn Tuffieħa under the management of the GAIA Foundation consists almost exclusively of Acacia species . . . Will the Foundation's acacia grove face the chop after the new regulations come into force? Not likely.'[21]

The document indicates that the FKNK (and hunters generally) contests the negative valuations of certain tree types by environmentalists (and the state, in this case). In practice, in the field, and away from the rhetoric of biological invasions, hunters value eucalyptus as fast-growing trees that attract birds and especially turtle doves. To remove them, or to replace them with slower-growing trees, would put the individual at a disadvantage in the zero-sum game described earlier. Eucalyptus, then, are excellent place-making trees, irrespective of their provenance and belonging. The FKNK document essentially defends this practice, in part by pointing out the various benefits of acacia and eucalyptus – and therefore locating hunters as stewards and benefactors of a productive and aesthetically pleasing environment. Recently, however, hunters themselves have increasingly adopted the value hierarchy of indigenous versus alien. Even as they water and tend to their eucalyptus trees, they talk about the benefits of indigenous species and emphasize that new planting tends to be in that direction. It is not all just lip service. Thus, for example, a recently planted stand of trees at Miżieb by the FKNK (tellingly, the planting was publicized and sponsored by a private law firm) uses species like the Sandarac gum tree and the holm oak, both of which fall squarely within the indigenous rubric, and a number of hunters have in recent years planted pines as readily as they have eucalyptus.[22] Increasingly, the FKNK is keen on representing hunters as the stewards not of any countryside, but one populated by indigenous species.

One of the reasons behind this shift is that it seeks to align hunting with dominant environmentalist narratives that appear to be backed by science and its prestige language of invasion and ecological incompatibility. Hunters in Malta today understand the political dynamics in which these notions are embedded. They know that advantage lies not in their negation, but rather in their appropriation. Besides, many hunters have taken to planting olives that, although relatively slow-growing, are attractive to birds and produce the side-benefit of fruit. The last is significant in at least two ways: first, it rehearses the classical bricolage of hunting and agriculture discussed earlier in this chapter; and, second, it locates hunting within an ascendent hierarchy that assigns great value to the olive as a timeless (ironically enough) product of the Mediterranean region. Local production of olive oil has shot up in the last twenty years or so, also in light of fashionable assurances as to the magical attributes of a Mediterranean diet based on olive oil, the economic possibilities of boutique production, added value in the tourist market and so on. By planting olives, hunters can align themselves with a broader narrative of national development, even as they make hunting place.

The significance of tree planting lies as much in the action as in the results. Ekers and Farnan (2010) have explored the cultural representations (in film, for example, and 'wilderness art' more broadly) of tree planting in the context of Canadian nationalism. In particular, the staple and romanticized images of white, middle-class young men and women who spend time in remote campsites and plant trees on logged-over land serve to link the action to a discourse in which the Canadian nation shares the demographic attributes of the planters. Because it signifies the ecological regeneration of the landscape and the righting of the 'historical wrong of industrial logging', planting roots the planters within a long-term narrative in which 'the nation's subjects look to the past and then rush through the obligatory national passage point of the Canadian tree planting experience in order to realize the promised future of the nation' (2010: 111). The emphases are on the value of cultural representations (rather than something innate to tree planting itself), the location of planters within a broader (environmental and nationalist) narrative and a broader (national) community, and the link between the (racial, class and other) characteristics of planters and the kind of nation that is imagined.

In Malta, the cultural representation of tree planting and its significance underwent an important transformation in the last quarter of the twentieth century. Prior to that, the planting of trees as a public spectacle was done for ceremonial purposes and on special occasions. Thus, for example, when Emperor (then Crown Prince) Hirohito of Japan visited Malta in 1921, his itinerary included the planting of a tree in a public garden. Two things happened to public tree-planting events in the late twentieth century: first, their frequency increased sharply as school and corporate events, annual occasions like World Environment Day and Arbor Day, or other private or public initiatives, were increasingly deemed at least as worthy as visits by Japanese princes; and, second, they became linked to an environmentalist double narrative of 'greening the nation' specifically and contributing to a greener and ecologically more sound planet more broadly. (At some point, the themes of climate change and carbon sinks were scripted in.) To plant trees was to become part of this two-pronged project of ecological redemption. Images of politicians 'doing their bit for the environment' and of company employees 'taking up their corporate responsibility' became a staple cultural representation that located those wielding the spade within a narrative of good citizen-ship, a 'greener' nation and environmental responsibility. In this vein, government's '34U' ('tree for you') campaign was launched in 2005 and at the time of writing is still in place. It 'gives an opportunity to individ-uals, NGOs and companies alike to plant indigenous trees in afforestation areas around the Maltese Islands'. To plant a tree is to contribute 'towards a better environment and will help us [the government] create greener and healthier places for people to enjoy for generations to come'.[23] The cost of sponsoring a tree includes the sapling itself as well as a dedication tag and a commemorative photo.

While both hunters and environmentalists participate in this increas-ingly powerful cultural representation, they do so in different ways. Tree-planting events have in recent years become a much-publicized aspect of the public image of hunters. For example, literature produced by the FKNK often features groups of hunters planting or tending to trees, usu-ally in one of the woodland areas reserved for hunting. Much the same is true of ENGOs: for example, BirdLife Malta's tree-planting events have their own special site online. In 1995, the organization came up with the idea of converting an area of abandoned fields close to the nature reserve at Għadira into a 'Mediterranean woodland'. Tapping into the notion of

Figure 4.7. Afforestation in progress at BirdLife Malta's Foresta 2000. Photograph by the author.

millennium projects, the place was christened 'Foresta 2000'. To date, about 20,000 trees have been planted there, including many at large-scale planting events hosted by BirdLife Malta. There are two points to be made here.

First, tree planting by ENGOs is usually represented as 'restoration' of a once-pristine environment in which Malta was thickly forested. This, for example, is how Foresta 2000 is described by BirdLife Malta: 'In the past Malta was covered in woodland, however when people arrived on the islands 7000 years ago, woodland was cleared to create agricultural land for growing crops. In 1995 BirdLife Malta came up with the idea of restoring this area of degraded woodland to its former glory.'[24] The time scale in which contemporary tree planting belongs includes the primordial past as well as the distant future. In this context, the stands of old trees that are thought to be 'remnant populations' of the thick forest that once covered Malta become very significant – so much so that their value is formalized in law and in officializing discourses. A prime example is Il-Ballut tal-Wardija, a stand of old oaks thought to be a remnant population that dates back around a thousand years. To environmentalists, these 'forest remnants' function as repositories of ecological meaning. To visit them is to step into a time continuum in which indigenous nature holds out against modernity and human agency. To plant trees is to work towards the restoration of that past and, by inference, to locate one's actions within a long-term eschatological narrative of pristine nature.

There are no such references in hunters' representations of tree planting; rather, the emphasis is on social responsibility and on hunters as good citizens who value nature and are ready to contribute towards a healthy environment in Malta. In this sense, tree planting serves as yet another example of the different frameworks and cartographies of meaning and practice discussed in Chapter 3. While environmentalists locate the practice, and its representations, within broad contexts of Nature and its redemption in Malta and globally (the latter through associations with carbon, climate change and so on), hunters tend to locate its moral bearings within the nation-state.

Second, the point about tree planting as a spectacle is rendered more forceful when one considers its opposite. In 2010, three young men were fined and sentenced to community service after they pleaded guilty to having destroyed 104 saplings at Foresta 2000. It turned out that the men were hunters and that they had destroyed the trees because they were 'angry at the decisions that had been taken regarding hunting'.[25] Many of the destroyed trees had been planted in 2007 to make up for a more serious act of vandalism in which up to 3,000 saplings were uprooted. Since the point is spectacle and its location within a politics of conservation, two things are worth noting: first, the images of sawn-off stumps quickly made the headlines in the Maltese press; and, second, a number of organizations reacted publicly to the news of the sentence. The warden of Foresta 2000, a BirdLife Malta member, said that the sentence was too lenient; the President of Din l-Art Ħelwa ('This Fair Land', an ENGO) said that the vandalism had been 'a destructive act that harmed the natural environment'; the President of Nature Trust called it a 'major environmental crime [because of which] all of the Maltese population had suffered'; and the President of Gaia, an ENGO, said that 'you cannot put a price on nature'. Significantly, the hunting organizations were equally vociferous. The FKNK 'strongly and unequivocally condemned such a cowardly act against the environment' and added that 'over decades, hunters and trappers have planted and cared for tens of thousands of trees all over Malta and Gozo, definitely much more than any other sector of the society'; the FKNK also proceeded to disown the hunters by suspending their membership, effectively making it legally impossible for them to renew their hunting licence. For its part, the KSU condemned the act and said that 'hunting issues should be resolved by the involvement of all parties concerned through democratic means around a negotiating table . . . unfortunately, certain malicious actions by fanatics from both sides of the fence prevent such dialogue being possible and only lead to more animosity'.[26] The action of uprooting or otherwise destroying trees, then, functions as a spectacle in much the same way as planting or tending to them: it sets up the doer vis-à-vis discourses of social responsibility and stewardship of nature, and embeds itself in a political dynamic in which different groups locate themselves within dominant discourses of morality and value.[27]

The transformation of land by hunters is not, of course, just about trees. Trapping, for example, requires the making and maintenance of the *mansab* (trapping site). In practice, if not necessarily legally, trapping sites may be situated anywhere, and that includes garrigue that has to be levelled, cleared of stones and vegetation, and prepared to accommodate the nets. Some trappers also encourage selective growth of plants that are known to attract finches; these include various types of thistles (*xewk*), amaranths (*għobbejra*), and mustard (*ġarġir*).[28] Every year in late summer, trappers maintain their sites in preparation for the autumn season. The term they use is *tnaddaf il-mansab* ('to clean the trapping site') and it is deceptively benign (see below). On the one hand, and as trappers see it, it is about keeping a place tidy and suitable for trapping. *Tnaddaf*, however, means 'to clean' generally. Hunters and trappers will point out that they spend much of their time cleaning up after Sunday afternoon trippers and the *ħmieġ* (dirt, rubbish) they leave behind, or that they rescue rubble walls from the destructive practices of people looking for snails (which is significant because rubble walls are considered a picturesque and desirable feature of the Maltese countryside). Therefore, as hunters see and represent it, their practice contributes to a clean and tidy countryside that can be enjoyed by a public that is often insensitive to the state of the countryside and to rural matters like hunting.

On their part, environmentalists point out that the images of a tidy countryside are a front. As they see it, the trapper's – and to a lesser extent the hunter's – *tnaddaf* actually means to clear the landscape of wild plants and nature generally in order to make room for what are essentially ecologically sterile wastelands. The principle is established at law and there is a long list of places where trapping sites are not allowed. Apart from nature reserves and places where no hunting or trapping may take place generally, they include areas within Natura 2000 sites that contain one of more specially designated habitat types (there are many), as well as scheduled 'Areas of Ecological Importance' and 'Sites of Scientific Importance'.[29] In effect, trapping is limited to cultivated agricultural land and relatively disturbed areas that are not classified as ecologically valuable in any way; scheduled garrigue and maquis are off-limits to trappers, and there is a system by which all registered trapping sites are GPS-located and matched with maps of habitat types and their respective ecological value. However, environmentalists are not convinced and oppose trapping also on account of its cavalier destruction of natural flora and fauna.

To hunters, the hyphenated being-there may be an intrinsic and fundamental part of the hunt. Yet, to bird protectionists and ENGOs, it adds another dimension to the arguments against hunting, namely that of the destruction of the landscape. It is in this context that the place-making practices of environmentalists that are the subject of the next chapter belong.

Notes

1. Ted Hughes, 'Hawk Roosting' in *Lupercal*. London: Faber & Faber, 1960.
2. Baker 2015: 31.
3. Until a couple of decades ago, it was common for trophies to be displayed in windows overlooking the street, among other conspicuous places. Increasingly, however, and due partly to the changes discussed in Chapter 3, taxidermy trophies tend to be locked away in homes, away from prying eyes. It is also the case that many people no longer consider them fashionable or in good taste. Internationally, taxidermy went out of fashion after the First

World War, only to experience a meteoric rise in popularity from the early 1970s (Turner 2013).

4. Some of my informants told me that, while at home domestic work was the preserve of their wives, in the field they readily took to 'housekeeping' tasks. As one hunter put it, *'id-dar ma mmissx xkupa, hawn 'il hin kollu niknes'* ('I don't as much as touch a broom at home, but here I spend my time sweeping'). Of course, the emphasis here was that this was not really domestic work and that cultural notions of gender and division of labour had not been transgressed.

5. Excerpt from an interview with a hunter published in *Il-Passa-temp*, Issue 35, August 2016.

6. In 2018, the total number of people (almost exclusively men) employed in construction in Malta was 12,595 or 9.6 per cent of the total employed population (source: Labour Force Survey, National Statistics Office, Malta, Q1/2018).

7. 1 tumolo (Malt. *tomna*) = 1,124 m².

8. Hierarchies work both ways. Thus, while *is-sinjur* might enjoy higher social prestige, tenants enjoy legal security of tenure for ridiculously low rents and without having to pay succession duties. In fact, offers by landowners to purchase are usually turned down or met with offers of deliberately risible amounts. This in part explains why the old landowning families have not, for the most part, sold up to tenants.

9. Members were allowed to enter the reserved land before sunrise to shoot turtle doves, but not quail (this ensured that quail would not be flushed and disturbed before the time was right); they were not allowed to shoot in a field or enclosure that was already occupied by another member; the use of *kwaljerin* (a device to call quail, that therefore gave an unfair advantage) was not allowed; and members were obliged to stop trespassing hunters from entering the reserved area. Members who did not observe these rules risked losing their membership of the syndicate.

10. Judgment of the European Court of Justice, Case C-76/08, 10 September 2009.

11. For a recent account by an insider, see Simpson (2017). Portia Simpson worked as a gamekeeper on deer-hunting and grouse- and pheasant-shooting estates at Invercauld, Ardverikie, Letterewe and the Isle of Rum.

12. It is not unusual for 'guns' to pay four- or even five-figure sums per session for the privilege of sitting in 'butts' and shooting grouse (Simpson 2017).

13. Such high densities are only achievable on managed moors, which means that grouse numbers are highest on shooting estates. Avery (2015) states that the management regimes produce grouse densities that are always ten times what they would normally be and that in some cases, that figure can go up to one hundred times. To opponents of driven-grouse shooting, these figures are an indictment of the practice as an unnatural aberration.

14. This, for example, is Waring writing in 1843: 'For some distance we followed the course of a little valley, which, though more fertile or, I should rather say, less barren than any part of the island . . . Almost the only trees we met with on this excursion were the fig, now without foliage, and the carob tree . . . We wished to have explored the south-west coast, and to have visited Citta

Vecchia and the "Boschetto". This place from its name and from the annexed view, appears to be more woody and pleasant than any other part of the island' (Waring 1843: 178–90).

15. Men of the Trees (Malta) was founded in the late 1960s as a branch of Men of the Trees, an organization set up in Britain in 1924 by Richard 'St Barbe' Baker. The first committee for Malta included British people as well as a Maltese senior civil servant and army officer. Arbor was set up by a university student in 1989, by which time Men of the Trees (Malta) was largely defunct. It later merged with other ENGOs to become Nature Trust (Malta).

16. A non-native organism (a tree species in this case) that was introduced in antiquity, that is, before Europeans became aware of the existence of the Americas and that became naturalized and integrated in the landscape (Lanfranco 2015).

17. Louis F. Cassar and Elisabeth Conrad, 'An Outline Strategy for Implementation of a National Restoration and Afforestation Project', unpublished report, October 2014.

18. Technically an archaeophyte.

19. They were, in fact, planted in ways that facilitate the setting up of the mist nets used by bird ringers.

20. 'Critique of the Draft Consultative Trees and Woodlands Protection Regulations, 2011', FKNK, 2011.

21. 'Critique of the Draft Consultative Trees and Woodland Protection Regulations, 2011', FKNK, 2011.

22. In some cases, pines are planted that are several years old and imported from Sicily. The costs are high compared to that of small saplings, but it is a means by which hunters circumvent the problem of slow-growing species.

23. Website of the Ministry for Sustainable Development, the Environment, and Climate Change, Government of Malta, www.msdec.gov.mt, accessed on 19 August 2016.

24. BirdLife Malta website, www.birdlifemalta.org, accessed on 20 August 2016.

25. 'Hunters Plead Guilty to Foresta 2000 Vandalism', *Times of Malta*, 24 August 2010.

26. 'Trees Vandalism Court Sentence Deemed Too Lenient by Park Warden', *Times of Malta*, 26 August 2010.

27. At the time of writing, there is a controversy in Malta over the removal of trees to make way for wider roads. To many, this represents the government's lack of environmental and social responsibility.

28. Various techniques are used. Amaranth, for example, grows in summer. What trappers do is cut and keep clumps of it in the dark until the autumn season, when they place them in specially dug holes around the trapping area.

29. Subsidiary Legislation 549.93 of 15 July 2014, Government of Malta.

CHAPTER 5

Watching over Migrants

But instead of linking city to city and runway to runway, the bird-migration maps linked wild place to wild place . . . The migrating birds did not shun humans; they were happy to live round them. What they did assess when choosing where to land, though, was wildness: how far the water and the land would allow them to follow their own instincts and fulfil their own needs. Where they could not do this, they did not land.
—Robert Macfarlane, *The Wild Places*[1]

Yet the middle-class professionals . . . eventually came to realise that their best means of safeguarding the wildlife was also to control the land.
—Mark Cocker, *Our Place*[2]

Late in the summer of 2018, a flock of ten flamingos set up home at Għadira, a BirdLife Malta nature reserve in the north of Malta. Special open days were held and the birds were seen by several hundred members of the public over the following weeks. However, one afternoon in November, three of the flamingos decided to stretch their wings outside the reserve. A few minutes later, only two returned, one of which had visible gunshot injuries on the neck. This is how the BirdLife Malta press release put it:

> The uniqueness of these birds complemented by their elegance left many amazed with their beauty, especially after the public began to understand the way they feed and get their pink colour, whilst also learning about their migration. All these added to the appreciation of nature's beauty . . . In a year to be labelled as the worst year for the illegal hunting of protected birds in the past six years, this incident just proves the sad reality that illegal hunting in Malta and Gozo is rampant.[3]

Bird protection activists routinely represent the Maltese countryside as a place that, if left to hunters' devices, would be a Gin Lane for birds. Among the antidotes into which they invest a tremendous amount of energy are places of conservation where birds and nature enjoy some degree of protection. In this sense, a reserve like the one at Għadira functions as a kind of laager within which birds like flamingos can be safe.

The place-making activities of bird protection ENGOs tend to be rooted in the routines of field observation of nature generally and birdwatching in particular. However, this does not mean that they are all about ornithology. Rather, as Zerner puts it, nature conservation and environmental management are inevitably projects in politics:

> Certain species, landscapes and environmental outcomes are privileged, while others are peripheralized or disenfranchised. Each park, reserve, and protected area is a project in governance: in drawing boundaries – conceptual, topographic, and normative; in implicating a regime of rules regulating permissible human conduct; in elaborating an institutional structure vested with power to enforce rules; and in articulating a project mission rendering the management regime reasonable, even natural. (Zerner 1999: 16–17)

In this chapter I explore the place-making projects – which are obviously of direct consequence to hunting and conservation – of bird protection activists in Malta. Using examples, I first look at how specific spaces are singled out, located and made into places of long-term ornithological and conservation significance. I then look in turn at two kinds of specialized places: the fenced reserve and the protected area. Finally, I describe and discuss the panopticization of the Maltese landscape more broadly, and the attempt to transform it into a place that is safe for birds and where hunters are disciplined.

Locating Birds, Nature and Conservation

The bird protection enterprise at hand is located squarely in Malta. It takes as one of its foundational principles the transformation of the national space into one in which birds are ornithologically appropriated and likely to stay alive. However, that is not to say that this space is a flat, straightforward or undifferentiated one; on the contrary, it is contoured, distorted, Escher-like and homes in on particular places as being of special significance. The process by which the cut is made is worth looking at in some depth and with the use of an example.

One such site of special significance is situated within Buskett, a wooded area in the west of Malta. Every year from late August to early October, birdwatchers congregate every afternoon on a patch of open rocky high ground called *fuq ix-xagħra* ('on open land'), specifically in one spot known as *ħdejn iċ-ċipressa* ('by the cypress'). As the names suggest, it is a fairly unassuming patch of garrigue where the only landmark is a lone cypress tree. However, the place is considered to be exceptionally valuable on account of the birds of prey that migrate through every autumn. On some days the experience can get intense, as hundreds (occasionally thousands) of the impressive birds converge on Buskett and often roost there. The phenomenon quickly came to the attention of the first Maltese birdwatchers in the 1960s and there has been an unbroken line of annual sustained effort ever since. By the standards of any bird-watching location, anywhere, Buskett has a long memory. To spend time there is to watch birds and hope for rarities and so on, but also to be part of a history of birdwatching. The point of congregation is the cypress tree that regulars have, year after year, watched grow from a tiny sapling into a fairly tall and dense tree that offers some shelter from the hot sun. On September afternoons, *ħdejn iċ-ċipressa* is *the* place to be, partly because of the promise of birds, but also in terms of socialization value. Apart from the regulars (typically a core of five to ten birdwatchers who go there every day for the duration of the season), people with a sporadic interest in birdwatching will usually visit once or twice in September as a kind of ritual of renewal. The constant rounds of texting and phoning also

Figure 5.1. Birdwatchers congregate *ħdejn iċ-ċipressa*, Buskett, on a typical September afternoon. Photograph by the author.

make the place a hub of information about what happens to be migrating, where.

However, the significance of *fuq ix-xagħra* and Buskett goes further. Hunting has been outlawed there for several decades, and in any case birds of prey have been fully protected in Malta since 1980, but bird-watchers over the age of thirty-five or so have vivid memories of the rampant hunting and targeting of birds of prey that took place every September well into the 1990s. Stories of dozens of honey buzzards shot in a single evening as they flew in to roost are routinely circulated at *fuq ix-xagħra*, especially on days when migration is good ('twenty years ago, it would have been a massacre'). Older birdwatchers will point out to younger ones the bush behind which an eagle fell, the place where hunters sat waiting for a flock of birds and so on. Yet this is only part of the story, because they also possess and circulate memories of police chases, public protests and efforts by BirdLife Malta to have the law enforced. The protection of birds of prey at Buskett was, in fact, possibly the highest-profile and most sustained bird protection campaign of the 1980s and 1990s. The year 1994 was a landmark one in that birdwatchers at Buskett were attacked, and some seriously injured, by a large group of hunters. Twenty years later, there was another, equally wounding attack. The cypress tree itself bears the scars of the struggle – it was vandalized at least once, but survived and flourished, a symbol of hope to activists. Buskett, then, is a longstanding birdwatching location, but it is also a site that tells the story of a long and bitter struggle, and eventually of a successful if fraught conservation outcome. As a direct result of BirdLife Malta's activism over the years, birds of prey can now fly over and roost at Buskett safely.

However, Buskett is much more than a site with privileged access to birdwatching and hostile hunters. Over the past few decades, its 'significance' has been formalized in a number of ways. First, the records of birds seen are regularly published by BirdLife Malta in its journal and eventually in the international ornithological press. In some instances, they were embedded in compilations that brought together regional or global sites in frameworks of comparative ornithological importance. In my activist days in the 1990s, for example, I was involved in adding up the facts for the Hawk Mountain Sanctuary Association, an ornithological organization based at the eponymous place located on the Appalachian flyway in Pennsylvania. At the time, the Association was compiling data on key sites of bird of prey migration around the world. This and many other exercises have put Buskett on the map of global significance for a particular order of birds. Birds of prey tend to migrate along well-defined leading lines and flyways, and to congregate at strategic sites during their biannual journeys. In Europe there are three main flyways, and large numbers of birds fly through the Bosphorus, the Strait of Gibraltar and the Strait of Messina (see, for instance, Bildstein 2006). The image of the three flyways, and of Malta's position on or close to the central Mediterranean one, is etched in the minds of birdwatchers as they wait for migrating birds to make an appearance at Buskett. To watch, count and record the phenomenon is to embed locality (Buskett in this case) within a universal cartography of ornithological significance.

Second, Buskett has been inscribed in various ways as a site of Natural (capital deliberate) and environmental importance. It is host to a number of EU designations and is a Natura 2000 site that includes both a Special Area of Conservation (SAC) and a Special Protection Area (SPA); each of these in turn subsumes a number of formalized habitat types (for example, 'Arborescent matorral with Bay Laurel, Habitat 5320') according to Annex I of the EU Habitats Directive. While the 'importance' of Buskett goes beyond birds of prey, their seasonal presence and the attention they attract have been key to its inscription. As the management plan states, the place is an SPA 'because of the importance of the site as a stopover for migratory raptors in both the spring and autumn migrations'.[4]

The process by which parts of the world are singled out and inscribed as being especially significant to nature and conservation has been discussed by, among others, Watson (2003). Using the example of Godlingston Heath in Dorset, he argues that when places become nature reserves, some of their select attributes are transformed into a text that can be circulated. In the case of Godlingston, 'lowland heath' is a type of habitat that is recognized in both national (Britain) and international (the Bern Convention, the Birds Directive and so on) legislation as being of 'biodiversity importance'. For a particular patch to be designated as lowland heath and afforded status and protection, it first has to 'exist as something that can be brought together with other entities, other habitats or species, in the limited spatial and cultural locales in which these decisions are made' (Watson 2003: 151). Further, the locality that is lowland heath has to be transformed into something mobile (Watson draws on Latour's notion of 'immutable mobiles') that can be transported between the different spaces and cultural contexts that give it its specially designated status. In order for this to happen, lowland heath has first to be fixed as text: as 'habitat descriptions, floristic tables, species lists, as statistics of coverage and quality. Being a small number of sheets of paper, or a few fields in a database, lowland heath can easily be handled, it can be compared against other habitat descriptions, and it can be attributed relative value within frameworks of evaluation that reach across continents'

(2003: 151). It is this kind of text that is located and travels so readily within the global space of conservation.

Watson's point on specialized texts invites inquiry into the dynamics of production, and the work of the producers, of these texts. In her work on the Gennargentu National Park in Sardinia, Heatherington (2010) points out that models of environmental governance in the Mediterranean are increasingly mediated by scientists, planners, entrepreneurs, activists and technical personnel with recognized special expertise. The discourses of environmental governance they produce are presented as objective scientific knowledge, even as the matrix of institutional partnerships, legitimate knowledge, funding priorities and forms of implementations to which they belong are a form of cultural production. Drawing on Gramsci's notion of 'organic intellectuals', she argues that a 'class of professional environmental experts is emerging to articulate and sanction the technical and moral discourses that both obscure and legitimate the political ecology of power' (Heatherington 2010: 37).

Buskett, then, presents a useful illustration of the dynamics involved in foregrounding parts of the national space as sites of special significance. While the roots may lie in birdwatching routines, the result goes far beyond that. In a place like Buskett, ornithological value, socialization possibilities, narratives of conservation, the politics of relevance within the EU and internationally, scientific study and histories of environmental legislation are imbricated into a complex dynamic.

The Fenced Reserves

I shall now explore the making and functions of some of the privileged places of conservation. In Malta, and with respect primarily to bird protection, the most distinctive of these are the fenced reserves that are managed as special sites for birds and nature generally; access is tightly regulated and unwanted guests are kept out by fencing, barbed wire and other security measures. If, as I argued for Buskett, places of conservation are the result of processes of transformation, fencing is an especially powerful manifestation of those processes. To follow up the case of Godlingston, the moment at which the alchemy was completed was when a fence was put up around the reserve. In that case, the main practical purpose of the fence was to keep sheep in as part of a conservation-linked grazing scheme and to prevent them from straying onto a neighbouring golf course and busy road. Case-specific purpose aside, the Godlingston fence served to section off a part of the landscape as special and distinct from its surroundings. Besides, the fence was:

> The material expression of a specific locale as a result of generic frame-
> works of description and evaluation. It is an effect of processes through
> which the generic uneasily becomes specific, where 'global' flows of texts,
> knowledge and meaning become material and static in a particular 'local'.
> The fence is a materialization of processes that constitute Godlingston as a
> scientific object, reduced to standardized mobile representations based on
> systematic and universalistic classifications. (Watson 2003: 152)

There are two fenced reserves in Malta. Għadira ('pool') and Simar
(named after a type of reed) are tiny – 11 ha and 5 ha respectively. As the
technical literature assures us, they are prime examples of coastal brackish wetland, an extremely rare type in an island where there are no rivers.
I shall take the former as my case study. Għadira was declared a bird
reserve in 1978. Old maps of Malta show that the place was originally
used for the production of salt, an activity that was discontinued when
the Knights built elaborately engineered saltpans further down the coast
in the seventeenth century. Prior to BirdLife Malta's intervention, the
pool would flood after the rains and all but dry up in summer. In winter,
it was a favourite spot for campers and Sunday afternoon picnickers.
A small group of hunters, most of who belonged to the gentry, held the
rights to shoot over the pool, which was considered one of the best places
for waterfowl anywhere in Malta; one of them had actually built a large
hunting lodge a few hundred metres away. The attractiveness of the place
to migrating waterbirds caught the eye of the first generations of BirdLife
Malta activists and birdwatchers, who throughout the 1970s campaigned
for its transformation into a bird sanctuary. Significantly, the campaign,
which was successful, involved the presentation of 'scientific data to the
government showing the ornithological value of the wetland'.[5] Shortly
after Għadira was declared a reserve and effectively handed over to
BirdLife Malta (then the MOS) in 1978, the RSPB's Bert Axell was roped in
to help create a 'proper' nature reserve. The RSPB was the natural choice
on account of its longstanding relations with BirdLife Malta, and Axell
himself enjoyed a strong reputation as a pioneer in the field of nature
reserves. The one he had established at Minsmere in Suffolk was famous
for its design (its birdwatching hides were some of the earliest to be built
anywhere in the world, for example) and its success at attracting large
numbers of birds. One corner of Minsmere consisted of a large shallow
lagoon dotted with islands. 'The Scrape', as it became known, proved so
iconic that many lagoon reserves around the world were modelled on it.[6]

The reserve at Għadira is a case in point. The main transformation
consisted in excavation works that ensured the year-round presence of
water, the salinity levels of which fluctuate considerably according to
the amount of rainfall. Trees, mainly tamarisk and pine, were planted

around the pool. Aerial shots show a close resemblance between it and 'The Scrape', in spite of the different contexts. (There is, at first glance, not much in common between the Suffolk coast and a bay in the Mediterranean dotted with hotels and beach contraptions.) The terminology too is telling: 'islands' were created, a 'ditch' and a 'reservoir' dug, 'hides' built, an 'embankment' raised and a 'warden' employed. Still today and thirty-odd years after the transformation, birdwatchers at Għadira still use these words in the English original to take their bearings; they might say, for example, '*Ir-russett qiegħed quddiem l-embankment, eżatt wara l-island ta' ħdejn ir-reservoir*' ('the heron is in front of the embankment, just behind the island near the reservoir'). Such situations are common in a bilingual context (Malta) characterized by lexical promiscuity, but the case of Għadira is particularly telling, in that a whole jargon of British wetland reserves was imported wholesale and attached to a landscape transformed in the manner of those reserves. It is also relevant to note that when a new wetland reserve was established at Simar in the 1990s, exactly the same scheme and language were employed.

Which brings me to the fence, predictably referred to as '*il-fence*'. At Għadira, it was the very first thing that was put up the moment the bulldozers left the site. From a purely practical perspective, this is hardly surprising, given that the reserve attracts its fair share of the kind of birds that are deemed desirable by collectors of taxidermy specimens. It follows that the maintenance and policing of the fence, and of its associated defensive works that include barbed wire, a flooded ditch and a raised embankment, should be a priority on the warden's tasklist. The reserve also employs round-the-clock watchmen. Even so, break-ins were something of a standard fixture well into the 1990s and are still not entirely unknown today, especially when some rare and eye-catching bird decides to pay a visit. The point is that there is a very real practical reason for the fence to exist.

Certainly, however, there are other, more nuanced and symbolic reasons. As in the case of Godlingston, the fence marks the limits of a patch of land that has been transformed into a scientifically informed text that is comparable with similar texts located in other contexts. The production of this text started when Għadira was first inscribed as a birdwatching location in the 1960s. It gathered pace when the 'scientific data' on the 'importance' of the place were presented to the government in the 1970s, and then when the newly established reserve was grafted onto the RSPB-stewarded logic, design and terminology of wetland reserves. In various ways, it is a work in progress. For example, one of the warden's key tasks is to oversee the production and compilation of systematic records for

Figure 5.2. Għadira nature reserve, with its excavated pool and islands over-looked by a birdwatching hide (at the edge of the pool, centre right). Photograph by the author.

the site; observations of birds and other types of animals are recorded on standardized sheets that make up a growing collection of volumes. Bird ringing has been carried out on site on practically a daily basis since the early 1980s and a good number of specialist studies have been conducted on the hydrology, botany and zoology of the reserve. As BirdLife Malta puts it, 'as a result of the management and protection of the site, the reserve offers a stunning combination of biodiversity and natural beauty. Today the area is home to a variety of flora and fauna, some of which is rare and endangered and given special protection by the European Union'.[7]

Significantly, Għadira is also a Ramsar site. The Convention on Wetlands of International Importance, called the Ramsar Convention, is an intergovernmental treaty with a stated mission of 'conservation and wise use of all wetlands through local and national actions and inter-national cooperation, as a contribution towards achieving sustainable development throughout the world'. It was adopted in the Iranian city of Ramsar in 1971 and came into force in 1975. The list of sites and contract-ing parties (states) stood at 2,186 and 168 respectively in January 2015, and the sites covered a total area of 208,449,277 ha.[8] Malta currently has two Ramsar sites: Għadira (Ramsar site 410, established as such on 30 September 1988) and Simar (Ramsar site 789, established as such on 29 January 1996). The production of scientific records and data at Għadira falls into place in texts such as the official Ramsar description of the reserve:

Council of Europe Biogenetic Reserve; Mediterranean Protected Area, No Hunting Area. A brackish water coastal pool (once used for salt production) of carrying water level and salinity, bordered by dunes. Several rare plant species, salt-resistant vegetation, and a diverse invertebrate fauna, including endemic grasshoppers and wasps, are supported. The rare fish *Aphanius fasciatus*, endangered elsewhere on Malta, is present in good numbers. An important area for resting and feeding for numerous species of migratory birds. Human activities include intensive summer tourism and conservation education. The surrounding land is under intense cultivation.[9]

The fence at Għadira fulfils another function, and one that is particularly significant in the Maltese context. It effectively marks the place as a negation of the surrounding landscape, imagined and represented by BirdLife Malta and environmentalists generally as a den of shotgun-wielding iniquity and environmental degradation. A site like Għadira functions as a living representation of what Malta could be like if birds and nature were left to their own devices under the stewardship and care of ENGOs. The BirdLife Malta website spells it out in no uncertain terms: 'Għadira offers a taste of what the Maltese islands would be like if hunting and trapping were stopped . . . the reserve is a rare sanctuary.'[10] In particular, the establishment of six new breeding bird species for Malta – five of which are wetland species and therefore especially novel and significant in a country where wetlands are very scarce – is portrayed as living proof of this departure. The power of this representation derives not least from the fact that the fenced reserves operate a well-rehearsed system of guided visits. Hundreds of schoolchildren visit every year, and both Għadira and Simar are open to the public at weekends. Professional guides and volunteers take groups of people around the reserves and point out the birds from the hides. Visitors can make use of specially provided telescopes and binoculars, and there are small counters where books are sold and information leaflets are handed out. The pathways are carefully signposted with information panels on the various species of plants and animals that thrive on site. News of rare birds, and especially the more interesting breeding species, regularly makes it to the local press. Certainly the routines are not unknown in other protected areas. But it is only at the fenced bird reserves that BirdLife Malta can claim complete (or almost, give or take the occasional break-in) control and stewardship. Għadira and Simar constitute a paragon of the conservation work of BirdLife Malta and its outcomes. Writing about a similar situation at Loch Garten in Scotland, where the RSPB hosts thousands of people who go there to view breeding ospreys, Cocker marvels at 'what an impressive and slick piece of social theatre it is' (2018: 39).

Protected and Special Areas

The fenced reserves may be the most conspicuous type of sectioned, 'significant' place, but they are also by far the smallest. At the time of writing, 28.5 per cent of the land area of Malta is protected under some kind of designation (in the case of a number of places, multiple designations). The various types of protected sites fall into two categories. The first includes sites protected under national legislation, namely the Environment Protection Act (2016 – there were various antecedents). There are eight formal designations within this category: Bird Sanctuaries, National Parks, Nature Reserves, Protected Beaches, Special Areas of Conservation (National Importance), Special Areas of Conservation (International Importance), Special Protected Areas and Tree Protection Areas. Each is regulated by one or more formal legal instruments, typically a Government Notice or Subsidiary Legislation.

The second category includes sites protected under international legislation as established by multilateral agreements. The substantial number of designations include Wetlands of International Importance (the UN Ramsar Convention), Specially Protected Areas (Protocol Concerning Specially Protected Areas and Biological Diversity in the Mediterranean under the UN Barcelona Convention [Convention for the Protection of the Marine Environment and the Coastal Region of the Mediterranean]), Special Areas of Conservation (the EC Habitats Directive), Special Protection Areas (the EC Birds Directive), and Areas of Special Conservation Interest (the Emerald Network under the Council of Europe Bern Convention). The last three overlap with the Natura 2000 Network of protected areas designation, which in Malta accounts for 13.1 per cent of the land area.

It is beyond the scope of the present work to discuss the various designations in any detail. (The vast technical and other literature would easily fill a volume.) I will therefore limit myself to one that happens to be of particular relevance to the argument of this chapter. Important Bird and Biodiversity Areas (IBAs) represent a system of site monitoring that forms part of a 'global strategy' put in place by BirdLife International in 2004 (although the concept can be traced back to the 1980s). In October 2018, the list of IBAs stood at over 12,000 sites in over 200 countries and territories (including marine territories) worldwide. The assessment criteria and monitoring protocols are fairly complex and include standardized procedures for compiling data and evaluating their relevance (the emphasis throughout is on 'quantitative ornithological criteria'). A crucial variable is that of so-called 'trigger' or 'qualifying' bird species, technically defined as 'those for which the site has been recognized as an IBA under any of the global (or, where appropriate, regional criteria)'.[11] This refers to species whose status is deemed unfavourable (as in declining, threatened, or endangered global or regional populations). Malta currently has twenty-one IBAs that together cover an area of over 3,000 km². The only specifically noncoastal site is Buskett, which secured its status mainly on the basis of its importance for migrating birds of prey – itself established, as discussed earlier, as a direct result of the annual September birdwatching and counting exercise. The rest of Malta's IBAs are coastal or offshore (hence the vast area relative to the country's landmass). Three of the key trigger bird species are the Scopoli's and yelkouan shearwaters and the European storm petrel, and most of Malta's IBAs consist of the inaccessible coastal cliffs where these species nest, or the pelagic areas where they feed. As in the case of Ramsar sites, IBAs are described and classified in technical-scientific terms. The following, for example, is an excerpt from the IBA database description of Rdum il-Madonna:

> A promontory in the L-Aħrax area, where there is a 200m stretch of sea cliffs (25m high) at the base of which there is a lot of rock debris. The cliffs support one of the largest colonies of *Puffinus yelkouan* in the species's range. Notable numbers of *Calandrella brachydactyla* and *Sylvia conspicillata* (locally decreasing) breed along the cliff tops.[12]

The language and dynamics of classification are highly significant. The IBA designation and the various other national and international frameworks of classification and protection effectively locate Malta, and by inference the ornithological and conservation activities of local birdwatchers and bird protectionists, within structures of legitimacy underwritten by a technical-scientific prestige language of 'conservation status', 'trigger species', 'key biodiversity' and so on. A place that is designated as a Ramsar site or an IBA is one that has been consecrated as being of 'global importance', on a par with similar sites worldwide and located on the same horizontal plane of significance. For many designations and frameworks, there are online resources that include a world map that one can zoom into and click on in order to find country, site and information. There is a parallel with Google Earth in that these world maps double as informational spaces through which the viewer navigates and experiences the illusion of bodily presence and control, and implicitly partakes in a discourse of global awareness, in this case that of the significance of a tiny corner of a small Mediterranean island in the universalizing scheme of global bird conservation. It is hardly surprising that the ability to visualize the planet in this way has often been linked (for instance, in James Lovelock's idea of 'Gaia') to a kind of environmental sensitivity that is premised on the global as a horizontal plane of meaning where everything is interrelated and therefore equally significant. The United Nations Environmental Programme (UNEP), for example, provides data on the changing climate and environmental conditions across the planet to Google Earth (Jensen 2010). Clearly, this kind of global imaginary and discourse goes on to structure local valuations of specific sites. For example, on 30 August 2013, BirdLife Malta announced that the Malta–Gozo channel had been confirmed as Malta's first Marine Important Bird Area (a subtype of IBA). The press release, headlined in the local press, hailed this stretch of sea between the islands of Malta and Gozo as 'Malta's Galapagos' – it put Malta 'on the world stage alongside such iconic biodiversity hotspots as the Galapagos and the Azores as a refuge for threatened wildlife'.[13] IBAs, then, are a prime example of how 'collaborations among disparate knowledge seekers and their disparate forms of knowledge can turn incompatible facts and observations into compatible ones' (Tsing 2005: 89).

No Country for Hunters

This book is about how hunting and conservation intersect in Malta. Having looked at some of the dynamics of the making and location, physical as well as conceptual, of the places of conservation of environmentalists, I shall now discuss the contested presence of hunters and trappers in them. While only a few of the designations mentioned actually mean that hunting is not permitted, all set up a value system within which it is undesirable. I take as my first example the Majjistral[14] Nature and History Park, a 6 km² (extensive by Maltese standards) coastal area of open garrigue, cliffs, cultivated fields and sandy beaches in the northwest of the island. The site thus includes a number of landscape types ('habitats' in the language of significance) and has easy access to roads, which means that it is used by hunters, fishermen, tourists and so on, but also by ramblers, birdwatchers, nature photographers and other types associated with environmentalist valuations of the Maltese countryside. The centrepiece of the park is an area of garrigue known as Xagħra l-Ħamra,[15] which in the mid-2000s was proposed by the government as a site for a golf course. The proposal met with strong opposition from a resistance movement that was spearheaded by ENGOs and that enjoyed considerable public support.[16] In the event, the opposition prevailed and in September 2007, Xagħra l-Ħamra was legally incorporated into a new 'national park'. The park, which is managed by a Heritage Parks Foundation that consists of the representatives of three ENGOs, includes a visitors' centre and a stretch of protected coast designated as part of a larger Special Area of Conservation (International Importance) within the Natura 2000 network; it is also a member of the EUROPARC Federation of Nature and National Parks of Europe. The Majjistral Nature and History Park ticks all the right boxes. To Maltese environmentalists, it represents a rare ENGO victory over the threat of development, as well as a new departure in the direction of habitat protection and valuation. More broadly, and tellingly in the context of this discussion, it locates a site in Malta within a set of prestigious EU and international scientific, legislative and bureaucratic frameworks, and their perceived implications of progressive and desirable appropriations of nature.

However, not all types proved as easy to keep off the land as golfers. When the park was set up in 2007, the new management found itself with a slate that was anything but clean. The establishment of the park was premised on 'forward-looking' forms of appropriation of nature, landscapes and heritage: birdwatching, rambling, agro-tourism, environmental education and so on. The publicity materials showed unspoilt vistas, animal and plant species, key habitats and people taking photographs or enjoying sunsets. Yet this was a partial view, because the park was also home to a number of practices deemed undesirable by its makers. Visitors to the park were increasingly likely to perceive a dissonance between their expectations (nourished in part by a state-of-the-art visitors' centre) and the actual circumstances of the park. Three rogue practices in particular were singled out: off-roading, fly-tipping and hunting. Some teething problems and initial resistance aside, the first two were easy enough to bring to heel, partly through the installation of gates at the access points to the park that allowed for limited entry by locals.

Hunting and trapping proved much harder to tackle. Partly the reason was that, unlike fly-tipping for example, the practices were not generally illegal. Early attempts by the park management to banish them outright came up against strong resistance in the form of FKNK lobbying with government ministries and agencies. The area taken up by the park had a history as a hunting location of considerable value. In the long term, the open spaces and boulder screes had served for generations of (mostly) locals to combine small-scale agricultural production with the hunting and trapping of birds and rabbits. Some hunters had right of tenure over small leaseholdings that dated back several decades to when the British built barracks in the area and leased out plots of land to encourage settlement and therefore ensure the ready availability of agricultural products and domestic service. Others enjoyed rights to hunt and trap as part of long-term relations with landowners or through actual ownership (substantial tracts of what is now the park were and are privately owned). Yet another type, which included trappers in particular, had de facto rights rooted in their sustained use and transformation of public land. A related category was made up of hunters who had no other access to land and who hunted in the area on a more or less regular basis. The upshot was that the park management quickly discovered that the place was a tissue of different claims to the land and that it would not be so easy to dislodge hunters and trappers.

The reason why they were of concern at all is that, as the park management saw it, hunting was scarcely reconcilable with the newfound valuations of the place as a set of habitats where important species lived and to which people would be encouraged to relate. Visitors to the park complained that it did not make sense for the trapping and killing of birds to take place in a nature park that promised the opposite. According to the park manager, tourists were particularly vociferous in this respect. (The boundary of the park is metres away from a five-star hotel.) In the event, an uneasy compromise was reached in which hunting was first allowed until 9 a.m. and then, under pressure from the FKNK, 10 a.m.[17] The reasoning was that the needs of hunters and the expectations of visitors would balance out, since in any case most hunting took place in the early hours of the day. Hunters, however, were not convinced, and they continue to resist the restriction. A number of them told me – and this is also the official line taken by the FKNK – that they were apprehensive that their practice would be outlawed by stealth, as the government, under pressure from ENGOs and a public that was generally unsympathetic to hunting, took to designating swathes of public land as conservation areas, riding roughshod over the rights of hunters in the process. As someone who worked at the park put it, 'the first two years were not easy; people would spy on us from their hides and the first public meetings were a nightmare'. He added that one early form of resistance came in the form of spent cartridges left behind by hunters in a studied way.

Even so, a decade into the life of the park, hunting does in fact show some signs of outbound migration. The number of hunters using the park, especially of those who have no form of land tenure, is small at the time of writing. The main two reasons are the 10 a.m. curfew and the new forms of surveillance that came with park management. The number of CABS and BirdLife Malta teams (see below) that carry out onsite monitoring has increased, as have visits by the police. The park management employs rangers whose job it is to roam about the land and watch out for infringements. Perhaps most consequentially, the designation and marketing of the place as a park means a greater presence of people who are unsympathetic to hunters. The upshot is that the typical hunter at Majjistral gets more than his fair share of *sikkatura* (tightness). As I will argue shortly, this seriously compromises the hunting experience.

It was not just the presence of hunters that collided with the new understandings of space ushered in by the park. Hunters and especially trappers had over the years built and made use of a large number of hides, many of which were cobbled together from corrugated metal sheets, old oil drums and so on. When the park was set up, these were quickly deemed unsightly and, more importantly, dissonant with incoming notions of landscape as a repository of heritage and nature. To be sure, the area contained many types of built interventions. These were now allocated significance in terms of their perceived value with respect to history, heritage and harmony with the natural landscape. Corbelled stone huts (*giren*), for example, were classified as valuable on account of their location within a history of traditionally and typically Maltese vernacular rural heritage.[18] Likewise, a Second World War defensive 'pillbox' (a kind of concrete gun post) and an eighteenth-century tower were readily located within a narrative of national history and heritage, to the extent that the latter was eventually meticulously restored by the Maltese equivalent of the National Trust. It was in this emerging context that the hides that belonged to hunters and trappers proved a mixed bag. Some, typically those that were limited to undressed stone and deemed to have been built *b'sengħa* (with skill – this refers to the technique of dry rubble construction, a valued feature of the Maltese landscape in popular and officializing discourses, and one that enjoys considerable patronage by the state) were accommodated into notions of rural heritage; the rest, and especially those that contained bits and pieces of junk put together in a slipshod way, were not.

The park management identified and GPS-mapped about 175 such hides, which it then set about classifying with a view to dismantling.[19] Three categories of undesirable hides were established: those lying derelict due to disuse (itself partly linked to the process of passive eviction I describe above); those built of 'alien' materials and deemed an 'eyesore'; and those lying on public land and therefore technically illegal. Besides the hides, various bits and pieces of abandoned hunting and trapping paraphernalia – spent cartridges, pegs that served to anchor nets and so on – were earmarked for removal. Tellingly, the clean-up operation was choreographed into what may be described as a spectacle of eviction, itself part of the making of place for conservation. The dramatis personae included CABS volunteers (wearing their 'Anti-Poaching Operation: CABS Bird Guard' T-shirts, which are discussed later in this chapter), people from Nature Trust and BirdLife Malta, one or two employees of the neighbouring hotels, members of the public and, perhaps more revealingly, representatives of the FKNK.

For the anti-hunting complement of this cast, the process was to some extent a take on what they had always done. The urge to demolish hides or otherwise rough up hunting and trapping sites (when no one was looking) has long been a very real one to individual birdwatchers and activists in the field. What is straightforward vandalism to hunters and trappers is seen as a legitimate (if never sanctioned by the ENGOs themselves) means to fight back and reclaim the countryside for nature and its rightful inhabitants. As activists see it, it is worth sacrificing the wasted time and frustration of the people who have to rebuild the hides, in the interest of birds and nature. Such kinds of hunt sabotage are well-known internationally and were formally represented by the Hunt Saboteurs Association (HSA) that was set up in Britain in 1964 and has since become a worldwide network of considerable punch. Although no Maltese have ever been linked to the HSA in any way, the demolition of hides is a textbook case of the type of anti-hunting guerrilla tactics associated with it. A long-time birdwatcher told me how he would do the job whenever he could:

> My foremost aim was for trappers to have to waste time rebuilding their hides. That wasted time meant birds flying free that would otherwise be caught. But I also hated hunters and trappers with a vengeance. I had heard honey buzzards scream in pain as they were hit and fell to the ground, and that sound came to me every time I demolished a hide or tore up nets.

The 175 hides at the Majjistral Nature and History Park were a different species altogether. Their demolition was not intended as isolated action by faceless individuals venting their feelings of helplessness in the face of what they saw as the senseless killing of birds. Rather, it was a fairly high-profile initiative that was sanctioned and legitimated by being embedded into a narrative of legality, management and conservation. The language used was that of 'alien structures', 'clean-ups', 'eyesores', and 'constructive destruction'.

The public demolition event made its way to the social media, where the discussion by participants and their acquaintances included such comments as 'I bet that was great fun'; 'I will carry on until every one of these abominations are removed'; and 'Grateful Sea Squill[20] watches over clean-up at Majjistral, nodding its approval in the breeze'. The last is particularly telling, since it portrays nature itself, as represented by a flower, saluting an operation that would help it prevail over destructive human depredations at the park.

The (token, bird protection activists would say) presence of the FKNK at the event was especially significant. On the one hand, the event was about the destruction of structures built by fellow hunters and trappers and was directly linked to their practices; the members of the FKNK who took part will have had their own hides in other locations. Perhaps that explains why, during the clean-up, the environmentalists and FKNK people worked together, but very much at arm's length; as the park manager told me, 'I expected some fireworks but thankfully there were none'. On the other hand, the participation of hunters followed a studied rationale: first, it showcased the FKNK as an organization – and therefore hunters as a type – that cared about the welfare of the Maltese countryside; and, second, it rehearsed the link between hunters and the locality, and established the FKNK as one of the main stakeholders, with a measure of control over the transformation of the place into a 'nature and history park'. To not participate would have meant jettisoning that claim and the regulated access to the park that came with it. It would also have left the hunters and trappers at the park at the mercy of the managers and their ENGO associates. If, then, the demolition event was intended by activists as a spectacle of eviction, it equally functioned as a spectacle of admission to hunters.

It is equally crucial to note that, throughout the process, hunters and bird protection activists shared, in principle at least, a common understanding of what a nature park – and more broadly the Maltese countryside – ought to be. Although the hunters at the clean-up may well have had have their own corrugated metal and dressed stone hides elsewhere, within the context of the park, they saw the value of 'indigenous' rubble construction. It was relatively easy for the park management and the FKNK members to agree on which hides had to go and which (very few) could stay. This shows, first, the power of officializing narratives of landscapes of conservation (especially in the context of a national park) and, second, the process by which gentrifying hunters align themselves with and appropriate them.

Majjistral, then, was set up as a nature park from which hunters were to some extent evicted or where they found they had to adapt to new valuations of place. However, the making of places of conservation is not limited to fenced reserves, protected areas and parks; rather, bird protection activists work with a model of a national space that should ultimately be tamed in its entirety and where the laws that govern bird protection apply uniformly. This ultimately means that the place-making activities of bird protectionists often extend (or attempt to do so) directly to places that are strongly associated with hunting. A useful example in this respect is Miżieb. Measuring approximately 80 ha, it is a very extensive (by Maltese standards) wooded ridge that runs across the island from east to west. It is hemmed in by agricultural areas, hamlets, and coastal tourist and recreational developments. Other notable neighbours include Simar Nature Reserve, the Majjistral Park and a string of Phoenician archaeological remains. The earliest moves towards the afforestation of what used to be open land were made in the late 1950s, when thousands of saplings donated by the Israeli government were planted along the ridge. In the 1970s, ENGOs including BirdLife Malta held a number of tree-planting activities on site. By the 1980s, Miżieb had become a classifiable habitat – a Mediterranean woodland made up of young growth interspersed with patches of garrigue and maquis.

In 1986, the government abruptly handed Miżieb over to the FKNK as a hunting reserve. According to well-informed sources, the decision was taken by the Prime Minister at the time, who reasoned that one way to resolve the mounting tension between hunters and ENGOs was to contain as many hunters as possible within specially allocated areas. However, there were complications. Activists were quick to accuse the government of having traded public land and, indeed, the lives of birds for hunters' votes. With national elections a few months away, the point struck a chord with many, especially since Maltese politics at the time was shot through, especially among the Nationalist-leaning middle class, with a sense that the Labour government of sixteen years had become a corrupt edifice given to cultivating vote banks at the expense of the public interest. What was then a growing ENGO movement routinely accused the government of selling out to powerful lobbies such as hunters and land-hungry developers. In the event, and whether or not the Miżieb handover was a backroom deal with strings attached, both the accusation and the hunting reserve were there to stay. More than thirty years later, the popular drift is that the place is *tal-kaċċaturi* (belongs to hunters).

Miżieb is used mainly by hunters who do not have regular or reliable access to land elsewhere. It is managed by the FKNK and one cannot just turn up and hunt there. Rather, the system is for the FKNK to grant access and allocate shooting hides (clearly, some spots are more desirable than others) according to the extent of participation, by individual hunters, in the regular cleaning and tree-planting sessions held on site, usually in summer. The number of hours of participation are added up and hides allocated before the start of every season. It is thus essentially managed on a *res communis* principle, with preference of use going to those who show the most commitment to the place. Apart from the hides, Miżieb teems with signs of hunter occupation. There are many FKNK notices that remind the public (the area is openly accessible) that the place is reserved for hunting, that littering and fires are prohibited and so on. The regular tree-pruning and planting operations may be publicized, and thus function as a spectacle of presence and (de facto) ownership. Fences may be real, as at the nature reserves, but they may also be virtual.

It would be inaccurate to say that there is some kind of systematic or sustained programme by BirdLife Malta or activists generally to reclaim

Miżieb as a place of conservation; by and large, the feeling is that it will remain in the hands of the FKNK for the foreseeable future at least. However, there were two incidents that shed light on some of the politics and dynamics of the relationship between hunting, land and conservation in Malta. In the first, the facts as reported by BirdLife Malta were as follows. On the morning of 20 September 2009, members of the organization's Raptor Camp (see below) saw hunters shoot at protected birds of prey as the birds left their roosts at Miżieb. A short while after the shooting, two Camp members searched the area from where the shooting had come; they were joined by three members of CABS who were running a separate monitoring camp in Malta during the same period. A number of dead harriers were found and more members as well as the police were called in. Two mornings of intensive searches on 20 and 21 September resulted in 'the discovery of the largest wildlife crime scene in recent Maltese history, with the carcasses of over 200 protected birds discovered hidden under rocks, stuffed in crevices and old barrels, or under piles of rubbish within the woodland'.[21] The incident and its images reached the press within an hour or two of the first discovery and headlines were made that a 'bird cemetery' had been found at Miżieb; the reports were updated as the search unfolded. Following these events, BirdLife Malta went on to produce a detailed report and to claim that hunters had no legal claim on Miżieb. The only document that existed was a 1986 handover letter signed by the Prime Minister; no management plans or other legal instruments had ever been drawn up, as had happened in the case of bird reserves such as Għadira.

The second incident caused an even greater media furore. It involved BBC wildlife presenter Chris Packham who spent several days in Malta together with a small film crew in April 2014. Packham's project was to document the spring hunting season by uploading daily video blogs and YouTube videos under the heading 'Malta: Massacre on Migration'. For the fifth episode, Packham chose to film at Miżieb, which he described as 'one of the best habitats' he had seen on the island, but also one that was 'absolutely bristling with hunters'. Predictably, things got 'interesting', as Packham put it. Barely a few paces into Miżieb, a number of hunters accosted him and his crew, and warned them that the place was a hunting reserve and that they had no right to provoke hunters by shooting – the pun was delicious – there. When Packham insisted he had a right to be there, things escalated to a fairly physical level, at which point the police showed up and set things right. Some of what the hunters screamed at Packham is fascinating:

> Don't shoot . . . you're provocating [sic] me, he's filming me . . . this is not a public place . . . we are Maltese, we are not in your country, you are in our country, we don't come to your country and do what you're doing here . . .

disgusting, *'l Alla qażżiżtuh*[22] . . . you said we shoot millions . . . get the hell out of here . . . the gun is not loaded . . . I'm telling you, if you broadcast this, I'll sue you in court.

The filmed incident became one of the star sequences of Packham's documentary film. Packham went on to give several interviews to and write a number of articles in the British press, the drift of which was that Malta was a 'bird hell'.[23] Equally significantly, the BirdLife Malta member who had accompanied Packham was charged with trespassing. In 2017, the court cleared him of all charges on the grounds of lack of evidence: while there was no question that the activist was at Miżieb, no evidence had been presented that showed that hunters had exclusive rights over it. This was interpreted by BirdLife Malta, and by sections of the media, as a 'crucial blow' to hunters' claims on Miżieb.

Miżieb is not a place of conservation in the same way as the fenced reserves or the sites of scientific significance. In many ways, it is rather the antithesis. And yet it is not entirely beyond the reach of the activists. Its very inception as a place reserved for hunting is questioned and contested. It has also on occasion been the centre of attraction of a bird protection enterprise that constantly seeks to turn the national space into a space of conservation. An important part of that enterprise is surveillance.

The Making of a Panopticized Landscape

> Guy believes that the techniques used to kill Hen Harriers have changed . . . Gamekeepers used to think that they were pretty much inviolate themselves as they violated the law on remote hillsides, but now there is more of a feeling of fear that they may be being watched – and so killing birds at roosts is far commoner, as is distant rifle-shooting of birds.
> —Mark Avery, *Inglorious: Conflict in the Uplands*[24]

At first light on 26 April 2012, shots rang out in a field near Marsascala, a place known for its popularity with hunters. This was not an event that would normally have made the news, except the casualty in this case was a rather unusual species. It was a drone – a particularly sophisticated one built and operated by a Swiss engineer, in fact. The predictable joke was that a hunter had mistaken it for a turtle dove, but there was a more sinister streak. That morning, the drone was being used to monitor (illegal) trapping sites that would otherwise have been hidden from view behind high field walls. It was the latest chapter in a story that tells of how bird protection activists have sought to panopticize the Maltese countryside and of the chequered conservation outcomes of that effort. It is to that part of the story that I now turn my attention.

The association between conservation, hunting and technologized surveillance goes back to the early days of birdwatching in Malta. Two fundamental aspects of the practice of birdwatching are that it uses field optics that bring into magnified view and that it results in the keeping of records of sightings. The first involves looking in a particular way in particular places and systematically observing what one normally does not. Birdwatchers and their (cumbersome at the time) binoculars were a novel presence in the countryside in the 1960s and, in less well-trodden places, remained so until well into the 1980s. The earliest suspicions were that they were *nemmiesa* (voyeurs). This soon developed into a subversive and somewhat stale joke among hunters, especially in a place like Għadira where the hides overlook the nature reserve but also a popular beach. As I shall explain, the humour became less good-natured as hunters realized that binoculars could also be used to keep track of what they did from a safe distance.

It was not just binoculars that came to represent a threat. The telephoto lenses (typically 300 mm or more) used to photograph birds could equally be aimed at hunters. Over time, the growing portfolio of long-distance photographs of hunters holding protected birds they had just shot, or roaming in protected areas, became a key weapon in a one-sided war of images that also included the photographs of dead or injured birds discussed elsewhere in this volume. That the photographs were often cropped and grainy was added value – the idea was that they had been shot at a distance and clandestinely, but only because the practice they showed was itself illicit and potentially dangerous at closer quarters. As birdwatching and photographic technology became more affordable and portable (adapter kits can now be cheaply bought that enable telescopes to be coupled with cameras), the volume of these images increased. The point is that the birdwatching presence and 'gaze' was increasingly seen by hunters as a threat, especially when the results were inscribed on film and circulated in the media. 'Gaze', used here in Urry's (1990) sense, has multiple meanings. For example, tourists (notably British and German) roaming the countryside were readily enrolled in the surveillance enterprise. Being looked at through binoculars, photographed or filmed came to be construed as acts of hostility and provocation, whether they came from activists, tourists or tourist-activists (as indeed some were). This led to some intriguing situations – suffice it to say that many photographs exist of hunters mooning. There have also been incidents where angry hunters physically assaulted birdwatchers, and occasionally tourists, and specifically targeted their photographic equipment. The worst of these took place at Buskett in 1994 and 2014, when expensive cameras and lenses were smashed in premeditated vicious attacks by small

Figure 5.3. Trespassers, especially foreign ones, are not welcome here. Photograph by the author.

groups of hunters (who were not actually hunting on those occasions; it appears they went to Buskett solely to cause trouble). The significance of these acts as vivid illustrations of the public image of hunters as violent and lawless was discussed in Chapter 3; in the present context, they emphasize the growing resistance of hunters to the perceived threat of the presence of birdwatchers and their technologies of surveillance and inscription. The fact that actual violence was and is the rare exception does not undermine the argument.

One factor that contributed to the systematization of surveillance was that the gaze was very often also inscribed in the fieldnotes kept by birdwatchers. These took the form of tallies of birds seen, but also of those seen being shot. Sometimes notes would be added that described the behaviour of hunters as observed on the day, as well as the approximate number of shots heard. These records were not always systematic and they also depended in large measure on the disposition of the individual birdwatcher. Still, they were significant in at least two respects. First, BirdLife Malta increasingly urged birdwatchers to record observations of hunting activity more comprehensively and to pass them on to the organization. (Standardized sheets were prepared and distributed on a number of occasions throughout the years.) Second, the conversion of what was originally an incidental gaze into a more intentional, rigorous and inscribed one laid the foundations for the elaborate and specialized systems of surveillance that developed from around 2000 or so, and that had a profound effect on relations between bird conservationists and hunters, and hunters and the landscape.

The global model of organized hunt surveillance was not unknown to bird protection ENGOs in Malta. It had produced dividends in Sicily, for example, where LIPU (Lega italiana protezione uccelli, the main bird protection organization in Italy) had over the course of several years largely managed to bring to heel the illegal shooting of migrating birds of prey that took place every year around the Strait of Messina. In Britain too, the RSPB had successfully monitored and protected the nests of rare birds from the attentions of egg collectors, among similar initiatives (see, for instance, Cocker 2018). One of the reasons why Maltese bird protectionists were familiar with the model was that some of them had over the years travelled to take part in these and other initiatives as volunteers. This also explains the growing need felt by BirdLife Malta to systematize its surveillance operations.

The first and still the most consequential sustained and systematic hunt surveillance programme operating in Malta is that of CABS (Committee Against Bird Slaughter – Komitee gegen den Vogelmord). The organization was set up in Berlin in 1975. Its stated mission was to curb the illegal hunting of wild birds in Europe, with an emphasis on 'black spots' such as migratory bottlenecks where large numbers of birds were killed or contexts in which rare species were targeted. Its first ever campaign was to call on German tourists to boycott Italy in protest against the hunting of migratory birds in that country. Its operations, which target specific cases of illegal hunting and trapping, now include various countries. The organization is run by a small central committee, but places a premium on action on the ground and close cooperation with local ENGOs and police. It also actively lobbies national governments and, more importantly, the European Commission and various EU agencies.

The presence of CABS in Malta goes back to 2000, when initial contact was made by a Maltese person who was involved with both BirdLife Malta and International Animal Rescue (IAR – an animal welfare organization based in Britain). Malta had been on the CABS list of black spots for many years, and the contact came at a time when the organization had just come into substantial funding and was looking to expand its operations. The first visits to Malta were spent scouting locations, walking in the countryside, talking to people and otherwise building a basis of local knowledge: as a CABS activist put it to me, 'when you start working in a country you have first to spend time learning, otherwise you make big mistakes'. The first tangible action was the donation of a powerful outboard motor to the Malta police, to be used to patrol inshore waters for illegal hunting. This, among other measures, proved effective and inshore sea hunting was all but eradicated within a few years. Following this early success, CABS launched small-scale operations in Malta in the spring of 2004, with a fully fledged 'camp' held in the autumn of 2007.

'Camp' refers to meticulously organized biannual events held in spring and autumn, in which volunteers (up to around twenty-five at a time) spend a few weeks in Malta during the peak migration and hunting seasons. Typically, they represent a number of nationalities. Most are from Europe, with Germany and Italy being the strongest contributors, but there have been volunteers from as far away as the United States. While not paid for their time in the field (and the daily rounds of surveillance and briefings can be punishing), they are fully funded by CABS. In the main, the camps attract two kinds of people: people involved in bird conservation projects elsewhere who, as an organizer put it to me, 'don't want to see the result of their efforts there destroyed here in Malta', and animal welfare activists. CABS is able to draw on a sizeable pool of volunteers, and recruitment takes place by word of mouth within transnational networks of conservation and animal welfare activism. The organization, which at any one time is involved in camps and other forms of activism in various places, prefers to assign volunteers to the same location year after year so as to build up a capital of local knowledge.

The local knowledge that is most highly prized is that of the landscape and its contents. Camp participants who work in the same place for successive seasons gain the spatial fluency that is so essential to the work of CABS in Malta, that includes detective work on the ground to secure evidence of illegal hunting and trapping. A CABS team might try to locate the source of electronic bird callers, for example, or to take photographs of a hunter within the protected perimeter of a nature reserve. In some circumstances, the police are called in, or a team may accompany them in the field and supply them with intelligence. When that is not possible, the CABS teams try to produce photographic evidence in order eventually to secure a conviction. In the media run-up to the September 2010 camp, for example, spokesman Axel Hirschfeld said that the volunteers from Bulgaria, Germany, Italy, Sweden and Britain would be 'recording the shooting and trapping of protected birds and identifying and reporting those responsible to the police'. Video cameras would be installed on vehicles and all offences 'rigorously documented'.[25] One of the cardinal principles of CABS, as emphasized to me by organizers and volunteers, is that all their activities take place in conformity with the law of the land in which they happen to be, and in full collaboration with its agents and

Figure 5.4. The T-shirts worn by CABS volunteers make it clear what the intention is. Photograph by the author.

enforcers. That is why they focus exclusively on illegal hunting and also why a substantial part of their work in Malta has to do with building and maintaining good relations with the police. Partly this has obvious practical purposes. Perhaps more importantly, it preserves the public image of CABS as a legitimate and trustworthy player. In the words of a camp organizer: 'You cannot break the law yourself . . . you would lose your credibility, the support of the police, and that of the public.' CABS, then, is not involved in hunt sabotage.

One of the reasons why public credibility and support are so essential to CABS is that the photographs and films produced are not just used as evidence to secure convictions; they are also fed into what I have called a one-sided war of images. CABS is known for its media savvy, and the images of birds being shot or trapped quickly make it to the website of the organization as well as to online locations like YouTube, where they typically generate many thousands of 'views'. Further, and because CABS has over the years built good relations with the domestic media, the images also make the headlines in Malta, sometimes within hours of their origin in the field. Film clips of birds being shot or of the police chasing trappers about a field generate much interest and hundreds of online comments. They therefore serve a double purpose: as evidence in case of a prosecution, and as an important part of the work as of CABS an activist organization with an eye on public support and impact.

The work undertaken by CABS is rooted in highly organized forms of field surveillance. Methods vary, but the standard one is for small teams of observers to take up strategic positions in the countryside, preferably ones that enjoy high visibility and overlook intensively hunted places or ones that attract certain kinds of migrating birds (roosting birds of prey, for example). The teams proceed to meticulously record any illegal hunting activity, as well as things like the number of shots heard. These teams are equipped with telescopes (including, at the time of fieldwork, an extremely expensive high-magnification spotting scope donated to CABS by a benefactor in Germany) and cameras, and they try to secure photographic evidence if and when the occasion arises. When on surveillance duty, CABS teams wear T-shirts printed with the words 'Anti-Poaching Operation: CABS Bird Guard'.

The CABS camps are not the only initiative of their kind. In 2008, BirdLife Malta launched Spring Watch on the same model. It was the first year since Malta joined the EU in 2004 that spring hunting was completely outlawed and there was a palpable sense of anxiety among bird protectionists over whether or not the ban would be effective. What BirdLife Malta did was to tap into its transnational networks (at the time, the Executive Director of the organization was a Turkish former Greenpeace activist with solid international ENGO connections) to invite volunteers to 'monitor' the Maltese countryside during the two weeks of April when spring migration would be at its peak. There was also a public relations exercise in which members of the public were invited to join Spring Watch volunteers for a Sunday morning 'stroll in the countryside, while admiring the miracle of our natural heritage undisturbed'.[26]

Since then, Spring Watch camps have been held annually and are now one of BirdLife Malta's main activism events. Every year, around thirty volunteers spend two weeks in Malta to monitor the spring hunt. Recruitment is carried out through an international open call for volunteers, in close collaboration with the RSPB in Britain and other partner ENGOs of BirdLife Malta in other countries. The call for 2016 emphasized the IUCN reclassification of the turtle dove as 'vulnerable' and the part that the monitoring camp would play in the protection of the species:

> Our goal will be to collect data that can be used to challenge the derogation that allows spring hunting to happen . . . the opportunity to make a difference to bird conservation in the Islands and Europe. You will have a chance to get out in the field, see some fantastic birds, get experience with undertaking wildlife surveys and gathering material for media releases. This is a fantastic opportunity to meet fellow birdwatchers from all over Europe.[27]

The dynamics of recruitment mean that the majority of Spring Watch volunteers are British. Unlike CABS, BirdLife Malta does not fund their participation in the camp.

As is the case with the CABS camps, Spring Watch surveillance is tightly organized and follows fixed routines. At dawn every day, teams of three to five people wearing bright yellow T-shirts position themselves at strategic 'watchpoints', usually places on high ground that enjoy a great deal of visibility. Equipped with binoculars and telescopes, they keep detailed records using three kinds of standardized sheets. The first records all birds seen and details of type of flight, direction, height and so on; the second records the number of shots heard within a timeframe, the type of hunting activity observed, the bird species targeted and outcome, a description of the hunter and any hunting vehicles used, and the time and extent of police presence; the third is used in the case of a report to the police and records a description of the 'suspect', geographical coordinates and details of photographic or video evidence secured (most volunteers carry cameras). When not at their stations, the Spring Watch teams roam the countryside to watch over and monitor specific situations (a flock of roosting birds, for example, or a report of illegal hunting) and, perhaps more importantly, scout for watchpoints. As with CABS, spatial fluency and detailed intelligence on ground activity by hunters and trappers is of the essence. This information is exchanged and discussed during long briefing sessions held every evening at which the team members report on the day's work and decide on the best course of action for the day after.

Campbell and Veríssimo (2015) have discussed some of the ways in which the CABS and BirdLife Malta surveillance projects summon military discourse to represent their activities to the public. The vocabulary includes words like 'bird guards', 'monitor' and 'survey' the landscape, 'patrols', and so on. As they put it, 'depicting an unrelenting enemy who cannot be reasoned with, and whose lust for blood leads him to develop cunning ways of evading the laws of the State, NGOs maintain that their only recourse is to train volunteers in equally cunning tactics of conceal-ment and surveillance, and beat the hunters at their own game' (2015: 83). At first glance, this sounds rather like a case of the 'militarization of conservation' – the practice, that is, in places like elephant reserves and Africa and tiger reserves in India of waging literally armed and lethal war against poachers. However, and as the authors argue, the Maltese case is different because it does not include military operations that pursue and eliminate poachers; rather, it is all about the use of military metaphors by ENGOs to legitimize their involvement in the field and represent their work to the public (Campbell and Veríssimo 2015). In other words, the emphasis is on the discursive value of the work of CABS and Spring Watch.

It is clear that the surveillance camps feed into a discursive field that sets up hunting as a negative presence in the Maltese countryside and bird conservation ENGOs as its morally rightful opponent. And yet, this is only one aspect of what they do. A leading CABS activist and camp organizer I spoke to actually resisted the military associations. Lending credence to Campbell and Veríssimo's emphasis on metaphor and dis-course, he told me that if there was a battle at all, it was limited to the media. However, he added that the real thrust of the work of CABS was elsewhere – its main objective was to ensure that the hunting laws in Malta (and elsewhere) were properly enforced, partly by helping the police secure convictions and partly through surveillance work that would make hunters feel watched and less likely to break the law in the first place.

Writing about the 'Operation Osprey' conservation project in the Scottish Highlands, Cocker argues that the value of military metaphors was originally practical rather than discursive. As he puts it, 'the some-what paramilitary-style title now seems little more than a calculated appeal to our sense of the dramatic, yet at its inception in 1959 Operation Osprey's whiff of hands-on guerrilla action for nature had real substance' (2018: 38). As far as substance goes, CABS and Springwatch have been behind a significant number of convictions. More importantly, they have introduced to the Maltese landscape a palpable sense of systematic sur-veillance, the results of which go well beyond the discursive. It may be worth recalling that the surveillance teams wear conspicuous T-shirts, use heavy field optics and position themselves in places that enjoy high visibility. Visibility is choreographed to produce a conspicuous kind of seeing presence – they are seeing-seen, so to speak. The effect on hunting has been profound. As one team member explained, 'when hunters and trappers know we are on the island, it's a big deterrent. The effect of that is hard to measure – you cannot count how many birds are not shot because of our presence'.

The Gaze Resisted

By 2004 or so, hunters in Malta had to contend with a new presence in the field: that of parallel surveillance efforts run by BirdLife Malta and CABS. It is hard to overemphasize the importance of this innovation. A new word was added to the hunters' register: *sikkatura*. Literally, this means 'tightness', and in this case it refers to a tightening of enforcement. In part this was due to mounting pressure by the EU Commission on the Maltese government to get its act together. The presence of the BirdLife Camp volunteers and CABS, and of the police, turned the Maltese countryside into one vast panopticon that was ultimately underwritten by political and legislative power. For hunters, it was now no longer sufficient to moon and give the finger. The transformation of land by hunters had always taken into account leading lines, but now sightlines were added into the equation. Even as the watchers developed a set of what they call 'watchpoints' (strategic points from where large tracts of land can be monitored), the rubble walls around hunting locations got higher and CCTV became a not-uncommon fixture in country lanes. The point is that for hunters today, being-there is also something of an optical cat-and-mouse game of partial visibility. This *sikkatura* is probably also why it has become possible in recent years for birdwatchers to enjoy some semblance of undisturbed bird life. There is thus a parallel between the process of social and political corralling, and the partial retreat of hunters behind the walls and fences of privately owned land.

Military metaphors aside, the tangible effects of *sikkatura* are readily seen. For example, hunting by free roaming on public land is on the decline. Unless it is designated as a reserve or park, this type of land is technically open to hunters – but it also invites walkers, birdwatchers and members of the public generally. It is much more difficult to block the sightlines to and across it, and this makes it vulnerable to surveillance and police raids. Therefore, what CABS and similar surveillance efforts have done in their several years of work in Malta is to systematize and panopticize the gaze I discussed earlier. The innovation has had a profound effect on the dynamics of hunting and conservation in Malta. Partly this is because hunters do not just resignedly accept the presence of CABS and Springwatch teams. One of the ways in which they resist the gaze is through the twin process of spatial containment and the fortification of space.

The 2012 incident involving the shooting of the CABS drone made the news in more ways than one. A few days after the event, the FKNK called on the police to press charges against CABS, on grounds of harassment, breach of privacy, trespassing, spying, flying a 'spy aircraft' over private land and breach of air traffic control regulations. The FKNK also called on the Commissioner of Police to confiscate all footage and photographs 'in the interest of the protection of personal data of Maltese citizens'. It added that:

> This is not about hunting . . . During the Second World War, the Maltese Islands absorbed the heaviest, most sustained and concentrated of aerial bombing in history that was carried out by German aircraft. Yet the Maltese triumphed in the end. We are now faced with German-based CABS using an unmanned aerial vehicle, commonly known as a drone, the likes of which are mostly used in military operations, to film, spy and disrespectfully invade Maltese privacy and provoke Maltese hunters.[28]

On its part, CABS responded by describing the FKNK's press statement as a 'potpourri of ill-founded allegations, xenophobia, intimidation of those with other views and empty bluster'.[29] In many ways, this was a routine exchange of blows between the FKNK and a bird protection ENGO. However, the point is that hunters do not just accept the gaze, surveillance and *sikkatura*; on the contrary, they actively resist and counter it, in at least two ways.

The first way is discursively, by summoning the notion of privacy. The argument is that surveillance, particularly when it involves the use of field optics to gaze into private land, is an intrusion and a breach of privacy. It is usually illustrated using the hypothetical example of unwanted attention to sexual intimacy. As a hunter put it to me: 'It's my private land, why should I have drones flying over and cameras pointing at me? What if I decide to share a moment with my wife there?' The earlier humour of voyeurism is thus rehearsed, but also transformed into a more sombre argument for the protection of privacy. This shift towards a sustained case for privacy has been lent considerable weight by a context that increasingly values data protection. A relative newcomer to Malta (data protection legislation was first enacted in 2001 and was brought fully into force in 2003), the notion has since seeped into everyday discourse in contexts that range from market research to school noticeboards. Put simply, many people in Malta have at least some understanding of what data protection means and are aware that it is minutely regulated at law at the national and EU levels. Thus, when hunters complain about breach of privacy, they are not regurgitating a general and fuzzy notion; rather, they are invoking a set of emerging cultural, moral and legal norms. In so doing, they also attempt to effectively turn the tables on the observers – in watching out for illegal hunting, the watchers are themselves in the wrong, especially when they do not just observe but also record and publicize. Further, an essential aspect of the resistance discourse of hunters, both at the informal and public sphere discursive levels, is that the breach of privacy is especially unacceptable because it involves foreigners who use illicit means to pry into the lives of Maltese hunters on Maltese soil. The argument thus taps into the notion of *indħil barrani* (foreign interference) to considerable effect, but it also exposes hunters and the FKNK to accusations of xenophobia.

The second way in which hunters counter the surveillance gaze is more practical. There have been instances in recent years of hunters and trappers wearing improvised head coverings to make themselves unidentifiable to unwanted field observers. Roosting birds have been known to be targeted at night, and some hunters have bought shotguns that make less noise and therefore attract less attention. These, however, are more extreme cases and are usually linked to daringly law-breaking practices such as the trapping of finches in spring and the deliberate and planned shooting of rare protected species. In a more general way, surveillance and *sikkatura* have led to the fortification of rural space, to adopt a term from contemporary urban anthropology. Two-way radios and mobile phones are useful to generate real-time field information about migrating birds, but equally about the presence and movement of CABS, birdguards and the police. Watchers have been known to be employed in certain strategic locations as a form of countersurveillance. Perhaps most importantly, privately owned hunting places have tended to become increasingly inward-looking and protected against surveillance. As mentioned earlier, high walls and trees block sightlines very effectively, and surveillance technology such as CCTV is not uncommonly encountered in the countryside. There has even been talk of infrared motion sensors installed in country lanes as early-warning systems. Electronic bird callers, especially the kind that are left on at night on a continuous loop, tend to be concealed in ways that seek to outwit the surveillance teams and the police.

Concluding Remarks

In Chapter 4 I looked at the ways in which hunters in Malta make place for hunting. I argued that, increasingly, the surest way in which they do so is the outright acquisition of land that they then proceed to make into a hunting *post*, in part through a process of fortification. In other contexts, conservation ENGOs have done much the same and in some cases have become significant landowners in their own right. In Britain, for example, 407 acres of marshland at Cley were bought at auction by a wealthy doctor in 1926 and soon afterwards were incorporated into a wildlife conservation organization called the Norfolk Naturalists Trust. The mould had been set by the National Trust, which by 1919 already held sixty-three properties and 6,000 acres. A hundred years on, the RSPB alone owns 323,000 acres across the country (Cocker 2018).

In Malta, ENGOs have not to date sought to privately own land. The reasons have to do with the complications of land ownership in a small and densely inhabited place, as well as with the price of land, which makes it impossible for organizations on tight budgets to aspire to purchase anything beyond a couple of hectares. However, this does not mean that ENGOs have not actively pursued the project of making place for conservation. Reserves, designations and the panopticization of the landscape are the main thrusts of this continuing project.

This is a project that, as far as hunters are concerned, brings about a creeping dispossession and eviction. The model is well known in the scholarship. For instance, Cronon (1995) has written about the establishment of parks in North America according to an archetypal convergence of 'wilderness' and nation that proved seminal in many countries. The parks, myopically seen as last bastions of 'wilderness' within a dichotomous framework that opposed nature and culture, very often ended up dispossessing Native Americans. Likewise, and looking at how the inhabitants of highland towns in Sardinia struggled for decades against the establishment of a national park, Heatherington recounts how a local informant would 'sometimes explain ruefully that people in Orgosolo were just like the Indians, about to be closed up on a reserve when the park was made, and no longer allowed access to their traditional lands' (2010: 65).

In Malta, hunters are acutely sensitive to what they see as the spatial creep of conservation. In 2016, the Ornis Committee discussed the case of a place called Fra Ben, where hunters sat in hides metres away from a busy beach and summer resort. The suggestion (originally raised by the police, who report regularly to the Committee) was that the government ought to consider banning hunting at Fra Ben, partly on the grounds of safety. However, the FKNK strongly resisted the demand, arguing that its members had over the years suffered a steady decrease in hunting land as more and more places had been designated as reserves or otherwise protected. The FKNK saw this as a war on hunting 'by stealth' and said it would oppose any further decline in the space of possibility.[30] In a country where 28.5 per cent of the national space is covered by some type of designation, where surveillance teams roam the countryside armed with powerful optics and where urbanization and tourism close in on the countryside from all directions, it is hard not to see their point.

Notes

1. Macfarlane 2007: 292.
2. Cocker 2018: 47.
3. 'Flamingos Flying out of Għadira Nature Reserve Shot', BirdLife Malta press release, 3 November 2018.
4. 'L-Inħawi tal-Buskett u tal-Girgenti: Natura 2000 Management Plan (SAC/SPA)', Environment and Resources Authority, Malta, 2014, p. 5.
5. Retrieved 28 January 2015 from www.BirdLifemalta.org.
6. Source: obituary of Bert Axell in *The Telegraph*, 26 November 2001.
7. Retrieved 28 January 2015 from www.BirdLifemalta.org.
8. Retrieved 28 January 2015 from www.ramsar.org.
9. Retrieved 28 January 2015 from www.ramsar.org.
10. Retrieved 28 January 2015 from www.BirdLife.org.
11. 'Monitoring Important Bird Area: A Global Framework', BirdLife International, 2006.
12. BirdLife International, 'Important Bird Areas Factsheet: Rdum tal-Madonna', 2015. Retrieved 26 January 2015 from www.BirdLife.org.
13. '"Malta's Galapagos": Gozo Channel Malta's First Marine Important Bird Area', BirdLife Malta press release, 30 August 2013.
14. *'Majjistral'* means 'northwest'. It is not a historical toponym; rather, the name was first used when the park was set up.
15. *'Xagħra'* means a stretch of garrigue and *'ħamra'* means red, after the reddish soil that is found in this place and indeed in most of Malta – the Maltese word for 'soil' is actually *'ħamrija'*, which means 'reddish'.
16. The movement was based in part on a previous case, that of the *Front Kontra l-Golf Kors* (*Front Against the Golf Course*), which in the early 2000s had successfully campaigned to stop a golf course development in an agricultural area in a place called Rabat.
17. Legal Notice 217 of 2013 of the Government of Malta established that 'no person shall, prior to two hours before sunrise and after ten o'clock in the morning, hunt or attempt to hunt, take or attempt to take, in any area of the Park'.
18. *Giren* (sing. *girna*) were described as 'national heritage' in a dedicated and richly illustrated monograph researched and written by a Dominican friar who mapped them and proposed a typology. Some of the best examples illustrated and described in the book were located at what was to become the Majjistral Park (Fsadni 1999).

19. The process included a technical report ('Removal of Derelict Hides', Heritage Parks Foundation, 2012) that was submitted to the Planning Authority as part of the application for a permit to dismantle the hides.
20. The sea squill is a Mediterranean plant that produces stately white flowers in August. It grows in profusion at the park.
21. A. Raine and T. Temuge, 'The Mizieb Report', BirdLife Malta, May 2010.
22. Literally 'you have made God sick', an idiom used to express disgust at behaviour that is thought to go well beyond the normal standards of decency.
23. Patrick Barkham, 'Chris Packham: Malta is a Bird Hell', *The Guardian*, 28 April 2014.
24. Avery 2015: 42.
25. 'Birdwatchers Return to Look out for Illegal Hunting and Trapping', *Times of Malta*, 30 August 2010.
26. 'BirdLife Spring Watch Camp Kicks off', *Times of Malta*, 14 April 2008.
27. Retrieved 24 March 2016 from www.BirdLifemalta.org.
28. 'Hunters to Press Charges against German Birdwatchers over Drone Flights Filming Illegal Trapping', *The Malta Independent*, 29 April 2012.
29. 'Hunters' Drone Drama a Storm in a Teacup, Says CABS', *Malta Today*, 16 May 2012.
30. Minutes of the Ornis Committee meeting of 2 November 2016.

CHAPTER 6

How Many Fowl Is Fair?

This senseless slaughter includes 2,500 little bitterns; 16,000 herons and egrets; 3,000 honey buzzards; 10,000 marsh harriers; 6,500 hobbies (a total of over 50,000 raptors in all); 11,500 assorted owls; 16,000 hoopoes; 5,000 bee-eaters; 80,000 golden orioles to name a few. If that list doesn't make you sick then add 17 hundred kingfishers; 55,000 cuckoos; 100,000 robins; 200,000 skylarks and at a rough guess over 2 million finches.
 —David Bellamy, 'Foreword', in Natalino Fenech, *Fatal Flight*[1]

My feeling is that the green movement has torpedoed itself with numbers.
 —Paul Kingsnorth, *Confessions of a Recovering Environmentalist*[2]

Science and numbers figure prominently and increasingly in the dynamics of bird conservation in Malta. They capture the imagination of the press, lend support to or undermine arguments and form the basis of derogations from EU legislation. Above all, they are vigorously contested by a range of parties. It may seem a straightforward matter, on a small island where the word 'remote' has little substance and where hunting and the places where people live and work are cheek by jowl, to quantify the hunt. It turns out to be anything but. In fact, numbers are possibly the most fiercely contested aspect of the encounter between hunting and conservation in Malta. In this chapter I explore some of the dynamics of this busy intersection. I shall first describe the ways in which bird protection ENGOs established their stewardship of scientific ornithology, embedded themselves in a broader context of scientific knowledge practices and emerged as the prime producers of numbers that represented the scale of hunting in Malta. I then explore the contestation of these numbers, and their supposed implications, by hunters and hunting organizations. Finally, I trace the emergence of a full-blown enumerative modality that was the direct result of Malta's accession to the EU. Throughout, the emphasis is on the processes of production and the politics of scientific knowledge practices generally, and quantification in particular, and their location within the enterprise of conservation.

Numbers That Served a Cause

But the hunters and their decoys and semi-automatics couldn't be everywhere at once, so Stephen found plenty to count. Or count and revise: thirty-five dunlins that landed, seventeen dunlins that took off, six dunlins that
made it over the next ridge – an attrition rate that would clearly result in no
dunlins at all one stop later, but maybe the hunters are all on this side today.
—Nell Zink, *The Wallcreeper*[3]

In a recent court case, a respected ornithologist and BirdLife Malta activist (who has since passed away) testified that, while the numbers given
in *Fatal Flight* of birds killed annually in Malta 'may have been inflated',
he had still supported their dissemination. The reason was that they had
'served a cause he endorsed'.[4] His testimony is tremendously important
to the argument of this chapter. What the case suggested was that the
protectionists' estimates of the numbers of birds bagged by hunters were
(and are), to paraphrase Best (2012), entangled with the media, politics
and activists. They are also thought, by protectionists as well as hunters,
to be directly linked to conservation outcomes.

An important aspect of BirdLife Malta's output is that of publications.
It is beyond the scope of the present work to detail the various in-house
newsletters and magazines for members. Suffice it to say that their frequency as well as their generally high standards of production have
served to establish the ENGO as text-oriented and anything but paper-
shy, a factor that is significant to our understanding of its fluency with
the language, protocols and practices of national, EU and international
lobbying. However, the type of output that is more significant in this context is that of ornithological scientific publications. BirdLife Malta was
born as an ornithological society (MOS, the Malta Ornithological Society)
and one of its main activities has been to steward, centralize and regulate
the study of birds in Malta. From early on, all the records of birds seen
and ringed were fed into a central database, on the basis of which annual
'systematic lists' and 'ringing reports' were compiled and published. The
ENGO's extensive list of published books and pamphlets on the birds of
Malta were empirically based on that body of data. Besides, a number of
self-taught ornithologists with direct or indirect links to the organization
published research articles on bird migration, breeding and behaviour, in
in-house as well as international peer-reviewed journals. These empirical
and systematic data and publications established BirdLife Malta as the
(sole, to all intents and purposes) producer and purveyor of scientific
knowledge on birds in Malta, with two very relevant outcomes.

First, the value of these data derives from their origins in processes
of production (bird counts, ringing, record-keeping and so on) that are

standardized in international ornithological circles. This means that they are thought to be comparable to similar data produced by ornithologists elsewhere and thus to contribute to BirdLife Malta's location in a wide-ranging cartography of prestige and scientific legitimacy. Put simply, the valid and reliable – because they are produced using standardized and recognized procedures – data produced by BirdLife Malta mean that the organization is also known and respected internationally for the quality of the knowledge it produces. Second, the data produced have been used on numerous occasions as the basis for conservation projects, most notably the classification and sectioning of space as 'scientifically important', 'relevant' and so on. One example will suffice to make the point. *Bird Studies on Filfla*, which was published in 1970, presented the findings of a number of research visits to the islet in 1968 and 1969. It established the importance of the place as a major breeding site for a number of seabird species. However, the book also proved instrumental in terms of convincing the British (Malta was a British base at the time) to stop using Filfla for naval target practice.

With respect specifically to numbers, the bird conservation enterprise has always been keen on quantification. One might remark that there is a continuity between birdwatching as commonly practised, which involves lists of species and numbers seen on a particular day,[5] and the production of species-specific numbers about hunting. One of the basic rituals of birdwatching involves the keeping of records, and in Malta birdwatchers learn to list the type and numbers of birds seen and to bracket observations of the number of birds shot next to each species, sometimes followed by the total number of shots heard at the end of the list. In this way, Maltese birdwatchers are bird as well as hunt enumerators. The indirect result is that most of the contributors (especially post-1960s) to ornithology and conservation in Malta have also come up with lists of numbers shot and trapped by species and, perhaps more importantly, a total annual figure.

The first attempt to produce such lists was presented by two Maltese ornithologists at an International Council for Bird Preservation (ICBP, which became the BirdLife partnership in 1993) conference held in 1975. The focus was specifically on birds of prey and the numbers given were 2,458 to 4,508 shot annually as the total for an itemized list of twenty-four species (Sultana and Gauci 1977). It is relevant that these numbers were produced specifically for circulation at an international conference.

A second and more ambitious enumeration exercise followed soon after. The Woldhek report was commissioned by the Netherlands-based European Committee for the Preservation of Mass Destruction of

Migratory Birds, which had been set up in 1976 by the ICBP. The aim of the Committee was to coordinate fundraising activities in the countries of northern Europe, the proceeds of which would go towards bird protection in the Mediterranean. Accordingly, the Woldhek report was not about Malta specifically, but rather the Mediterranean generally, where 'although the available estimates are very rough, even the most optimistic ones indicate that hundreds of millions of migratory birds are killed annually'.[6] The report described Malta, together with Portugal, Spain, France, Italy, Cyprus and Lebanon, as 'very bad for migratory birds'. People in Malta were 'far from indifferent to birds'; on the contrary, they wanted to 'hold them in their hands, dead, stuffed, or alive'. Significantly in the present context, the Woldhek report included a section on the number of birds shot and trapped in Malta annually. Two Maltese ornithologists were invited to independently produce estimates, which were presented separately. For birds shot, the two estimates were 600,000, and 600,000–1.5 million; only one estimate, that of 1.5–3 million, was given for birds trapped. Although the two ornithologists were broadly in agreement, some of their numbers varied significantly: for example, 2,000–3,000 as opposed to 10,000 for the nightjar, 11,000 as opposed to 300,000 for thrushes, and 40,000 as opposed to 500,000 for robins. The Woldhek report was one of the sources used by two Maltese ornithologists to come up with their own estimates in 1982: 423,700–681,500 for birds shot, and in excess of 1.5 million for birds trapped annually, for the years 1972 to 1982. The authors were cautious in at least one respect: 'due to this fluctuation (the result of variable migration patterns) the numbers of birds shot or trapped vary correspondingly. It is very difficult to estimate properly the numbers taken annually and the estimates given . . . could be higher or lower in some years' (Sultana and Gauci 1982: 26).

The next instalment was the Magnin report, which was commissioned by the ICBP and was based on a visit to Malta by the author in October and November 1985.[7] It included a detailed list, itemized by species or family, of the number of birds shot and trapped annually. The list was based on a survey conducted among fourteen active members of BirdLife Malta (then MOS), many of whom were active birdwatchers. According to Magnin, the figures ranged from 680,458 to 981,930 for birds shot and 3 million to in excess of 4 million for birds trapped.

However, it was Natalino Fenech's *Fatal Flight*, published in 1992, that really set new standards. As discussed elsewhere in this volume, there are many reasons why this was such a landmark book. In the context of this chapter, its most significant aspect was Fenech's attempt at enumeration, which sought to go beyond the guesstimates of earlier authors. Consider the following excerpt:

7.1 million cartridges are loaded each year. To these one must add 2.5 million ready-made cartridges which are imported. This means a total of about 10 million cartridges are used each year. If one million cartridges are used for clay pigeon shooting, while the other 9 million are used for shooting birds, and if one assumes that a bird is killed for every three cartridges used, then a minimum of 3 million birds are shot each year. To these one must add the number of birds which are trapped. (Fenech 1992: 2)

Besides cartridges, Fenech made use of the hunting bag records of ten informants, records kept by taxidermists, official statistics of hunting and trapping licences, and time spent by hunters in the field in order to come up with a range of estimates using basic formulae of mathematical proportionality. Sections of *Fatal Flight* are dense with all manner of numbers and statistics. Fenech's conclusion was that the number of birds shot in Malta was over 3 million annually, while that for trapped birds was 1–2.8 million; he added that the latter figure was a conservative estimate.

Fenech's figure of 3 million proved tremendously consequential, in that it appeared to fix the scale of hunting in Malta and became a rallying cry for bird conservation. There were a number of reasons for its evangelical success. First, it was produced in the context of a widely publicized popular book with a catchy and provocative title, as opposed to a report or a specialized bird guide, as in earlier cases. Second, it was based on an attempt to generate data based on sampling, actual counts and extrapolations – in other words, data based on the scientific principle of tangible evidence. Third, because it had the blessing of BirdLife Malta and could therefore draw on the cartography of the organization, it was actively taken up and circulated in the field of international bird conservation, where it really mattered. The quote given at the start of this chapter is taken from David Bellamy's Foreword to *Fatal Flight*. Bellamy was a well-known British author, broadcaster and campaigner. It was through brokers like him that the number became so widely known and apparently self-evident. Finally, one might suppose that nothing captures

Table 6.1. The various estimates of the number of birds shot and trapped annually in Malta (some totals compiled by the author).

Source	Numbers shot annually	Numbers trapped annually
Sultana and Gauci 1975	2,458–4,508*	Not applicable
Woldhek 1980	600,000–1 million	1.5–3 million
Sultana and Gauci 1982	423,700–681,500	At least 1.5 million
Magnin 1985	680,458–981,930	3–4 million
Fenech 1992	1,501,800–2,853,650	1–2.8 million

* Estimate specifically for raptors.

the imagination like a seven-figure number. The upshot is that the figure of 3 million (birds shot annually in Malta) became a key device in the campaign for bird protection. Twenty-seven years after the publication of *Fatal Flight*, the number still regularly crops up in popular and news pieces that describe hunting in Malta. Fenech's book remains influential where it matters. For example, the section on the turtle dove in Mark Cocker's recent and acclaimed *Birds and People* (2013) is based almost entirely on it. Malta, according to Cocker, retains its top perch as the place most notorious for dove hunting. The cumulative bag for Maltese hunters and trappers (between 2.6 and 5.8 million birds) is the one estimated by Fenech, of which 160,000–480,000 were turtle doves. Cocker does add that since that time, those numbers have declined substantially.

The most recent attempt at general quantification was carried out by BirdLife Malta in 2015.[8] The initiative came from BirdLife International and was intended to produce systematic, quantitative data on the illegal killing of birds in the Mediterranean. The guidance notes for the exercise emphasized the lack of 'systematic, coordinated monitoring', as a result of which it was 'not currently possible to compare the scale of the impact of illegal killing in different countries, nor for different types of illegal activity . . . this limits our ability to tackle the issue effectively, through raising funds, prioritising actions and targeting interventions and to monitor the effectiveness of interventions'. There was therefore a need for 'more robust information' that would underpin BirdLife International's lobbying with the European Commission, the Council of Europe and AEWA-CMS.[9] BirdLife Malta used three different methods to come up with estimates. For most species, estimates were based on the 'taxidermy value' of each; this was calculated as 'the ratio of the number of individuals killed or found dead from 2011 to 2014, plus the birds confiscated by the police in 2014, divided by the number of individuals observed in Malta in 2006/2007'. For species that could be hunted by derogation, estimates were based on national bag limits and extrapolated *carnet de chasse* figures (see below). With respect to species for which no data whatsoever were available, a default number of 1 was given as the estimate.

A short time after the study was published, the FKNK commissioned Natalino Fenech to conduct an 'independent expert review' of it. One might suggest that this was Fenech's chance to get back at the BirdLife Malta activists who had questioned his own numbers in the 2008 court case. Be that as it may, he discussed why, in his view, the BirdLife Malta estimates were spurious and based on flawed methodologies. He also questioned the inclusion of species like the turtle dove and finches, which, given that derogations were a legal instrument within the Birds Directive, could not be said to be illegally hunted. The details of BirdLife Malta's estimates, and Fenech's contestation of them, are beyond the scope of the present work. However, four things are worth pointing out on account of their relevance to my argument.

First, the inherent uncertainty of this sort of quantification is evident in the estimate range: the BirdLife Malta report concluded that a minimum of 51,324 and a maximum of 256,186 individual birds across all considered species were killed illegally in Malta every year. This is a broad and presumably accommodating range, and yet Fenech took issue with the estimates and ultimately concluded that the BirdLife Malta report inflated the number of illegalities beyond what was actually happening on the ground. It is hard not to conclude that no estimate of birds hunted and trapped in Malta, no matter how self-declaredly approximate, is safe from contestation, or perhaps the more approximate and cautious a number is declared to be by its producers, the more open it is to contestation. Second, such numbers are always located within narratives of conservation. The BirdLife Malta report concluded that the results 'suggest a moderate (<25%) decline of illegal killing of birds in Malta in the past ten years'. A moderate decline is just that, and BirdLife Malta's numbers dovetailed with the ENGO's drift that the surest route to effective conservation was law enforcement, which, notwithstanding some improvement, was still in short supply. However, Fenech argued that the decline in illegal hunting was much sharper than that, that Malta was 'fast becoming a normal place for birds' and that the transformation was in significant measure down to a 'change in mentality' among hunters. He went on to suggest a number of ways forward, many of which included working with hunters towards self-regulation. The point is that these were not just two different sets of numbers, but also radically divergent conservation programmes. Third, the dynamics of the contestation suggest that it was also about the rightful stewardship of numbers and their methods of production. In this case, BirdLife Malta's stewardship (itself rooted in the history discussed earlier) was challenged by Natalino Fenech, himself commissioned by the FKNK. Further, Fenech's description of his report as an 'independent expert review' suggests that he – and, by inference, the FKNK – considered BirdLife Malta to be neither an independent nor an expert producer of data. The fact that BirdLife International relied on BirdLife Malta's data for its own final report (Brochet et al. 2016) indicates that, at least in that international bird protection circle, BirdLife Malta's stewardship was unaffected by the FKNK-Fenech challenge. Finally, this attempt at general quantification was an exception for its time; BirdLife Malta had not carried out such exercises for very many years.

Hunters' Own Numbers and the Refutation Enterprise

As expected for such a politically charged field, it is not just the bird protection lobby that produces and otherwise relates to numbers. On the contrary, hunters too have routinely and increasingly challenged bird protectionists over the numbers they produce, as well as their (mis) appropriation of the enumerative enterprise more generally. Less regularly, hunters have also produced their own competing figures.

Traditionally, hunters enjoyed a dubious reputation as yarn-mongerers. By 'traditionally', I mean of a broadly defined past up until the time when growing numbers of people began to think of hunting as a questionable if not downright unacceptable practice. Roughly speaking, the shift took place during the 1970s as the natural history and conservation societies set up a decade earlier began to make their presence felt. Until that time, hunters had been known as tellers of tall tales involving vast numbers of game birds (typically quail and turtle doves) or encounters with some *tajra* (*tajra* is the generic word used for nongame birds that are however desirable as stuffed trophies) of great size. There was much humour in these notions, and old songs and ditties still circulate that poke fun at hunters and their stories.[10] Besides, old hunters today reminisce about the spring days when 'the walls were lined with nightjars, the trees crawled with owls, and turtle doves kept coming in constant streams'. *Kif Dieb il-Gemiem* (*The Turtle Doves Have Melted away*) is a recent book that brings together a number of interviews with old hunters. They invariably talk about the large numbers of birds that migrated over Malta in the past, and of the ample bags that Maltese hunters once enjoyed (Fenech 2016).

There are two points to be made here. First, the tendency in the past was to inflate the numbers seen or shot. As I shall argue shortly, this is diametrically opposed to the present situation, in which hunters are likely to talk about the scarcity of birds and therefore meagre catches. Second, and more importantly, contemporary stories about the vast numbers of the past are a way of talking about a mythical golden age when the quantity of birds was limitless and hunters could take as they wished, without the pressures and *sikkatura* (meaning here the constraints of laws and their enforcement) that plague them nowadays.

These, however, were largely aspects of oral culture. As far as writing is concerned, the keeping of records has never been an intrinsic part of the hunting experience, as it is for birdwatching. There are some exceptions to this and some hunters, especially ones with a higher educational background, do in fact keep notebooks in which they record their catches. Yet, there is one important difference. Unlike birdwatching records, there has never been any attempt to pool notes and convert them into systematic and disseminable data; they are, to all intents and purposes, intended as private personal memories. The result is that the hunting lobby cannot draw on a legacy of record-keeping and data production. Nor has it produced, in any sustained way, specialized knowledge and numbers that could serve to locate it within international currents. In fact, enumeration by hunters developed as a limited and reactive enterprise intended to compete with or refute the data produced by bird protectionists.

Turning away from a (real or imagined) legacy of number inflation, hunters eventually started to systematically contest the big numbers produced by conservationists. What fuelled this shift was the realization that there was more to numbers than humour; in fact, they were a consequential aspect of a burgeoning conservation enterprise that threatened the legitimacy and therefore the future of hunting. Science and numbers were being used to raise the profile of the Maltese case internationally, especially in Britain and Germany – both powerful players in international bird science and conservation. The attention spawned regular coverage in the British press and, with it, pressure on the Maltese government to do something about hunting; it also brought resources (funds, for example, and specialist consultancy) to the local bird protection lobby. Indeed, it was the coupling of numbers ('millions') and images of dead or injured birds that served, and to some extent still does, as one of BirdLife Malta's sturdiest forms of capital.

The numbers produced by the campaigners, then, were increasingly contested by hunters, who accused the activists of magnification and outright deception. *Fatal Flight* and its millions came under particularly heavy fire. The word *'miljuni'* ('millions') became a standard joke among hunters, as well as a byword for the perceived unreliability and duplicity of bird conservationists. Thus, a hunter might reply *'miljuni'* when asked how many birds he had shot in a morning. BirdLife Malta is often referred to as 'Birdlies' by hunters; Steve Micklewright, who was the organization's director from 2012 to 2016, was nicknamed 'Micklewrong'. Besides, my hunter informants told me, there was a key contradiction in the numbers argument: it seemed that the more millions of birds were shot by Maltese hunters, the more there were to shoot (because the claims to large numbers shot were always coupled, by activists, with claims to continuing indiscriminate slaughter).

On a formal level, the FKNK has consistently contested the millions claims. It has also occasionally come up with numbers of its own. For example, a few months after the publication of *Fatal Flight*, the FKNK published a polemical pamphlet – in English, tellingly – that tore into Fenech's arguments, and especially his numbers and methods of quantification. The most memorable line was that 'he [Fenech] uses statistics as a drunk uses a lamppost, for support, rather than for illumination'.[11] The pamphlet accused Fenech (and, by implication, the whole edifice of activist science and quantification) of what Best (2012) has called 'number laundering' – the process by which numbers based on guesses or guesstimates take on a life of their own and, through repetition, come to be treated as straightforward fact, accurate and authoritative. Number laundering is especially rife, Best argues, when activists find themselves defending the 'dark figure' – that part of a social problem that is not represented by official statistics (2012: 33–34). This point will be taken up later in this chapter.

One of the most recent attempts by the FKNK to counter the numbers argument was a pamphlet published in 2012 – again, in English – with the title '*The Facts* about Maltese Game-Shooting and Live-Bird Capturing' (emphasis added). The overall annual average bag for Malta, itemized by species and apparently based on bag counts for the years 2001 to 2004, is given as rather less than 3 million – under 130,000, in fact. The authors go on to explain that this works out at an average of thirteen birds per hunter per year. It is significant that the formal FKNK quantification exercises have tended to be in English. Clearly, the intention was to counter BirdLife Malta's numbers internationally, where it mattered. One instance stands out in this respect. In 1991, the FACE commissioned Heribert Kalchreuter, a researcher at the European Wildlife Research Institute (EWRI, to my knowledge a one-man show that did not outlive Kalchreuter), to conduct a study on hunting and trapping in Malta. The circumstances of the commission are relevant to the present context. In 1990, a meeting was held between delegations from the FKNK (at the time the Association for Hunting and Conservation) and BirdLife Malta (then the MOS) under the auspices of the Naturopa Centre of the Council of Europe and FACE. The meeting had a conciliatory objective (it was hailed by the Director of Environment and Local Authorities at the Council of Europe as a 'new cooperation between the two parties')[12] and the parties agreed to have Kalchreuter look into the situation as an 'independent expert'. The study that resulted was based on two brief visits to Malta that included interviews with the main stakeholders and a small number of organized field sessions.

The part of the Kalchreuter report that is most relevant concerns his observations on the lack of quantitative and systematic data. In particular, it pointed out that there were none on the size of the populations of birds being hunted, the proportion of these populations that was being 'harvested' in Malta and the extent to which the losses due to hunting were compensated for by lower natural mortality and higher reproductive rates. Kalchreuter lamented the spuriousness of the annual bag data, which he described as 'vague' and 'ornithologists' guesstimates'. Kalchreuter went on to recommend the systematic keeping, by hunters themselves, of quantitative data by means of bag statistics. Only in this way could the 'real impact' of hunting on bird populations be ascertained. Further, such data would provide concrete evidence against 'exaggerated allegations'.

The Kalchreuter report turned out to be anything but conciliatory. BirdLife Malta was deeply upset by its use of terminology like 'harvested' and 'wise use'. As the organization saw it, this was hunter doublespeak coming from someone who after all had been commissioned by FACE and who was clearly sympathetic to hunters. Perhaps more importantly, Kalchreuter had questioned the veracity of the estimated figures for annual bags as cited by the MOS, as well as the significance of these figures in any case:

> The likelihood of a noticeable impact of shooting and trapping on migrant populations is rather small ... even the 'estimated' Maltese harvest of 3 million birds still comprises a tiny fraction of less than 1% of the total bag of birds taken during their migration through the Western Palearctic.[13]

For the hunters' association, on the other hand, the Kalchreuter report was a godsend. It was the first time that someone who ostensibly had the credentials to be described as a 'foreign independent expert' – Kalchreuter had a doctorate and ran an institute – had challenged the numbers produced by BirdLife Malta and its associates. The fact that the expert was also a foreigner did not go unnoticed: as hunters saw it, it was a providential reversal of roles, in that the bird conservation lobby had traditionally pitted enlightened foreigners against Maltese hunters who had no regard for science. Further, the wording of the report had tacitly represented hunting and trapping in Malta as legitimate practices that had both a rich past and a promising future. In spite of the fact that Kalchreuter was critical of the rampant poaching that took place in Malta, the departure from the standard way in which hunting in Malta was represented by foreigners was too welcome to be affected by such details.

Hunters as Conservationists: Discourses of Sustainability

The 'K' in FKNK, it is worth remembering, stands for *konservazzjonisti* ('conservationists'). In principle, it proposes that hunting and trapping are also about conserving birds. In contrast, to bird protectionists, 'hunter conservationists' is the gold standard against which all other oxymorons are measured. This was discussed in Chapter 3, but it is equally relevant here because of a notion it implies that has to do with science and numbers: sustainability. The effects of hunting on wildlife populations and the regulation of hunting is one of the deepest-rooted topics in applied ecology. In the United States, a pioneer in the field, bag limits were introduced around 1878 when Iowa limited prairie chicken catches to twenty-five birds per hunter per day. Leopold (as cited in Mills 2007: 14) linked the move to an American viewpoint – itself in part a reaction to European models of hunting that were perceived to benefit the elite – that saw game laws as 'essentially a device for dividing up a dwindling treasure which nature, rather than man, had produced'. Still, it was early days yet, and there was little connection with enforcement or with expected population response – by the late nineteenth century, extinction loomed for a number of species (including the iconic passenger pigeon). For most of these species, hunting was only one of several causes that led to decline. In the case of the passenger pigeon, for example, hunting – even if practised in astonishingly intensive and destructive ways – was not necessarily the most critical factor that led to extinction. The clearance of vast areas of forest east of the Great Plains, as well as the fact that the species could only survive in vast flocks, were equally consequential (Fuller 2015).

Be that as it may, the relationship between hunting and sustainability is complicated. Numbers killed do not necessarily imply population decline; in fact, a number of variables ought to be taken into account when assessing hunting outcomes. The first is the percentage of quarry population killed, known as the 'predation rate'. Second, it is necessary to establish whether the mortality is compensated for (for example, via lower mortality rates in other parts of the year, or immigration). Third, the effect on quarry populations depends also on *who* gets killed – it is well known that large-scale killing can occur in specific age classes with little impact on populations as a whole (Mills 2007). Sustainability, then, is not an exact science, and it is also one in which precautionary principles ought to play an important part: 'the trick with managing a population for sustained yield is to play it safe' (Caughley and Sinclair, as cited in Mills 2007: 297). As I will show shortly, the precautionary principle is of much consequence to hunt enumeration and sustainability models in Malta.

One of the FKNK's key claims is that hunting in Malta – by which is meant hunting according to the law – is fully sustainable.[14] This term, which was transposed from global environmentalist discourse and population ecology, as well as from global sustainable hunting discourses represented by FACE and other hunting circles to which the FKNK belongs, means that the number of birds taken by hunters and trappers is low enough not to negatively affect bird populations. The associated word 'harvesting', with its connotations of renewability and long-term preservation of resources (sustained yield), is equally significant in this respect. The FKNK uses it to try and locate hunting in Malta within a dual discourse of sustainability and wildlife management. Consider the following quote from the official website:

> Maltese hunters utilise the basic principals [*sic*] of hunting . . . which is the method of wise use of renewable natural resources and adapt European and International standards to the unique situation prevailing in the Maltese Islands. Unique, since the Maltese bag depends solely on migratory birds, there being no resident species. By such methods one can identify those species that can withstand harvesting, even the limited bag of Maltese hunters and trappers in Spring and regulate accordingly.[15]

The use of the word 'unique' is central to our understanding of how hunting and sustainability are brought together by Maltese hunters. It suggests the use of an exceptionalist model in which hunting in Malta is special because it is fully dependent on migration, and that the normal parameters of the science of sustainability cannot be applied in a straightforward way. To bird protectionists, this model is not just flawed, but is actually an underlying alibi of the general idea that hunters in Malta lack a logic of conservation. The argument is that, dependent as they are on migration, Maltese hunters fail to make the connection between the quarry and its breeding and population dynamics. In other words, and because Maltese hunters do not see the bigger picture, hunting in Malta cannot be sustainable. Mark Cocker sums it up neatly:

> For his part, the Maltese hunter on the ground applied much the same logic. 'If I don't shoot it, someone else will, so I'd rather shoot it myself', one individual explained when asked why he killed as he did. The argument is revealing for drawing its primary meaning from competition among the hunters, and also for its utter lack of reference to the prey itself. It is, in truth, not a rationale for hunting. That surely requires some imaginative transaction, some ecological linkage, between the hunter and his target. To justify the killing as a means to pre-empt one's predatory competition is little more than a charter for the quarry's eventual extinction. (Cocker 2013: 245)

To my mind, Cocker's understanding is partial. On the one hand, it is true that competition among hunters is especially likely to be an important source of meaning in a situation of free gathering. On the other hand, throughout my fieldwork, I worked with hunters whose transactions between their target and themselves were far from nonexistent – in fact, they were very imaginative indeed. Once again, the turtle dove presents us with a useful case study.

Figure 6.1. Uncertain future: a turtle dove. Photograph by Aron Tanti. Published with permission.

It is hardly possible to be in the field with hunters (especially in spring) and not talk about the drastic decline in the number of doves that migrate over Malta. Even if we make allowances for selective memory and shifting baselines, it is clear that the average hunter today can consider himself lucky if he sees, let alone bags, in a whole season what a hunter would commonly have seen in one morning forty years ago. The linear flocks (*sriebet*) and layers (*saffi*) that could number hundreds of doves are a fading memory; nowadays, the bird is usually encountered singly or, on exceptional passages, in very small flocks. The decrease is evident in the ornithological record from Malta, as well as in wider official sources. The IUCN estimates the current European population at 3.15–5.94 million pairs, which equates to 6.31–11.9 million mature individuals. IUCN data show that the species has undergone a rapid decline in much of its European range, as well as in Russia and Central Asia. The decline is thought to be driven by a number of factors, including loss of foraging and nesting sites, disease and hunting along its migration routes.[16]

Hunters are aware that the bird they value so highly as a quarry is in trouble. And yet, I never met a single hunter who thought that the turtle dove should be fully protected, or at least protected in spring: the general picture is of people taking, and wanting to continue to take, from a dwindling wild resource. There are a number of ways in which hunters in Malta resolve the contradiction. The first line of reasoning is that there are in fact plenty of turtle doves left in many parts of Europe and North

Africa. Maltese people who worked in the Libyan desert (usually with petroleum companies) in the 1980s and 1990s brought back vivid descriptions of vast flocks of turtle doves at watering holes, at a time when numbers in Malta had already dwindled significantly. Nowadays, hunters often talk about, and sometimes visit, places like Bulgaria, Romania and Morocco, where the flocks appear, to them at least, to be unaffected. The reasons given as to why numbers have gone down in Malta are many. They include changing migration routes (*il-gamiem bidel ir-rotta*), possibly to do with a shrinking Maltese countryside, changes in weather patterns or even conflict in Libya (the last was a popular explanation during the events of 2011). Sometimes, hunters use local topography to explain these changes. I once had a conversation with a hunter who owned land in what used to be traditionally one of the best hilltop locations for migrating turtle doves; the place now overlooks a sprawling coastal town. 'See all of that down there?', he told me, 'it's directly across what used to be the flight path of doves coming in from the sea; when that place was built up, the doves stopped coming.' Another localized explanation is that, as the number of trees increased over the past decades, turtle doves tended to disperse (*il-gamiem jitferrex*) all over the islands rather than follow the old routes.

Even so, there are many hunters who are prepared to concede that turtle dove numbers have indeed gone down globally. However, the reasons they give for this have nothing to do with hunting; on the contrary, they resolutely absolve it. Pesticides (*il-bexx*) are the most commonly blamed factor for the decline. This and other explanations are not necessarily entirely spurious, nor are they conjured up out of nothing. First, they are backed by a considerable volume of data. In Britain, for example, the population of the turtle dove declined by 97 per cent between 1970 and 2013. It is the sharpest decline of any species in that country and, while adverse pressure during migration and in wintering grounds cannot be ruled out, it is clear that by far the primary cause has been changes in farming practices. The turtle dove and the corn bunting are the only two species that obtain almost all their food from arable land; the former declined by 97 per cent and the latter by 90 per cent for the given period (Newton 2017).

More popularly, hunters will often refer to wildlife documentaries and pieces in the international press to support their arguments. They also draw comparisons between turtle doves and other bird species to make their point. 'Take wagtails or wheatears', a hunter told me, 'they haven't been hunted here for as long as I can remember, but their numbers have gone down catastrophically nonetheless – so why should the decline in doves be blamed on us?' The converse argument apparently works equally well: one hunter mentioned the example of woodcock, which had increased in recent years in spite of the fact that it was heavily hunted and that bags had got bigger and bigger. The argument is that even if wild birds are declining, the numbers taken by Maltese hunters are too small to matter. In support, it is often pointed out by hunters that Malta is not really located on a main migration route between Europe and Africa, simply because it makes more sense for birds to fly across the 150 km or so that separate the Tunisian from the Sicilian coast. (On very clear days, the North African coast can be made out from high places in western Sicily.) The birds that do migrate over Malta, so the reasoning goes, are a minor trickle and do not represent European populations in any significant way. In addition, most birds migrate at night or, if during the day, at great height and make no attempt to alight in Malta; these doves are automatically inaccessible to hunters. Besides, the turtle doves that migrate through the Malta route do not exclusively represent European populations, but also others from neighbouring areas (Russia, for example) where populations are healthy. These and other arguments are frequently encountered in the field when talking to hunters, as well as in the public sphere in opinion pieces and letters to the editor. A booklet published by the FKNK, for example, concludes that 'Maltese hunting and trapping do not appear to have any negative effect on the European populations of this bird'.[17]

Theodossopoulos (2003) describes a similar scenario among hunters on the Greek island of Zakynthos, and indeed in modern Greece generally, where turtle dove hunting is a big deal that occupies most men in April and from August to September. At the time of his fieldwork, the April hunt was banned following an agreement between the state authorities and the Zakynthian Hunters Society. However, the ban had no effect whatsoever and the April hunt was reported by Theodossopoulos to be proceeding normally, except for one factor: year after year, the doves were decreasing. On the one hand, this did nothing to diminish the zeal of hunters, who shot incessantly from their positions in the olive groves around the villages. On the other hand, the same hunters were aware of the decline of turtle doves and at times appeared apologetic to be hunting them; yet, none of them accepted that they had anything to do with the decline. The real reasons, they argued, were elsewhere. Poor people in Africa were destroying doves to protect their crops and the use of pesticides was devastating all manner of wild animals, including turtle doves. The latter explanation was so prevalent and formulaic that Theodossopoulos calls it 'pesticide rhetoric'. It was also lent considerable potency by a number of supporting narratives, which included the parallel decline of sparrows: sparrows were not considered game and not hunted, so their decline in numbers was treated as evidence that hunting was irrelevant to the decline of turtle doves and other birds.

The evidence suggests that hunters in Malta and Zakynthos are not alone in looking elsewhere for explanations for the decline of birds, in particular turtle doves. In 2008, I spent some weeks in the field with hunters in Lampedusa, the largest of three islands that make up the Pelagie archipelago (Italy) that lies about 160 km southwest of Malta. My informants there invariably talked about a sharp decline in the number of migrating turtle doves; as one hunter put it, the days were gone when the island would be *impestata* (teeming) with the birds. At the most, I was told, hunting was a *minima ragione* (minor reason) for the decline. Rather, the main culprits were pesticides used elsewhere (there is very little agriculture in Lampedusa), air pollution that included a coal-burning power station and the open-air burning of household waste, and quite possibly electromagnetic waves emitted by a radar installation that kept the migrating doves away. Likewise, two hunters I interviewed on the Aegean island of Chios (Greece) in 2017 told me that turtle doves had declined and that the main reason was transformations in agriculture in places like Britain; this, however, was not the case everywhere and healthy stocks existed in some places. This also explained why the IUCN classification for the species was so dismal: it had been drawn up by 'some person in England'.

Explanations for decline that absolve hunters of responsibility are well known in the literature. In the case of the passenger pigeon, and at the time of its catastrophic decline, they included a popular theory of mass drownings that suggested that billions of birds were being driven off-course by bad weather and drowning at sea; alternative explanations were a curse by a Christian minister, epidemic avian disease and white eggs laid by the pigeons. Others thought that the pigeon flocks had simply moved elsewhere, possibly to Chile (Fuller 2015). The point here is not whether these explanations, and the ones described earlier for turtle doves in the Mediterranean, have any scientific value (most of them are obviously canards); rather, it is that they all feature hunters who do not lack a logic of conservation. On the contrary, in fact, their explanations are based precisely on the principle of sustainability ('hunting in Malta/Zakynthos/Lampedusa does not affect populations'). To refer back to Cocker's point, these hunters *do* in fact engage in an imaginative transaction between hunter and prey, but that transaction tends to be more imaginative than Cocker imagines.

The word play is intentional. One might argue that, while hunters who hunt sedentary species experience population dynamics directly and within the context of familiar localities, those who hunt migratory species can only do so imaginatively and with reference to an elsewhere that is in any case often fuzzily defined and poorly known. The various explanations for decline discussed earlier, and the shifting locations they refer to, are examples of this latter kind of experience. The hunting of migratory birds in Malta and the Mediterranean may be a particularly problematic case, but it is not unique.

Possibly the best-developed conservation model that takes into account the relationship between hunting and migration is that of waterfowl (ducks, geese and swans) in the United States. Into the early decades of the twentieth century, waterfowl were considered effectively infinite in number and were taken without regulation. The birds' general movements were unknown – as Willock (1991: 73) puts it, 'they appeared seasonally from parts largely unknown and disappeared in a similar manner. It was not altogether surprising that sportsmen and market gunners took what they could get when they get it'. In 1916, however, and under pressure from conservationists, the United States and Britain (the latter acting on behalf of Canada) signed a Migratory Birds Convention that resulted in the Migratory Birds Conservation Act (Canada) in 1917. The United States followed with the Migratory Bird Treaty Act of 1918, which established a management mandate that still holds today: to protect migratory bird populations (including waterfowl) with the secondary objective of providing hunting opportunity compatible with protection. There was, to be sure, local resistance. In Missouri, for example, the state challenged the rights of the US government's enforcement regime. The Supreme Court ruled in favour of the latter in a sentence whose wording is relevant to the argument of this chapter: 'The whole foundation of the state's rights is the presence within their jurisdiction of birds that yesterday had not arrived, tomorrow may be in an other state, and in a week a thousand miles away . . . To put the claim of the state upon title is to lean upon a slender reed' (as cited in Willock 1991: 74).

By the 1950s, the systematic ringing (known as 'banding' in the United States) of waterfowl was being conducted and winter survey data were methodically collected and coupled with population models to determine how waterfowl populations responded to hunting mortality. By the 1970s, waterfowl data collection and population modelling had matured into one of the best monitoring systems in the world. It included winter surveys, harvest surveys, ringing programmes and aerial ground surveys. At present, around 13 million waterfowl are taken annually in the United States by 1.5 million hunters. Despite the high numbers, the geographical spread of hunters and the strongly migratory nature of the quarry, most populations are considered healthy, hunting is carefully monitored and regulated, and habitat is protected: 'the keys to success lie in successful legislation and curtailment of commercial hunting, combined with a management philosophy that eschewed the maximum harvest idea and supported the development of excellent science' (Mills 2007: 303–4). The case of waterfowl hunting in the United States, then, illustrates the complex relations between hunters and migratory birds, and the ways in which these relations can be incorporated into a successful conservation outcome that promises long-term sustainability.

'Small' Numbers: The Enumerative Modality

BirdLife Malta, and bird conservation in Malta generally, have by and large moved away from the strategy of total annual computations of the number of birds shot and trapped. As a BirdLife Malta official put it to me, the organization 'is now into verifiable numbers, the ones we have in hand (*ta' dak li għandna f'idejna*) . . . for years we haven't quoted millions figures, because it is hard to be accurate'. Correspondingly, hunters and the FKNK tend to put less effort into contesting total annual calculations. The production and contestation of numbers now follows two routes: it is based on the principle of actual counting of some kind (rather than estimates) and it is very specific both with respect to what is counted and why. The reason behind this shift is that numbers have come to occupy a different structural and institutional position. Whereas previously they were largely what we might call activists' figures (see Best 2012) – that is, numbers produced and disseminated as parts of conservation campaigns – they now function as a key device of hunting legislation. To paraphrase Cohn (1996: 8), bird conservation has come to be seen by its key stakeholders – if not necessarily by the public – as a vast collection of numbers.

The single most important factor that led to the development of a full-blown 'enumerative modality' (Cohn 1996) was the accession of Malta to the EU. As hunting and conservation were embedded into multilevel governance, the production and contestation of numbers took on an increasingly technical and pivotal aspect, even as they were incorporated into a new politics. Two key practices in particular have come to depend on enumeration: the spring hunt and trapping.

The Birds Directive (79/409/EEC, amended as 2009/147/EC) of the European Parliament and of the Council concerns the conservation of 'the species of wild birds occurring naturally in the European territory of the Member States'. Its premise is that many species of wild birds are declining, in some cases very rapidly. Because spring is considered part of the breeding season for resident birds as well as migrants that would have survived the autumn migration and wintering in Africa, the directive bans the hunting of birds in spring; it also bans trapping, in any season. That, however, is only part of the story, because the Directive also stipulates that Member States may apply derogations, provided there is 'no other satisfactory solution' (Article 9.1). Derogations may be applied for reasons of public health (air safety, for example) or research, but the part that concerns us is that they may also be applied by EU Member States to 'permit, under *strictly supervised* conditions and on a selective basis, the capture, keeping or other judicious use of certain birds *in small numbers*' (Article 9.1.c, emphasis added). The 'small numbers' precautionary qualifier is particularly consequential. What it means is that Member States that apply derogations must be able to empirically demonstrate that only small numbers of birds are involved, and then only under strictly supervised conditions, as part of a programme of judicious use. Two things need to be explained at this stage.

First, derogation is a process that involves the government of the Member State, hunting and conservation lobby groups, and various EU bodies. Under EU legislation, a Member State may derogate without prior notification. However, following a derogation, the Member State is bound to report to the European Commission, technically and through a formal reporting mechanism, and within a definite period of time. Typically, derogation reports are elaborate documents that detail the method of implementation and make the case for judicious use, small numbers and strictly supervised conditions. If the Commission is not satisfied with a report, it can do one or both of two things: institute an informal inquiry and ask for informal clarifications by the Member State, and/or launch a formal inquiry known as an EU Pilot, which is essentially a list of questions to which the Member State has to reply by a given date. If those clarifications and replies are still not satisfactory, the Commission draws up a dossier and, provided it is approved by the College of Commissioners, proceeds to formal infringement procedures. There are two steps to these procedures. The first is a Letter of Formal Notice by the Commission to the Member State that sets out the problems and requests the Member State to clarify or to take remedial action. Failing a satisfactory solution, the Commission issues a Reasoned Opinion – a detailed legal and policy document explaining why the Member State is in breach of EU legislation. The Reasoned Opinion is a kind of final warning and call for remedial action. If the Member State complies with this to the Commission's satisfaction, procedures may be dropped following the approval by the College of Commissioners. If, however, it does not, the Commission institutes litigation procedures by notifying the European Court of Justice, which is the highest EU court in matters of EU law. (The Commission can also request an injunction by the Court.) The case is then in the hands of the Court, which requests a statement of defence from the Member State. The Commission submits its reply to the statement of defence, following which the Member State has a last opportunity for a written rejoinder. When the written procedures are closed, either party can request a hearing. It is then up to the Court to decide the case. If the case is lost by the Member State, the provisions of the Accession Treaty come into force and that state has to take the necessary measures, failing which there is a final Court injunction that imposes daily financial penalties on the Member State by way of sanction.

Second, there cannot be a single fixed value for 'small numbers'. Numbers can only be described as 'small' in the context of the population of a given species and the impact that hunting is likely to have on that population. In this sense, 'small' is a byword for sustainable. What this means is that, following Malta's accession to the EU, a whole industry developed that sought to define 'small' for each species affected by derogations and effectively make the case for sustainable hunting. This is what I meant earlier by 'enumerative modality'. At the time of writing, Malta applies a number of derogations that allow the hunting or trapping of certain species in autumn or spring. For each, bag limits have to be set that fall within the 'small numbers' rubric, and procedures have been put in place that ensure that the bag limits set are actually followed. Both parts of the equation are as complicated as they are intensely contested by both conservationists and hunters.

Quantifying the Spring Hunt

The Government of Malta derogated to open a limited spring hunting season for turtle dove and quail from 2004, the year of EU accession. Both species are listed in Annex 2 of the Birds Directive, which means that they may be hunted, but not in spring. Soon after, the Commission initiated inquiry procedures (2006) and eventually a Letter of Formal Notice (2007), a Reasoned Opinion (2007) and Court proceedings (2008). Throughout the pre-litigation procedure, and eventually in Court, the Commission argued that Malta had not satisfied the conditions for derogation as set out in Article 9(1); besides, there could be no case at all for a 'no other satisfactory solution', since turtle doves and quail migrated in good numbers in autumn as well as spring. For its part, the Government of Malta maintained that the number of birds that migrated in autumn was too small and localized; turtle doves in particular kept to the west coast, which meant that for hunters whose land was elsewhere, there was no other satisfactory solution to hunting in spring.

When the Court delivered its judgment in September 2009, both bird protectionists and hunters claimed victory. The former pointed out that the Government of Malta had unequivocally lost the case. (Malta was clearly described in the judgment as the unsuccessful party and was ordered to pay the costs of the case.) Thus, and because it had failed to comply with Article 9(1) that established the parameters for derogation, the country was in breach of the Birds Directive. However, there was a complication. In its findings, and based in part on *carnet de chasse* numbers produced by hunters (see below), the Court noted that Maltese hunters generally had access to a very limited number of birds during the autumn migration. Further, the two species in question were classified by the IUCN as being of 'least concern' and their populations were at satisfactory levels. The Court thus accepted that the autumn season could not, in Malta, be regarded as constituting a satisfactory solution. This finding was read by hunters as a clear victory and a legal mandate for Malta to continue to derogate for spring hunting. But there was another thing the Court said. It is so crucial to my argument about the establishment of an enumerative modality that it is worth quoting in full:

> The prolongation of the hunting season for those two migratory species by authorisation of hunting for approximately two months in spring, during which the two hunted species are returning to their rearing grounds, which results in a mortality rate three times higher (around 15,000 birds killed) for Quails and eight times higher (around 32,000 birds killed) for Turtle Doves than for the autumn hunting season, does not constitute an adequate solution that is strictly proportionate to the Directive's objective of conservation of the species.[18]

In other words, the Court, while recognizing that autumn was not a satisfactory solution for hunters in Malta, argued that the numbers of turtle doves and quail shot in a hunt that included both autumn and spring was too high. It could hardly be contested that the spring hunt swelled the numbers, particularly since one argument that had been used by Malta to defend the derogation held precisely that it was in spring that most hunters stood any reasonable chance of significant catches. Besides, the Court's estimates for the number of turtle doves and quail that would be shot in a spring hunt were based on *carnet de chasse* figures for the period in question.

Ambivalent as it was, the 2009 Court judgment proved a watershed in the history of the spring hunting issue. It established that since autumn hunting was not a satisfactory solution for Maltese hunters, some sort of spring hunting arrangement was in principle possible, provided the numbers hunted were small enough for the practice to be consonant with the conservation parameters of the Birds Directive. However, the Court sentence had not absolved Malta of its legal obligations to the Directive; on the contrary, it was now up to the government, whenever it made the specific case for a derogation, to show that the logic was consonant with the judgment. In any future derogation, and to avoid further infringement and litigation procedures and possibly sanctions, the Government of Malta would have to show: first, that the bag statistics for the autumn hunt supported the 'no other satisfactory solution' principle; second, that the numbers of turtle doves and quail shot in spring were small enough to be acceptable; and, third, that the total number of these birds shot in combined spring and autumn hunts was small enough so as not to be a threat to the populations of the two species. Any future derogation report would have to show that these criteria had been met and that the terms of the derogation had been strictly supervised. The stage was set for science and enumeration.

The parameters set for derogations for the spring hunting seasons that followed are best seen as a work in progress. The details are copious, fairly Byzantine and mostly beyond the scope of the present work, but some basic aspects are central to my argument. The response of the Maltese government to the possibilities opened up and the constraints imposed by the Court judgment was to draw up a formula that, in principle at least, followed up on the 'satisfactory solution' point made by the judgment in a way that would be consonant with the 'small numbers' parameter of the Birds Directive. The formula is crucial because it represents an attempt to apply hard science to the field and to convert potentially vague terms into measurable quantities.

The initial stages of the process were not wildly successful. In April 2010, a few months after the Court judgment and right at the time when *namra* begins to peak, the government published a legal notice that announced that there would be a derogation and a spring hunt. It was the first in three years, since the 2008 and 2009 spring hunts had been called off due to the Court case. The 'Framework for Allowing a Derogation Opening a Spring Hunting Season for Turtle Dove and Quail'[19] established, among many other measures, that the spring bag limits would be set according to total (spring and autumn) limits of not more than 1 per cent of the total annual mortality rate for each species; however, they would not exceed a certain number of quail and turtle doves. Hunters could only hunt in spring if they were in possession of a special spring hunting licence. Perhaps most controversially, the number of special spring licences would be capped at 2,500 irrespective of how many hunters applied; if the number of applicants was larger than 2,500, licences would be assigned by means of a lottery drawn from among the applicants.[20] The FKNK condemned this limitation as discriminatory and instructed hunters to boycott the season, resulting in much media coverage and controversy. The boycott was successful: in 2010, 98 per cent of hunters did not apply for a special spring licence and the spring hunt effectively did not happen.

In response to the boycott, the capping was revoked for the 2011 season. This was the first in a series of changes that have seen the Framework amended a number of times in various ways between 2010 and 2017. For example, Legal Notice 221 of 2010 stipulated, among other things, that hunters were required to wear an armband in the field; this was revoked in Legal Notice 122 of 2013. The current version of the Framework takes as its point of departure the fundamental principle of the Birds Directive, that is, the conservation of wild bird populations in Europe. The first step of the derogation process is to establish the conservation status of the species concerned. This is carried out by a population scientist at the Wild Birds Regulation Unit (WBRU) and consists of a detailed technical report for each species. The reports are based on population data and conservation parameters produced by BirdLife International, the IUCN, EU agencies and other scientific sources. Assuming that the reports indicate no drastic downward trends, the next step is for the government (through the WBRU and the Ornis Committee) to refer to the bag statistics for the previous autumn. According to the Framework, the spring derogation can only be considered if the numbers of birds reported hunted in the previous autumn do not exceed 21,000 in the case of turtle doves and 20,000 in that of quail. (Autumn hunting is permitted for both species under the Birds Directive.) If that condition is met, the bag limits for each species for spring may be established. These are calculated at 1 per cent of the total annual mortality rates of each species. In any case, however, the bag limits may not exceed 5,000 birds for quail and 11,000 for turtle doves. There are two further conditions: first, the maximum bag limits are subject to revision in accordance with any changes in the international conservation status of each species; and, second, the maximum bag limits may only be allowed if the number of birds shot in the previous autumn does not exceed 10,000 birds for each species – if it does, the spring bag limit is reduced in inverse proportion to the number of birds bagged in excess of 10,000 for each species. So, for example, if 12,000 turtle doves are shot in autumn, the maximum bag limit for the species the following spring would be 9,000 (rather than 11,000).

In order to satisfy the Commission that the bag limits and other derogation conditions were being put into practice in the field, the government stipulated a number of supplementary conditions. For instance, it established the minimum number of enforcement personnel that would be in the field during hunting hours at any given time during the season;

this number was set at seven police officers for every 1,000 hunters holding the special licence. Also, a self-reporting system was introduced that required hunters to immediately report any birds shot by means of a text message. In principle, this ensured prompt reporting of catches and made it possible to establish a rolling total figure for overall catches; if the maximum bag limit for a species was reached before the end of the derogation period, hunting would be stopped for that species. Finally, a private consultancy company was hired to produce detailed surveys of migration of turtle doves and quail over the islands, the idea being to be able eventually to cross-match the data with those of reported catches and establish the veracity of the latter. This is discussed in more detail later on in this chapter.

In principle, therefore, and as a result of the Court judgment of 2009, the spring hunt in Malta was reduced to scientific data, mathematical formulae and a pointillistic quantification of populations and hunting bags. The amount of facts and figures, and counterfacts and counterfigures, produced by the government, the FKNK and BirdLife Malta since 2009 is truly staggering – the annual conservation status reports alone typically run into dozens of pages and masses of tables and graphs for each species.

However, in practice, even as numbers mattered more and more, they became increasingly irrelevant. Formally, virtually every aspect of the bag limit calculations has been contested by the FKNK, and to a lesser extent by BirdLife Malta, in a string of technical reports and memos. For example, the FKNK has taken issue with the calculations and figures for the annual mortality rates, the geographical extent (and therefore size) of the reference populations on the basis of which the mortality rates are calculated, the fact that the calculations are based on minimum (rather than average) population estimates, and the government's interpretation of the terms 'considerable numbers' and 'small numbers'. The upshot is that the FKNK has consistently argued that the calculations are flawed and that all three bag limits (national-seasonal, individual-seasonal and individual-daily) are ridiculously low; as a 2011 report by the organization put it, the figures for these limits were based on a 'mathematical formula which had no basis in science or law, thus reducing the corresponding spring hunting derogation to an absurdity'.[21] For its part, BirdLife Malta has said that the calculations of the technical note on which mortality rates are based are flawed and involve inflated numbers.

In practice, on the ground, none of the figures involved in the enumeration matter much, either to hunters or to conservationists. Rather, it is two things that really make a difference in terms of actual practice: whether or not there is a spring derogation (and hunt) at all, and the number of days and hours in the field established by the derogation. Even as they resent the situation, hunters realize that Malta has obliga- tions as an EU Member State and that the spring hunt is only possible by derogation; they also know that the country is under international pressure on spring hunting and that the future of the practice is at best a probability. Every year, as spring approaches and *namra* begins to mount, hunters find they have to deal with the uncertainty of a derogation that may or may not materialize. Further, even if it does, shifting parameters have been applied to successive spring hunts since 2009: the changes have involved the length of the season, its timing, bag limits and times of day when hunting is allowed. The ones that really matter to hunters are the duration of the season and times of day when hunting is allowed. On paper, these parameters exist to convince the Commission that spring hunting in Malta involves small numbers and is strictly limited and sus- tainable. To hunters, however, every day in the field is a battle won, par- ticularly when the timing of the season happens to coincide with good migration. It is being in the field that matters rather than the bag limits imposed by the derogation parameters. It is clear that this has to do with the fact that bag limits are very hard to effectively police, a point that is taken up in the next section.

Even so, it would be inaccurate to say that numbers are simply a front. One set of numbers that does matter very much is that on which the data for the conservation status of species are based. In May 2016, and just a few weeks after the end of the hunting season, the government declared a moratorium on the application of the spring hunting derogation for the turtle dove. The moratorium would 'remain in force until such time that the maintenance of the population of this species at satisfactory level is scientifically ascertained at EU level'.[22] The background to the mora- torium went back to 2015, when the IUCN reassessed the conservation status of the turtle dove. The status had been changed from Lower Risk/ least concern (LR/lc) to Least Concern (LC) in 2004; subsequent assess- ments in 2008, 2009 and 2012 confirmed the LC status. In 2015, however, the conservation risk was upgraded to Vulnerable (VU) – two notches up from LC and one short of the ominous-sounding Endangered (EN). The IUCN's justification for the reclassification was that the species had 'undergone rapid declines in much of its European range whilst in Russia and Central Asia it is thought to have experienced more severe declines'; tellingly, the decline was 'thought to be driven by a number of factors including loss of foraging and nesting sites as well as disease and hunting along its migration'.[23]

The IUCN reclassification was significant and quickly made headlines in Malta. Here was a species for which hunting had been allowed, by means of a derogation, for a number of years. Now, however, the status of that species was being deemed severely unfavourable by an international technical-scientific body that enjoyed and wielded tremendous prestige and lobbying power. In addition, hunting along the migration routes was listed emphatically as one of the causes of decline. The reclassification could not be ignored, and yet hunters had a year earlier won a national referendum that supported the spring hunting of the turtle dove (and quail). The first question would be whether or not to derogate for a hunting season in the spring of 2016. In the event, the Ornis Committee voted by five votes (including those of the government nominees and the FKNK) to one (BirdLife Malta) to recommend to the government to apply a derogation. However, the first vote was qualified by a second in which the Committee recommended to the government that 'in view of the recent reclassification of the turtle dove as a "vulnerable" IUCN Red List species and a "near-threatened" species at EU27 level, government apply special measures to further reduce the impact of spring hunting on the population of that species'.[24] Surprisingly, this qualifier was approved unanimously, which shows that, apart from BirdLife Malta's clear position on spring hunting, both the government and the FKNK were under pressure to take cognizance of the IUCN reclassification. The result was that, when the 2016 season was officially announced a couple of weeks later, it was three days (19 per cent) shorter than the previous year's, with a maximum turtle dove bag (that for quail was unaffected) being reduced from 11,000 to 5,000.[25]

And yet, beyond the territory of the Ornis Committee and the Government of Malta, the matter was far from settled. Even as hunters were halfway through their cherished spring hunt in 2016, the IUCN formally called on the Commission to immediately request that the Government of Malta protect the turtle dove. In a strongly worded letter to the EU Environment Commissioner, the IUCN reminded the Commission that a derogation for (especially recreational) hunting should not be granted for a species with an 'unfavourable conservation status' or with 'very low population levels'. Until further research showed otherwise, the spring hunting of the turtle dove was 'questionable'. Finally, and very significantly, the letter said that 'in order to save the turtle dove from a real threat of extinction, IUCN has requested the Commission to apply an urgent moratorium on spring hunting of the species in Malta'.[26] The words 'extinction' and 'moratorium' had been used for the turtle dove by an organization that was not a Maltese bird protection ENGO and that had the full weight of international science behind it – that was a kind of ulama of science, one might say.

The significance was not lost on the EU Commissioner, who responded to the IUCN letter by urging the Maltese government to impose a moratorium as recommended. (The Birds Directive does not make pro-vision for such a moratorium to be imposed by the Commission.) The situation was intriguing, because the EU Commissioner at the time happened to be one Karmenu Vella, a Maltese Labour Party politician who had been nominated for the post by the very Labour government that had defended and applied the spring hunting derogation. A few months earlier, Vella had been accused by a section of the Maltese press of long-distance partisan politics by 'dodging questions' about the turtle dove reclassification.[27] This time, and following the formal IUCN letter, there was no room for such accusations, which made Vella's call for a moratorium even more significant in Malta. The IUCN letter had another effect: the Commission, which had closed spring hunting infringement procedures against Malta in May 2015 (following the referendum and the sudden closure of the season), now sent the Maltese government a fresh EU pilot that requested clarifications on the 2016 spring season.

The combined heft of an IUCN reclassification, pressure by bird pro-tection ENGOs, a call by an EU Commissioner and the prospect of fresh infringement procedures was too much for the Maltese government to ignore. It was clear that something had to give and, even as the spring hunting season was under way, government officials were holding infor-mal and closed meetings with hunting organizations. The surprise (to outsiders at least) came at a press conference held by the FKNK on 21 May 2016, in which the organization formally suggested to the gov-ernment that a moratorium on the spring hunting of the turtle dove be applied; an hour after the press conference, the KSU followed suit. The proposals were discussed at a government Cabinet meeting and, six days later, the moratorium was announced.

The moratorium may have placated the IUCN, the Commission and to some extent BirdLife Malta, but it was an extremely tricky manoeuvre for both the FKNK/KSU and the government. For the FKNK, the risk was that hunters would interpret the proposal for a moratorium as being an initiative against their interests and a sign of weakness by the very organization that represented them. For its part, the government risked being seen by hunters as privileging the interests of bird protectionists and foreign organizations – in other words, giving in to *indħil barrani* (foreign interference). The prospect was especially unsavoury given the political direction of the Labour government in favour of spring hunting in principle, as well as the results of a democratic referendum in which the majority of Maltese citizens had voted to retain the right to apply a derogation for spring hunting.

In the event, things were choreographed in such a way as to make the hunting organizations seem like the movers and the government the moved (by a *local* force). Although it was well known in inner circles that it was the government that had initiated talks about a moratorium, it was ultimately the FKNK that made the formal recommendation to the government in a press conference; the government's reaction was to say that it would discuss and analyse the proposal at Cabinet. The choreographed chronology thus absolved the government, but it also saved the face of the FKNK and the KSU as organizations that cared about sustainability and that did not take their orders from anyone's initiative but their own. A couple of months after the moratorium was announced, the government went a step further and published a glossy pamphlet that was distributed to all hunters. It reminded them of all the work that the government had done in their favour; this included the simplification of controls and the application of a derogation in the face of adverse pressure by the EU. The government, the booklet reminded hunters, was 'prepared to defend Malta's right to derogate to the end and in an unprecedented way'. The 'mature' proposal by the FKNK and the KSU for a moratorium had come at a time when infringement procedures were looming, and the government had considered it carefully and ultimately accepted it. The government was also committed to contribute to the production of 'technical and scientific' knowledge that would 'secure the sustainable hunting of the turtle dove by Maltese hunters in spring, in the long term'.[28]

For its part, the FKNK held a press conference at which it qualified its recommendation for a moratorium. It accused the Commission of 'bullying' the smallest EU Member State, accused the majority of IUCN scientists of being BirdLife International activists and the IUCN of 'bullying' both the Commission and Malta, accused the IUCN of having postponed the reclassification of the turtle dove until after the referendum in Malta, argued that the IUCN had scaremongered on the issue of extinction – there were 'between 19,300,000 and 71,400,000' turtle doves in the world and 'between 6,310,000 and 11,900,000' in Europe alone, accused the Commission of inconsistency in that, even as it condemned the hunting of 5,000 turtle doves in Malta, it was happy to accept the 3 million shot every autumn by hunters in other EU Member States, emphasized that the small numbers hunted in Malta could never have any effect on the population dynamics of turtle doves, and said that the FKNK would draw on its connections in international scientific circles to establish that the spring hunting of turtle doves in Malta was ecologically sustainable. The importance of the contents of the press conference goes well beyond the specific circumstances of the moratorium. In fact, they read like a blueprint of the newfound vocation of the Maltese hunting lobby to position itself within the contexts of international conservation organizations, the EU, Maltese and international bird protection ENGOs, national

politics, conservation science, international power hierarchies, the morality of political representation and the Maltese public sphere.

Not surprisingly, hunters did not necessarily accept the IUCN reclassification as a disembedded scientific fact; rather, they saw it as part of a
greater and longer-term project, by conservationists, to eliminate spring
hunting. As one hunter told me with reference to the fact that the reclassification came a year after the referendum, *'ma daħlux mill-bieb, iridu
jidħlu mit-tieqa'* ('the front door was locked, so they're now trying the
back door'). In a similar vein, the KSU issued a press release accusing
BirdLife International of 'ulterior motives': 'Malta's right to apply a derogation in spring has never been accepted by BirdLife International, and
they have now sworn to have it their way. The classification of bird species is entrusted to BirdLife International, who have no one who can
contest them. The European Union takes their research to be the Gospel
truth.' The KSU went on to list three things in support of its argument.
The first two were the ECJ judgment, which had given Maltese hunters the right to hunt turtle doves in spring, and the referendum result.
The third and most relevant in the context of this chapter pointed out a
'contradiction'. Whereas BirdLife International's figures showed that 2–3
million doves were shot in Europe in autumn, it had never suggested
that turtle dove hunting be banned in that season: 'it is only the 11,000
birds that we try to shoot under the spring derogation that are the problem'. BirdLife International's move was finally described as *'qerq ieħor'*
('another example of deceit').[29]

The moratorium represents the latest chapter in the story of spring
hunting in Malta since EU accession and especially since the Court judgment of 2009. However, there was an epilogue, because the moratorium
made no mention of quail (which was still favourably classified as 'Least
Concern' by the IUCN). In 2017, a derogation was applied to allow the
hunting of quail in spring. Given the difficulty of enforcing the law in the
field, hunters saw this as a tacit victory. Yet, and apparently in accordance
with the migration patterns of quail, the dates for the season were set for
25 March–14 April. These dates overlapped, but did not neatly coincide,
with the migration of the turtle dove. (The peak of turtle dove migration
is mid-April to early May.) As it turned out, 2017 was a very good year
for turtle dove migration – the best season in many years, according
to my hunter informants. Hunters found themselves having to stay at
home, or hunt illegally, just as the migration season peaked in late April.
Informally, they lobbied to avoid another spring of discontent and, in
2018, the government shifted the quail hunting season by a week to 1–21
April. For conservationists, the new timing, and the quail derogation
generally, was an outright and deceitful attempt by the government and

hunters to bypass the IUCN classification. As they saw it, an open season for quail was simply a front intended to make it possible for hunters to be in the field during the turtle dove migration. BirdLife Malta condemned the extended 2018 hunting season as a 'gamble' that placed the turtle dove 'at an enormous risk'.[30] The government had ignored its own environment protection agency (the Environment and Resources Authority), which had recommended a 15 March–4 April season, and had given in to pressure from the hunting lobby. It pointed out that the new Parliamentary Secretary[31] for bird protection was a hunter himself and said that hunting hides and towers were being prepared that could not conceivably be used to hunt quail, but were intended for turtle doves.[32] On 22 March 2018, a few days before the start of the season, BirdLife Malta and Chris Packham were the main guests at an event in Brussels hosted by Anja Hazekamp, a Dutch MEP for the Confederal Group of the European United Left – Nordic Green Left. Packham said that '400 million birds have been robbed from us, 90 million in the UK, since the 1970s' and that the corruption plaguing Malta meant that 'the bird lobby in Malta was very powerful, and the government gave in easily to its requests to maintain its support and win election votes'.[33] On 21 April, the last day of the 2018 season, BirdLife Malta declared that it had been 'one of the worst spring hunting seasons in recent years'. Eight out of seventeen illegally shot birds retrieved by the public had been turtle doves. in other words, the quail season was a 'smokescreen' for hunters to be in the field and go after the real target.[34]

Troubles with Self-Reporting

Clearly, the bag limits, and indeed the possibility of derogation based on a formula, are merely the prescriptive part of enumeration. The counting itself depends on the actual number of birds shot or trapped and on the bag records produced by hunters in the field – in other words, on self-reporting. The scholarly record for the efficacy of self-reporting is at best ambivalent. For example, a study carried out in Germany followed the dramatic population collapse of the grey partridge as a result of exceptionally unfavourable weather conditions between 1978 and 1981 (Tillmann et al. 2012). The unfavourable conservation status of the species varied from 'critically endangered' to 'vulnerable' across the federal states and was categorized as 'vulnerable' at a European level. Status notwithstanding, nine of the sixteen states continued to make provision for a hunting season. In the context of the apparent contradiction, enumeration became important and hunting associations were roped in to produce data about the numbers of breeding pairs in their hunting districts. At the same time, and based in part on the hypothesis that the data were being 'adjusted to assuage political pressures' (Tillmann et al. 2012: 114), ornithologists were brought in to 'ground-truth' the hunters' estimates. In fact, it turned out that the data produced by hunters erred on the side of caution and tended to underestimate the numbers of breeding pairs. The study pointed out that one advantage of enumeration by hunters was that it encouraged them to be 'sensitised to the ecology of the grey partridge and follow the fate of "their" population in their hunting district'; this added to the wisdom of 'establishing reasonable monitoring programmes in cooperation with hunters' (Tillmann et al. 2012: 118).

In the same vein, Noss et al. (2004) argue that whatever form community wildlife management takes, a fundamental element is the participation of local hunters in, among other things, monitoring: self-monitoring (of number and type of animals hunted) is thus one way in which hunters can participate in community wildlife management. They take as their case study the Izoceño Guaraní people of the Bolivian Chaco, who became involved in conservation in the 1990s through their political organization, the Capitanía del Alto y Bojo Izozog (CABI). In 1995, they secured the co-management of the 3.4 million ha Kaa-Iya del Gran Chaco National Park and became part of a hunting self-monitoring programme that involved the active participation of outside (US) agencies. However, subsequent comparative research based on direct observation and household visits established that underreporting was rampant. With respect to subsistence hunting, bird catches especially were underreported in hunter self-monitoring, with small birds killed by children being missed completely. In the community of Ibasiriri, for example, Saavedra (as cited in Noss et al. 2004) recorded 1,074 bagged birds of twenty-five species, while self-monitoring during the same period recorded only ninety-five birds of six species. Extrapolating these figures to the entire region suggested a self-monitoring reporting rate of about 6 per cent, a figure that appears especially low when one considers that the case study involved high-participation voluntary self-monitoring. Noss et al. (2004) draw four conclusions from their exercise: first, that high participation rates alone are no guarantee of success for hunter self-monitoring programmes; second, that factors such as literacy rates, support from local leaders and organizations, and outside technical support affect the implementation of self-monitoring programmes; third, that self-monitoring alone cannot be relied on to supply data for specific research questions; and, fourth, that the value of self-monitoring programmes goes beyond their use as data collection tools and instead derives from their ability to foster a sense of participation and responsibility among hunters.

In Malta, self-reporting and the veracity of hunters' own numbers has emerged as one of the most contentious issues in the hunting–conservation encounter. In part, the reason is that the quarry of Maltese hunters and trappers is physically small (typically; birds up to the size of a pigeon), which tends to present greater difficulties for law enforcement. As Kaltenborn et al. show for the case of ptarmigan hunters in Norway, 'small game hunters can get away with exceeding quotas, hunting in areas outside what is covered by the permit, or even outside the legal season, without getting caught or penalised' (2012: 3381). This, however, is only part of a complex intersection.

The FKNK website hosts an open forum where users (mostly members of the organization, although anyone can register and contribute) raise and discuss topics related to hunting and trapping. In February 2012, a comment appeared that came from the 'Administrator' and therefore directly from the FKNK. It read: 'Keep in mind that each Turtle Dove and Quail that is reported bagged in September could be deducted from the bag limit for the following April. Let us know if you have trouble filling in the booklet.' What this referred to was the formula described earlier in this chapter by which bag limits for spring are established in inverse proportion to the numbers hunted in the previous autumn. The post did not go unnoticed by bird protection activists, who have since used it to support the argument that hunters routinely cook the bag record books and, by implication, the further argument that hunting in Malta involves numbers that are unsustainable and, in the case of derogations, in breach of the 'small numbers' and 'no other satisfactory solution' criteria. The claim is soundly rejected by the FKNK, which has defended the post as a simple exercise in information. Earlier, I discussed the significance, production and contestation of science and numbers from above, as used by official bodies to regulate hunting. In this section I shall look at the process from below.

There are two ways in which hunters (and more recently trappers) have systematically and formally quantified their catches. The first is the *carnet de chasse* (lit. hunting record book), a booklet that was designed for field use and in which hunters entered the type and number of birds bagged, as well as the approximate location, for each hunting session. The initiative came from the FKNK in 1995, at a time when tightening national legislation and enforcement encouraged the production of numbers that would counter the activists' *miljuni*; indeed, the first mention of bag statistics was in the 1992 Kalchreuter report[35] – the *carnet de chasse* was first mooted in an FKNK pamphlet published a few months later specifically to refute Fenech's claims in *Fatal Flight*. As the use of French suggests, the idea was an adaptation of similar systems used by hunters elsewhere in Europe – the FKNK, it is worth remembering, was and is a member of FACE. The *carnet de chasse*, which became popularly known to hunters as *'il-ktieb'* ('the book'), was soon embedded in national legislation and, via that route, eventually into the functioning of the Birds Directive legislation as applied in Malta. In this way, what started as a response to activists' numbers became an essential part of the annual quantification exercise required for the Government of Malta to derogate effectively, and to make the case for sustainable hunting more generally. The system required hunters to submit their completed booklets to the environment protection agency at the end of each year; the numbers would then be added up and compiled into an annual report.[36]

The second means by which catches are recorded is by text message. As a result of the 2009 Court judgment and its emphasis on accurate data, all hunting and trapping that involved derogations required hunters to send a text message from the field for every bird bagged. In principle, the advantage of the system was that it made possible a rolling tally of bags in real time. Thus, if and when the number of messages received indicated that the national bag limit had been reached, the season would automatically be closed; in principle, the text message system would also see to it that daily and seasonal individual bag limits were enforced.

At first, the text message and *carnet de chasse* systems coexisted; thus, a hunter who shot a turtle dove in spring would send a message *and* input the catch in the *carnet de chasse*. In 2016, however, the *carnet de chasse* was discontinued altogether and replaced with a 'game reporting system' based on the text message model, irrespective of whether or not the type of hunting or trapping involved a derogation. At the time of writing, all hunting and trapping bags are quantified using the text message system, itself coupled with a bespoke data management programme developed by a Maltese IT company. Two advantages were cited for the change: first, the new system would alleviate the bureaucratic burden of distributing, collecting and processing the thousands of *carnet de chasse* booklets; and, second, it would allow the real-time collection and compilation of bag statistics. Hunters were provided with a personalized booklet that contained their identity details and assigned a code number for each species. The rules required hunters to telephone and input codes into an automated system before leaving the hunting area (usually at the end of a hunting session, that is). All data would automatically be fed into the real-time database, and the system was also set up for hunters to receive an automated message that would serve as proof of report. A regime of on-the-spot fines was put into place for hunters who failed to report catches. The new system was presented by the government as by far the most sophisticated and detailed bag reporting system in any EU state. Aware of potential tacit resistance by hunters, the government produced an information video-film in which the new system was described as important on at least three counts: for the government to be able to uphold sustainable hunting; to 'show that Maltese hunters could act responsibly'; and to 'put paid to the long-peddled myth of millions of birds taken by Maltese hunters, by means of data provided by hunters themselves'. Throughout, the emphasis was on truthful self-reporting as necessary within the framework of Malta's EU membership, as well as the potential of accurate data as a means to undo the '*miljuni* myth' (by showing, presumably, that the real number was actually in the few thousands).

As expected, the link between theory and practice came under the scrutiny of conservationists. The main criticism has been that, whichever system is used, hunters and trappers have an incentive to underreport catches, according to at least three lines of reasoning. With respect to the post-2009 formula, national autumn bags of over 10,000 birds each for turtle dove and quail would mean a reduced size, by inverse proportion of bags for the following spring. Therefore, it is not in hunters' interests for autumn bags to reach the 10,000 figure – hence the FKNK forum post mentioned earlier. Second, a hunter whose text messages indicated that he had reached the individual daily or seasonal bag limit would automatically be barred from the field for the rest of that season. Third, if the total number of messages sent by hunters showed that the national bag limits had been reached before the end of the season, that season would be cut short. (This, in fact, was the main logic of a rolling tally system.) As such, whichever way one looks at it, it is in the interests of hunters to keep reported numbers low enough for the hunt to take place for the longest possible duration established at law. This, as conservationists see it, is a recipe for disaster when coupled with the great difficulty of enforcing bag limits in the field. It is too easy, they argue, for a hunter who exceeds his daily bag limit to squirrel away the surplus birds into a hole in a rubble wall and collect them later. As a CABS activist put it to me, 'bag limits are not enforceable, either for us or for the police – proper enforcement would require the police to follow each hunter around for the entire season, which is ridiculous . . . the system depends on hunters telling the truth, when they have every incentive not to and every means to get away with it'.

Sound though this reasoning may be, it is still theoretical, which is why BirdLife Malta and its associates have consistently sought to produce 'proof' that underreporting is the rule rather than the exception. Perhaps paradoxically, the proof is thought to lie partly in the reported numbers themselves. For example, BirdLife Malta has pointed out that, for both the spring hunting and the autumn trapping derogations, the (in any case too small) numbers reported tend to be clustered in the last two or three days of the season; this ostensibly shows that hunters only report catches when the season is about to close anyway.[37] For a number of years now, BirdLife Malta have correlated the bags as reported with the number of shots recorded by Springwatch observers; here, the reasoning is that, given the discrepancies, hunters must be very poor shots indeed. (The exercise is carried out separately, but to much the same end, by CABS.) The organization also points out that there is circumstantial evidence of underreporting. The FKNK forum post is one such example. Another goes back to 2011, when a prominent member of the FKNK wrote a letter to the *Times of Malta* in which he asked 'who, in the right frame of mind, would declare a bird caught at 6am, knowing that he then has to pack and leave? Who would record the fourth bird knowing that the season is over?'[38] The upshot – by hunters' own tacit admission, BirdLife Malta argues – is that the whole business of reporting catches, and therefore the sustainability of the derogations, is a sham. The point has been made every season in the derogation reports that BirdLife Malta and CABS produce jointly and send to the Commission, in part to counter the official reports produced and filed by the government. In 2012, BirdLife Malta proposed that the *carnet de chasse* and text message reporting systems be replaced by one in which all birds caught are tagged; hunters would be allocated tags according to bag limits. The proposal was dismissed by hunters and the government as unwieldy and impractical.[39]

The sense that self-reporting is mired in mistrust and inaccuracy is, to conservationists at least, lent support by the statistics themselves. A case in point was the plover trapping season of 2016. A total of 997 trappers held a licence to trap the species under a derogation from the Birds Directive; the season ran from 20 October to 31 December. A total of 297 live plover captures were reported. This was less than the 321 reported in 2015 and the 418 reported in 2014, and only 42 per cent of the established national annual overall bag limit of 700.[40] As officially reported, therefore, the 2016 season was a lean one in which 997 trappers caught 297 birds – one bird for every three trappers and well below the maximum permitted number. These numbers jarred with the fact that plovers migrated in unusually large numbers during that season. Word among trappers and hunters – and this kind of information percolates and spreads readily in Malta – was that 2016 was in fact one of the best seasons in recent years. Plovers migrated in unusually good numbers and many trappers caught relatively large numbers of birds. Stories circulated of trappers who caught dozens of plovers in a single day, sometimes whole flocks in a single sweep of the clap nets. The migration study commissioned by the government appeared to confirm this trend. A total of 227 plovers were counted in the sampled sites and extrapolated to a total estimated influx over the survey (and trapping season) period of 20,522 birds. Tellingly, only eighty (extrapolated to 7,233) were recorded in 2015, which was the first year in which the study had been commissioned for the species.[41]

The data producers themselves are more ambivalent about self-reporting. Certainly, the FKNK, which was behind the introduction of the *carnet de chasse* system, consistently supported its results as the 'best available data'. The terminology lends itself to a rich interpretation. For one thing, it rejects all other bag data as guesstimates: as the FKNK sees it, *carnet de chasse* data are the 'best available' because they are based on actual catches, on birds in the hand so to speak, rather than estimates of catches. Of course, the argument is stood on its head by BirdLife Malta, which argues that the *carnet de chasse* records are worse than estimates – they are actually numbers that are engineered to make the case for derogations and have no basis in reality. (The reasoning here is while the intention of an estimate is to arrive at a true figure, that of engineered numbers is to achieve some other outcome.) Further, the tacit point made by the FKNK is that *carnet de chasse* data are the best because they are produced by a reliable source – that is, hunters. Again, BirdLife Malta uses the same logic to make the opposite point: hunters' numbers are in fact the least reliable because it is hunters who are the most affected by the outcomes of quantification. Another point made by the FKNK is that, rather than being rewarded for their initiative and effort at producing reliable data, hunters and their organizations have been under increasing pressure from tightening legislation.

On the ground, hunters tend to approach self-reporting pragmatically, if with considerable suspicion. When the *carnet de chasse* was in force, many were concerned about how the data would be used. They did not quite trust the government with the final calculations, to the extent that some hunters told me that they would put a cross or cancel out blank boxes (days with no catches), just in case someone should add a number or two to inflate the final figures. There was also a feeling that the paperwork jarred with the general hunting experience. The following quotes illustrate this feeling: 'Before I left home this morning I felt as if I was about to sit for an exam, checking I had the armband, pen, *carnet de chasse*, licence and mobile'; 'out hunting with all those papers in hand, I feel like an architect rather than a hunter'; 'I'm considering carrying a briefcase like Gawdenz' (Gawdenz is a popular comedian who pokes fun at white-collar workers); 'very soon I'll be leaving my gun at home and carrying a laptop instead'. The text message system has met with less resistance due to its leaner bureaucracy, but few hunters I spoke to had anything good to say about it. In brief, hunters feel that self-reporting and enumeration have generally been used against them by a collusion of conservationists, government agents and the apparatus of the Commission. On occasion, this has led to friction between hunters and the FKNK: 'we were the ones who insisted on accurate self-reporting', an FKNK official told me, 'but look where it has got us . . . hunters complain with us that it has worked against them'.

At this stage, it is worth taking a detour to the complex and contentious science of fishing catch data. Like hunting, fishing involves the use of a finite natural resource. Whether or not that use is sustainable for particular fisheries is a matter of profound economic, cultural and social consequence; one need only consider the long, chequered and often painful history of North Atlantic cod stocks (see, for instance, Rose (2007) and Bolster (2014) for a historical account). Not surprisingly, the quantification of catch data has developed into a parallel industry that involves scientists, politicians, organizations and of course the fishers themselves.

One of the highest-profile and most recent exchanges involves the Food and Agriculture Organization of the United Nations (FAO) and Daniel Pauly, a leading marine biologist and the principal investigator at the Sea Around Us, a research initiative based at the University of British Columbia. The issue is the FAO's overall assessment that global catches peaked at 86 million tonnes in 1996 and have been stable since. Instead, Pauly holds, catches peaked at 130 million tonnes in 1996 and have since been in sharp decline. Pauly's main argument is that the annual catch statistics provided to the FAO by member countries tend to omit or underreport the takings of artisanal, subsistence, recreational and illegal fisheries, as well as discarded bycatch. The result is that the FAO's global dataset of fisheries statistics, which is widely used by policy-makers and scholars, contains a systemic underestimation. While the FAO acknowledges as much and stops there, Pauly recommends that datasets be adjusted using a technique known as 'catch reconstruction'. The technique uses a wide variety of data and information sources to derive estimates for all fisheries components missing from the official reported data. Catch reconstruction rests on two principles: first, that the value 'NA' (which is later turned into an 'elegant zero') is not an appropriate entry when no data are available; and, second, that in these cases, a best estimate should be used that is 'based on the fact that fishing is *a social activity that is bound to throw a shadow on the society in which it is embedded*' (Pauly and Zeller 2016: 5, emphasis added). The 'shadow' that Pauly has in mind consists of variables like the amount of seafood consumed, the number of and average catch by vessels involved in particular fisheries and so on. And, while quantifying the shadow must be an 'approximate' science, it is better than entering (invalid) zero values. (By coincidence, one of the FAO Member States that does take into account the shadow is Malta, recently held up by a Pauly-associated team of scholars as a country that is a step away from becoming a 'world leader in comprehensive marine catch data reporting' (Khalfallah et al. 2017: 247)). The FAO's response to Pauly's critique is that its own datasets are 'the best they can possibly be' (Ye et al. 2017: 402).

There are at least two reasons why the FAO–Pauly exchange is relevant to the present context: first, its references to catch reconstruction and 'shadow' echo the attempts made by bird protectionists in Malta to systematically undermine self-reported numbers by hunters; and, second and more importantly, the FAO–Pauly matter highlights the potential significance of underreporting in the sustainability equation, as well as the politics of taking that underreporting into account. It would appear that large institutions tend to be reluctant to tread the marshy ground of estimates and approximations, and prefer instead to stick to the safety of reporting methods (and their results) as formally agreed upon by their main constituents. In this case, the FAO is an intergovernmental agency that relies – prescriptively in fact – on data supplied by nation-states. While the FAO does to some extent seek to ensure the production and supply of valid data (Pauly acknowledges as much), the politics of inter-governance work against the adoption of reporting systems other than those run by individual countries. For their part, academics, independent researchers and activist groups are not usually hemmed in by intergovernmental politics; rather, they are in a position to question the numbers produced by nation-states and to suggest alternative formulas. In their rejoinder to FAO's response, Pauly and Zeller assert that they are 'academic scientists who reject such absolutist statements from authority' (2017: 2). They argue that working only with or through member countries does not prevent errors creeping into a database – in other words, the FAO's 'primary' statistics are as risk-prone as 'secondary' ones that are based on catch reconstruction techniques by non-FAO scientists. (Pauly and Zeller conclude that there is an urgent need for the FAO to collaborate with academics who are not necessarily part of national reporting regimes.)

With respect to the case at hand, conservationists argue that the Commission and the Government of Malta prefer to stick to official numbers, in spite of the overwhelming evidence that those numbers are widely off the mark. As a BirdLife Malta official put it to me:

> The calculations are all wrong. In any case, the numbers are of no consequence, since out there in the field it's a free for all [*kulhadd jaghmel li jrid*]. I'm amazed the Commission accepts the situation. There's a lack of political

> will, and the Commission anyway doesn't have the resources to ground-truth the numbers. It's clear that hunters, who have this passion for hunting turtle doves, will put two and two together and play about with numbers.

The hunters I worked with in the field were equally unimpressed. One of their constant grievances was that double standards beset the enumerative practices of conservationists and of the Commission. 'Why', I was told, 'do we have to be hounded for the few turtle doves we shoot in spring, when official figures show that millions of the birds are shot every autumn in France and other countries? Is the turtle dove declining only in Malta, in spring?' Besides, they argued, the numbers imposed by individual and national bag limits were insensitive to the dynamics of hunting when the birds concerned were migrants on unpredictable journeys. 'A couple of years ago I went out one morning when the conditions were perfect', a hunter told me, 'a minute into the hunt, my dogs flushed a quail and I shot it. That was my daily bag limit, and technically I'd have packed up and gone back to my car. I did nothing of the sort.' The point is that the bag limits and complex calculations are far removed from the reality of hunting in a context where good days are few and far between, and are keenly anticipated by hunters. It is not just the politics of underreporting that matter, but equally the dynamics of practice on the ground that make underreporting the sensible thing to do.

What Numbers Don't Flatten

'Statistics', Arjun Appadurai argues, 'are to bodies and social types what maps are to territories: they flatten and enclose' (1996: 133). While he makes the point in the course of a discussion on enumeration as a site where colonialism encounters the two-dimensionality of orientalism, the notion of enumeration as a flattening device may usefully be transposed to the present context. Throughout this chapter, I have shown that enumeration and science do not, in fact, flatten the enterprise or the outcomes of conservation. Both hunters and conservationists draw on empirical evidence, and on essentially the same models of enumeration and ecological science (sustainability, for instance) in order to reach entirely disparate conclusions. Jasanoff makes the point in his discussion of the notion of 'threatened species', which, he argues, brings into play the science of environmental risk and its measurement. Environmental risk should not be seen as 'real and physical if hard to measure, and accessible only to experts', but rather as 'constructed out of history and experience by experts and laypeople alike . . . risk in this sense is culturally embedded and has texture and meaning that vary from one social grouping to another' (1999: 150). Risk assessment is therefore necessarily a social and political exercise, even when the methods employed are the seemingly technical and ironclad routines of quantitative science. Further, 'judgements about the nature and severity of environmental risk inevitably incorporate tacit understandings concerning causality, agency, and uncertainty, and these are by no means universally shared even in similarly situated western societies' (1999: 150). The role that politics and social and cultural bearings play in conservation science is acknowledged even by conservation practitioners who see it as a hindrance to the real business. Mills, for example, describes it as a form of 'human perturbations'; as he sees it, 'politics, economics, bureaucracy, and apathy; all of these and more will play a role, and complicate decisions far beyond the guidance of applied population biology' (2007: 309).

Among the things that resist being rendered two-dimensional by numbers are populations, politics and morality. With respect to the first, I have shown how the iron necessities of daily and national bag limits, among other forms of enumeration, soften and distort considerably when they encounter the ground truths of hunting in the context of something as fluid and unpredictable as bird migration and the multisited populations it represents.

Take, for example, the trapping of golden plovers. The FKNK has consistently complained that the national annual bag limit is too small and that the populations of the species are healthy. At first glance, the science and numbers seem to uphold the grievance – the species is classified as Least Concern by the IUCN, the range is broad and the population numbers are high. However, there is a complication. The species is divided into two subspecies, *Pluvialis apricaria apricaria* and *P. a. altifrons*. The former (the nominate) is confined to the British Isles and northern Europe through southern Fennoscandia to the Baltic States; the latter has a much wider distribution that stretches from Greenland through much of Scandinavia to the Taymyr Peninsula in Siberia.[42] The national bag limit for Malta assumes that the subspecies that migrates through the central Mediterranean, and that may be taken by Maltese hunters and trappers, is *P. a. altifrons*, but this is contested by bird protectionists. If it could be shown otherwise, the implication would be that hunting in Malta targets a small and more vulnerable source population. The matter has been the topic of much discussion at the Ornis Committee, as well as some debate in the media.[43] At one point, it was suggested that DNA samples be taken from birds caught in Malta to settle the matter (the subspecies are otherwise all but inseparable). However, it seems unlikely that population science, however technical and advanced, will flatten this field any time soon. Even if it did, the scientific outcome would not necessarily matter on the ground. There are other target species – notably turtle doves – for which similar arguments from uncertain source populations are made.

A second point to bear in mind is that the production of science and numbers is embedded in multiple and competing moralities. Take my earlier discussion on self-reporting. It is not just BirdLife Malta that has an issue with the self-reported bag figures for hunting under derogation. Following the ECJ case, when quantification became all-important, the government undertook to commission, seasonally, an independent scientific study on the migration of turtle doves and quail. The study is carried out by a leading environmental consultancy company (EcoServ) and involves pairs of field observers (plus a dog for each pair for flushing quail) stationed at key sites around the coast for several hours a day, keeping detailed records of the number of birds seen. The numbers are then extrapolated and compared with the bag statistics as reported by hunters. The details are beyond the scope of the present context, but the crucial word here is 'independent'. It refers here to the fact that the EcoServ numbers are produced neither by hunters nor by BirdLife Malta; as such, they are thought to be disinterested and free from particular moorings. It is worth mentioning that originally the idea was to put teams in the field consisting of pairs of one BirdLife Malta member and one hunter; this would have kept it balanced, and in any case the enumeration process depends on identification and related competences that are assumed to belong to hunters and birdwatchers alone. However, BirdLife Malta was not really interested, possibly because it was busy producing its own numbers. Even so, it would not have done to appoint hunters alone as enumerators. EcoServ therefore hit on the idea of having one hunter and one independent person per counting station.

The EcoServ results have been contested on various grounds that include the lack of night-time observations (it is known that birds commonly migrate at night), the dubious nature of systematization (numbers of quail flushed depend, for example, on how good a given hunting dog happens to be) and so on. Here, however, the point is elsewhere. The emphasis on disinterested parties suggests that it is only enumerators who are not hunters or conservationists who have the moral legitimacy to produce truthful numbers. This is how a hunter and FKNK official put it to me: 'Why is it that what CABS and BirdLife say is taken to be true, and what is said by hunters isn't?' On a separate occasion, the same person told me that the real reason why BirdLife Malta had chosen not to take part in the EcoServ study was that if the true numbers came out, 'their whole argument would fall apart like a house of cards [*jaqa' kollox*]'. For its part, BirdLife Malta makes much the same arguments about the (lack of) moral legitimacy of hunters. It taps into the history of indiscriminate hunting, cases full of stuffed birds and violent demonstrations (see Chapter 3) to argue that hunters cannot be trusted. What is at stake are not just numbers, but rather the entire morality of the practice that the numbers seek to quantify. Theodossopoulos makes a similar point about the hunters of Vassilikos. As he puts it:

> the hunters of Vassilikos have reason to feel threatened by the rise of the ecological discourse, not because the 'ecologists' have the power to restrict hunting in practice, but because hunting is deprived of its positive moral connotations. A cultural practice traditionally considered as positive, is now treated by a growing number of urban neighbours as undesirable, destructive behaviour with a negative moral stigma attached to it. (2003: 151)

The third thing that science and numbers do not quite flatten is politics. Take the derogation mechanisms, on paper the most technical and objective aspect of hunting in Malta. The mechanisms for trapping are in many ways similar to those for hunting. However, in other respects, they offer fresh insights into the rounding effect of politics on science and numbers. Soon after the Labour Party was elected to power in 2013, the new government made it known to the Commission that it intended to derogate to allow limited finch trapping in autumn. Malta was not bound to notify the Commission prior to derogating, but it did so as a precaution. Finch trapping had been outlawed since 2008, when a transitional arrangement in the Accession Treaty to gradually phase out finch trapping expired. The decision to re-enable it was based on the political direction of the new government. In spite of the fact that the prederogation talks were inconclusive, Malta went ahead and applied a derogation in the autumn of 2014. Even before the derogation was applied, an EU pilot was received by the Government of Malta in June 2014. The case quickly ended up in the ECJ and was lost by Malta in 2018, following which the derogation to trap finches was not applied and finch trappers were left with a *namra* but no *delizzju*.

The case is telling for various reasons, one of which is the relatively short time taken by the Commission to refer the matter to the ECJ. A comparison may be drawn with the trapping of ortolan buntings in France for consumption as a delicacy. This has long been a contentious practice. The species has declined by 75 per cent in France in the last three decades; in 1979, it became illegal to trap ortolan buntings in that country and in 1999, the species was declared protected. And yet, BirdLife International estimates that around 30,000 birds are trapped and killed annually on their autumn migration through the southwestern regions of the country. As part of a campaign launched around 2006, the Ligue pour la Protection des Oiseaux (LPO – BirdLife in France) sent a complaint to the Commission. It took the Commission two years to inform the

LPO that the French government had satisfactorily replied to all its informal questions for clarification and that the complaint would be closed. However, the LPO kept sending the Commission complaints based on field evidence (produced in conjunction with CABS) of ortolan bunting trapping. In June 2016, the Commission announced that it had served France with a reasoned opinion over the matter; in December of that year, France was referred to the ECJ.[44] A few months later, the French Minister for Ecology stated his intention to definitively end the taking of ortolan buntings in the country.[45]

Government officials I spoke to gave me a list of reasons why the Commission was relatively swift and decisive in its action on finch trapping in Malta. First, there was the argument from precedent. Allowing trapping in Malta, or even being soft on the matter, would set a dangerous precedent, especially in a region (the southern part of the EU) where trapping was a fairly major issue in bird conservation. The fear was that Malta would set in motion a domino effect, especially since the forms of strict surveillance pledged by the Maltese government would be very difficult to effectively apply in larger-scale contexts such as France and Spain. Second, and beyond the confines of Member State obligations, Malta was conceptually thought of as a Mediterranean country and therefore prone to endemic and serious problems related to bird trapping. The case of Egypt, with its hundreds of kilometres of trammel nets that line the coast to trap migrating birds, looms large in this regional imaginary. Third, trapping was not a main concern of the powerful hunting lobbies of northern European countries and therefore is more vulnerable to EU measures to stop it.

The fourth reason is perhaps the most revealing of the way in which conservation is caught up in all sorts of complex political intersections. Unlike in the French case, Malta presented no regional complications. Ortolan bunting trapping is concentrated in the Landes, one of the ninety-six regional *départements* of metropolitan France. *Départements* enjoy a degree of autonomy from the central French government on a number of issues, which means that dealings between the Commission and France on regional matters of conservation are politically complicated. Another well-known example is that of duck hunting in spring in the Åland Islands, an autonomous region of Finland. The islanders have used their regional autonomy to resist the Commission on the issue, at one point in 2006 even threatening to veto Finland from ratifying an eventual EU constitution.[46] The trapping of thrushes in the Comunidad Valenciana in Spain is yet another example (Murgui 2014). What these examples mean in practice is that the work of the Commission is rendered tremendously complicated in the case of conservation matters that are rooted in regional identity and

216 | *Birds of Passage*

politics. Since finch trapping in Malta is a national issue and since in any case regional autonomy is not part of the Maltese political landscape, the Commission finds it much easier to deal with: the equation involves two clearly defined parties and is much more straightforward.

The author, poet and environmentalist Paul Kingsnorth has written about a deep divide, among activists, between the 'poets' and the 'quants'. The former, among whom Kingsnorth classifies himself, embrace and advocate an environmentalism based on narratives of a deep and meaningful relationship – in the manner of John Muir, for example – between humans and their environment. Quants, on the other hand, 'find themselves caught in a narrative of their other people's making' (2017: 46). Obsessed with numbers rather than narratives, they are hostage to a culture where nothing is thought to be 'real' unless sanctioned by a sort of ecological accounting: 'this is the kind of culture that produces an environmental movement made up of frustrated, passionate people who feel obliged to act like speak-your-weight machines in order to be heard' (2017: 45). Increasingly, then, environmentalists seem to accept that it is only arguments that are based on quantification that stand a chance of influencing policy. 'This, demonstrably', Kingsnorth concludes, 'is how radical movements die' (2017: 47). In this chapter, I have argued against this facile dichotomy. Whether or not the bird conservation movement in Malta is terminally ill, there appears to be much poetry in quantification.

Notes

1. Foreword to Fenech's *Fatal Flight* (1992: vii).
2. Kingsnorth 2017: 44.
3. Zink 2014: 136.
4. Sources: 'Bird Culling Figures "Exaggerated", Says Ornithologist Witness in Libel Case', *Malta Today*, 26 January 2015; and Court of Magistrates of Malta published case notes, Case 190/08 FDP.
5. For a useful critique of the dynamics, strengths and shortcomings of list-keeping and enumeration among birdwatchers, see Kaufman (2011). Liep (2001) has discussed the keeping and circulation of records among bird-watchers as a form of appropriation and gift exchange (as he insightfully puts it, 'airborne *kula*').
6. S. Woldhek, 'Bird Killing in the Mediterranean', European Committee for the Prevention of Mass Destruction of Migratory Birds, ICBP, October 1979.
7. G. Magnin, 'An Assessment of Illegal Shooting and Catching of Birds in Malta', ICBP, April 1986.
8. The following sections are based on the following four sources: 'Review of the Scale, Impact and Geography of Illegal Killing of Birds in the

Mediterranean: Guidance Notes for Completing the Template', BirdLife International, 2015; 'Review of the Scale, Impact and Geography of Illegal Killing of Birds in the Mediterranean', BirdLife Malta draft report presented to the Ornis Committee, 2015; 'The Illegal Hunting Situation in Malta: A Review of the Report by BirdLife Malta Entitled "Review of the Scale, Impact and Geography of Illegal Killing of Birds in the Mediterranean"', Natalino Fenech, 16 June 2015; and Brochet et al. (2016).

9. The Agreement on the Conservation of African-Eurasian Migratory Waterbirds (AEWA) is an intergovernmental treaty on the conservation of migratory waterbirds and their habitats across Africa, Europe, the Middle East, Central Asia, Greenland and the Canadian Archipelago. It was developed under the framework of the Convention on Migratory Species (CMS) and was administered by the United Nations Environment Programme. It entered into force in 1999.

10. For example, 'Martin il-kaċċatur' ('Martin the Hunter') is a well-known old song that mocks, among other things, the protagonist's unerring aim and the tremendous shooting that went on that made the trees tremble. The twist is that a 'large bird' shot by the bumbling Martin turns out to be his own donkey's ears.

11. 'Fatal Flight: The Facts', FKNK, Malta, 1992.

12. Preface by Ferdinando Albanese to the Kalchreuter report (Heribert Kalchreuter, 'On Bird Hunting in Malta', report published by FACE, Brussels, 1992).

13. Kalchreuter report, p. 9.

14. For example, a colour brochure produced by FACE MED (the Mediterranean branch of FACE) for Malta is called 'Hunting in the Mediterranean: Management and Sustainability for Future Generations' (FACE MED n.d.)

15. www.huntinginmalta.org.mt, retrieved on 26 April 2014.

16. IUCN Red List of Threatened Species, 2018.

17. 'The Facts about Maltese Game-Shooting and Live-Bird Capturing', FKNK information booklet, 2012.

18. European Court of Justice judgment, Case C-76/08, 10 September 2009.

19. Legal Notice 221 of 2010, Government of Malta (subsequently amended by Legal Notices 83 and 113 of 2011, 122 of 2013, 86 of 2014 and 90 of 2016, and 82 of 2017).

20. Legal Notice 221 of 2010 of the Government of Malta.

21. 'A Critical Analysis of the "Technical Note" in Respect of the Spring 2011 Hunting Derogation', FKNK report, 2011.

22. Government Notice 538, 27 May 2016.

23. IUCN Red List of Threatened Species, 2016.

24. Minutes of the Ornis Committee meeting of 25 February 2016.

25. Legal Notice 113/2015 of the Government of Malta.

26. 'IUCN Calls for the Commission to Protect the Turtle Dove against Spring Hunting Season in Malta', *IUCN News*, 26 April 2016.

27. 'Commissioner Vella Dodges Questions over Turtle-Dove Listing', *Malta Today*, 11 January 2016.

28. 'Il-Futur tal-Kaċċa fir-Rebbiegħa' ('The Future of Spring Hunting'), published by the Parliamentary Secretariat for Agriculture, Fisheries, and Animal Rights of the Government of Malta, 2016.
29. Kaċċaturi San Ubertu (KSU), press release of 10 February 2016.
30. 'The Hunting Period Extension is a Gamble That Will Backfire', BirdLife Malta press statement, 6 March 2018.
31. A kind of junior minister.
32. There are differences in the ways in which the two species are hunted: quail are usually flushed, while turtle doves are usually shot on the wing from strategically positioned elevated hides.
33. 'Hunting in Malta under the Spotlight in Brussels Discussion', *The Malta Independent*, 22 March 2018.
34. BirdLife Malta press statement, 21 April 2018.
35. It is worth quoting the relevant section in the Kalchreuter report: 'Bag statistics are required, both to calculate the real impact of hunting on bird populations *and to provide concrete data against exaggerated allegations*' (Kalchreuter report, p. 12, emphasis added).
36. As regulated by Legal Notice 79 of 2006 of the Government of Malta.
37. See, for example, 'Overview of Hunting Bag Statistics for Common Quail (*Coturnix coturnix*) and Turtle Dove (*Streptopelia turtur*) in Autumn and Spring as Declared by the Carnet De Chasse/SMS System', document presented to the Malta Ornis Committee, BirdLife Malta, March 2014.
38. As quoted in the report referenced in the previous footnote.
39. BirdLife Malta used as an example 1991 legislation from Scotland that required the tagging of wild salmon and trout.
40. 'Report on the Outcome of the 2016 Autumn Live-Capturing Season for Golden Plover and Song Thrush in Malta', Wild Birds Regulation Unit, Ministry for Sustainable Development, the Environment and Climate Change, Government of Malta, March 2017.
41. 'Report on the Outcome of the 2015 Autumn Live-Capturing Season for Golden Plover and Song Thrush in Malta', Wild Birds Regulation Unit, Ministry for Sustainable Development, the Environment and Climate Change, Government of Malta, March 2016.
42. Relevant entry in *Handbook of the Birds of the World* online, https://www.hbw.com/species/eurasian-golden-plover-pluvialis-apricaria (retrieved 26 December 2019).
43. For example, 'CABS Appeals to Prime Minister to Ban Trapping, Hunting of Golden Plover', *Times of Malta*, 12 December 2013.
44. BirdLife International, 'Can the European Commission Save the Ortolan Bunting?', 7 July 2016. Retrieved 9 August 2016 from www.BirdLife.org.
45. BirdLife International, 'In France, the Ortolan Bunting May Soon Be off the Menu', 22 September 2017, www.BirdLife.org, accessed on 20 April 2018.
46. 'Tiny Island That's Ready to Stop Europe in Its Tracks', *The Telegraph*, 15 February 2006.

Conclusion

I believe that for his escape he took advantage of the migration of a flock
of wild birds.

—Antoine de Saint-Exupéry, *The Little Prince*[1]

On the second day of 2017, a flock of twelve mute swans landed in a
reservoir near a fairly busy country road in Gozo. Within half an hour,
a small crowd of people had gathered to see them. Most were curious
onlookers, but there were also men in camouflage and people with cameras and binoculars. The event quickly made the headlines. As the newspapers reminded their readers, it inevitably brought to mind another
flock of swans that had settled in a bay in the south of Malta exactly
fifteen years earlier. The soft landing of the 2017 flock told a story of
progress and of bad habits that belonged in the past. Certainly the images
of birdwatchers and hunters standing side-by-side watching the swans
were a powerful testimony to this fresh air.

It soon became clear that both hunters and bird protectionists were
keen to embrace the winged messengers of transfiguration. What started
as a comment by BirdLife Malta that the swans were suffering from mal-
nutrition quickly escalated into a vitriolic war of words between it and
the FKNK. On 13 January, and reportedly as a result of 'reconciliatory
discussions', BirdLife Malta, the FKNK and the KSU reached a 'collaboration agreement' on a feeding regime. A few days later, the President of
the FKNK led a delegation of committee members to officially feed the
swans in a blaze of media attention.[2]

The occasion has all the makings of the proverbial storm, which raises
questions about this book, because it may not be entirely clear what circumstances in Malta might tell us about the bigger picture – especially the
far, far bigger picture traced by the migratory journeys of birds. Migratory
birds and, by implication, their conservation are a classic example of a
multisited object that appears to call for multisited field research (see
Falzon 2009) – at any rate certainly not research conducted on an island
that scarcely figures on a map of Europe. However, while there can be
no doubt that migratory birds are indeed a multisited object, the hope is

that the manageably small and bounded fieldsite retains its potency as a 'window onto complexity' (Candea 2007: 167). A partial and incomplete view it may afford, but hopefully not a useless one.

The ethnographic material presented in this book shows how Maltese conservationists draw on cultural lineages that enable them to study and protect birds *in* Malta, rather than *the* birds *of* Malta – in other words, to embed the birds that inhabit (through breeding and in particular migration) the islands into the much broader field of universalizing science and conservation. To apply Tsing's thought, they do this by tapping into a 'large space of compatibility among disparate particular facts and observations'. Migrating birds are 'collaboratively agreed upon Natural objects . . . convincing universals [that] travel with at least some facility in the world' (Tsing 2005: 89). Malta is imagined and made not as a unique case of interest to locals alone, but rather as one among a number of 'black spots' on a broad geographical map and therefore of much broader import. Albeit in a partial and incomplete way, an ethnography of hunting and conservation in Malta sheds light on the larger-scale issue of the conservation of mobile nonhuman objects (such as tuna and whales). This is very evident in the 'elsewhere' arguments put forward by Maltese hunters in their understanding of turtle dove ecology, in the ways in which science and enumeration are articulated by a government that persists in playing 'derogation games', and in the discourses and practices concerning biological invasions.

Nor is an exceptionalist framing particularly applicable to an understanding of hunting itself. I have shown how the passions and practices of hunting in Malta are often put down to localistic-regionalist models premised on supposedly atavistic and timeless forms of (mis)appropriation of nature. And yet, my ethnography takes the witness stand for transformations on at least four counts. First, it is clear that hunting in Malta has changed fairly profoundly. In terms of numbers, it appears to be in gradual decline. Even if the number of licence holders has not gone down dramatically, it certainly has not kept pace with the growing population of the country and is now at less than 3 per cent. This is comparable to the situation in Italy, where a gradual differentiation from rural everyday life has brought about a decrease of more than 50 per cent in the number of licenced hunters over the past thirty years (Barca et al. 2016). Perhaps more importantly, the kind of indiscriminate and wholesale hunting and trapping that used to be an undifferentiated aspect of daily life is a thing of the past. Second, the structures within which both hunters and bird protectionists operate are in a constant state of flux. The most significant change was Malta's accession as an EU Member State, but there were others. Thus, for example, both BirdLife

Malta and the FKNK have developed ways of engaging with specialized forms of knowledge and bureaucracy. Third, while hunting is underwritten by passions and practices that may at first glance appear to be Mediterranean relics, both *namra* and *delizzju* are in fact parties to broader political, social and economic forces. *Namra* is located within discourses of restraint and 'progressive' gender norms, and *delizzju* involves ways of engaging with changing understandings of the landscape, forms of access to land and surveillance. Fourth, there are important and current conceptual self-transformations in the way in which hunters increasingly oppose hunting game to poaching protected birds, for example, or in the parallel distinctions between 'real' and rogue hunters. Crucially, none of these transformations is unilateral; rather, they implicate hunters and protectionists, but also birds themselves, in 'multispecies' (van Dooren 2014) processes and outcomes. If van Dooren's little penguins of Manly, Sydney, 'do' place in meaningful complicity with humans – that is, in historical and 'storied' ways that bring together both human and nonhuman long-term sequences of events – there is no reason why the same cannot be said of turtle doves winging their way along leading lines transformed by urbanization and afforestation projects.

The ornithological record is depressingly rich in examples of extermination or outright extinction of sedentary (and often flightless) birds. Zooarchaeological work in the Pacific, for example, shows how the arrival of the Lapita people resulted in the direct extermination of most of the islands' indigenous birds, in many cases within decades of arrival (Steadman 2006; see also Hume (2017) for a discussion of avian extinctions). Migratory species are more complicated: even as they 'escape', local certainties escape with them.

Notes

1. Antoine de Saint-Exupéry, *The Little Prince* (London: Mammoth, 1991).
2. See 'Wild Birds Do Not Belong to BirdLife Malta Alone', FKNK press release, 8 January 2017; 'Time to Join Forces to Protect Birds', BirdLife Malta press release, 10 January 2017.

Glossary of Species Mentioned in the Book

Birds

As given in the text. Where necessary, full English names as currently accepted by the IUCN are given in brackets. Scientific names as currently accepted by the IUCN.

Bee-eater (European bee-eater)	*Merops apiaster*
Birds of prey (also 'raptors')	Accipitriformes
Bustard (great bustard)	*Otis tarda*
Chaffinch (common chaffinch)	*Fringilla coelebs*
Chats	Muscicapidae
Corn bunting	*Emberiza calandra*
Cuckoo (common cuckoo)	*Cuculus canorus*
Ducks	Anatidae
Dunlin	*Calidris alpina*
Eared dove	*Zenaida auriculata*
Egrets	Ardeidae
European storm petrel (European storm-petrel)	*Hydrobates pelagicus*
Finches	Fringillidae
Flamingo (greater flamingo)	*Phoenicopterus roseus*
Gannet (northern gannet)	*Morus bassanus*
Golden oriole (Eurasian golden oriole)	*Oriolus oriolus*
Geese	Anatidae
Greenfinch (European greenfinch)	*Chloris chloris*
Grouse (willow grouse)	*Lagopus lagopus scotia*
Gulls	Laridae
Harriers	Circinae
Hawfinch	*Coccothraustes coccothraustes*
Hen harrier	*Circus cyaneus*
Herons	Ardeidae
Hirundines	Hirundinidae
Hobby (Eurasian hobby)	*Falco subbuteo*

Honey buzzard (European honey buzzard)	*Pernis aviporus*
Hoopoe (common hoopoe)	*Upupa epops*
Icterine warbler	*Hippolais icterina*
Kestrel (common kestrel)	*Falco tinnunculus*
Kingfisher (common kingfisher)	*Alcedo atthis*
Larks	Alaudidae
Linnet (common linnet)	*Linaria cannabina*
Little penguin	*Eudyptula minor*
Little tern	*Sternula albifrons*
Montagu's harrier	*Circus pygargus*
Nightingale (common nightingale)	*Luscinia megarhynchos*
Nightjar (European nightjar)	*Caprimulgus europaeus*
Ortolan bunting	*Emberiza hortulana*
Osprey	*Pandion haliaetus*
Pallas's leaf warbler	*Phylloscopus proregulus*
Partridge (grey partridge)	*Perdix perdix*
Passenger pigeon	*Ectopistes migratorius*
Passerines	Passeriformes
Peregrine falcon	*Falco peregrinus*
Pheasant (common pheasant)	*Phasianus colchicus*
Plover (Eurasian golden plover)	*Pluvialis apricaria*
Prairie chicken	*Tympanuchus* spp.
Ptarmigan (rock ptarmigan)	*Lagopus muta*
Quail (common quail)	*Coturnix coturnix*
Rails	Rallidae
Robin (European robin)	*Erithacus rubecula*
Sardinian warbler	*Sylvia melanocephala*
Scopoli's shearwater	*Calonectris diomedea*
Senegal thick-knee	*Burhinus senegalensis*
Short-eared owl	*Asio flammeus*
Skylark (Eurasian skylark)	*Alauda arvensis*
Song thrush	*Turdus philomelos*
Sparrow (Spanish sparrow)	*Passer hispaniolensis*
Spoonbill (Eurasian spoonbill)	*Platalea leucorodia*
Swallow (barn swallow)	*Hirundo rustica*
Swan (mute swan)	*Cygnus olor*
Starling (common starling)	*Sturnus vulgaris*
Thrushes	Turdidae
Turtle dove (European turtle dove)	*Streptopelia turtur*
Waders (also 'shorebirds')	Charadriiformes
Wagtails	Motacillidae

Wheatears	*Oenante* spp.
Woodcock (Eurasian woodcock)	*Scolopax rusticola*
Yellow wagtail (western yellow wagtail)	*Motacilla flava*
Yelkouan shearwater	*Puffinus yelkouan*

Plants

Acacia	*Acacia* and *Vachellia* spp.
Amaranth	*Amaranthus* spp.
Carob	*Ceratonia siliqua*
Cypress	*Cupressus sempervirens*
Eucalyptus	*Eucalyptus* spp.
French daffodil	*Narcissus tazetta*
Maltese centaury	*Cheirolophus crassifolius*
Mediterranean buckthorn	*Rhamnus alaternus*
Mustard/Wall-rocket	*Diplotaxis* spp. (Mustards also belong to genera *Brassica* and *Sinapis*)
Oak (holm oak)	*Quercus ilex*
Olive	*Olea europaea*
Pine (Aleppo pine)	*Pinus halepensis*
Sandarac gum tree	*Tetraclinis articulata*
Sea squill (maritime squill)	*Charybdis pancration*
Sulla	*Sulla coronaria*
Tamarisk	*Tamarix africana* (Several other species are native to the Mediterranean region. In Malta, apart from the native *T. africana*, *T. gallica* and *T. parviflora* are commonly grown and also naturalized.)
Thistles	*Asteraceae* spp. (sub-fam: Carduoideae spp.)

Other

Deer	Cervidae
Elk	*Alces alces*
Fallow deer	*Dama dama*
Fox (red fox)	*Vulpes vulpes*

Freshwater crab — *Potamon fluviatile* (in Malta the subsp. *lanfrancoi*)

Hare (brown bare) — *Lepus europaeus*

Rabbit (European rabbit) — *Oryctolagus cuniculus*

Tiger — *Panthera tigris*

Turtle — Cheloniidae

Wild boar — *Sus scrofa*

References

Anderson, B. 1991. *Imagined Communities: Reflections on the Origin and Spread of Nationalism*. New York: Verso.

Angas, G.F. 1842. *A Ramble in Malta and Sicily in the Autumn of 1841*. London: Smith, Elder, & Co.

Appadurai, A. 1996. *Modernity at Large: Cultural Dimensions of Globalization*. Minneapolis: University of Minnesota Press.

Avery, M. 2015. *Inglorious: Conflict in the Uplands*. London: Bloomsbury.

Azzopardi, A.E. 1985. *The Maltese Shooter's Handbook*. Malta: Midsea.

Baker, J.A. 2015. *The Peregrine, the Hill of Summer & Diaries: The Complete Works of J.A. Baker*. London: William Collins.

Baker, R.R. 1984. *Bird Navigation: The Solution of a Mystery?* London: Hodder & Stoughton.

Bannerman, D.A., and J.A. Vella-Gaffiero. 1976. *Birds of the Maltese Archipelago*. Malta: Museums Department.

Barca, B., A. Lindon and M. Root-Bernstein. 2016. 'Environmentalism in the Crosshairs: Perspectives on Migratory Bird Hunting and Poaching Conflicts in Italy', *Global Ecology and Conservation* 6: 189–207.

Berthold, P. 2001. *Bird Migration: A General Survey*. Oxford: Oxford University Press.

Best, J. 2012. *Damned Lies and Statistics: Untangling Numbers from the Media, Politicians, and Activists*. Berkeley: University of California Press.

Bildstein, K.L. 2006. *Migrating Raptors of the World: Their Ecology and Conservation*. Ithaca: Cornell University Press.

Bloch, M. 1991. 'Language, Anthropology, and Cognitive Science', *Man (N.S.)* 26(2): 183–98.

Bolster, W.J. 2014. *The Mortal Sea: Fishing the Atlantic in the Age of Sail*. Cambridge, MA: Harvard University Press.

Bowen-Jones, H., J.C. Dewdney and W.B. Fisher. 1961. *Malta: Background for Development*. Durham: Department of Geography, Durham Colleges.

Braudel, F. 1975. *The Mediterranean and the Mediterranean World in the Age of Philip II*. London: Fontana.

Briguglio, M. 2015. 'The Bird Hunting Referendum in Malta', *Environmental Politics* 24(5): 835–39.

Brincat, J.M. 2011. *Maltese and Other Languages: A Linguistic History of Malta*. Malta: Midsea.

Brochet, A.-L., et al. 2016. 'Preliminary Assessment of the Scope and Scale of Illegal Killing and Taking of Birds in the Mediterranean', *Bird Conservation International* 26: 1–28.

Brockman, E. 1961. *Last Bastion: Sketches of the Maltese Islands*. London: Darton, Longman & Todd.

Bryans, R. 1966. *Malta and Gozo*. London: Faber & Faber.

Bye, L.M. 2003. 'Masculinity and Rurality at Play in Stories about Hunting', *Norsk Geografisk Tidsskrift – Norwegian Journal of Geography* 57(3): 145–53.

Campbell, B., and D. Veríssimo. 2015. 'Black Stork Down: Military Discourses in Bird Conservation in Malta', *Human Ecology* 43: 79–92.

Candea, M. 2007. 'Arbitrary Locations: In Defence of the Bounded Field-Site', *Journal of the Royal Anthropological Institute (N.S.)* 13: 167–84.

Cartmill, M. 1993. *A View to a Death in the Morning: Hunting and Nature through History*. Cambridge, MA: Harvard University Press.

Cassar, C. 2018. 'Hunting and Game in Malta in the Sixteenth to the Eighteenth Centuries: A Historical Anthropological Approach', *Journal of Mediterranean Studies* 27(1): 35–48.

Chambers, I. 2008. *Mediterranean Crossings: The Politics of an Interrupted Modernity*. Durham, NC: Duke University Press.

Choy, T. 2011. *Ecologies of Comparison: An Ethnography of Endangerment in Hong Kong*. Durham, NC: Duke University Press.

Cocker, M. 2013. *Birds and People*. London: Jonathan Cape.

———. 2018. *Our Place: Can We Save Britain's Wildlife before It Is Too Late?* London: Jonathan Cape.

Cohn, B.S. 1996. *Colonialism and Its Forms of Knowledge: The British in India*. Princeton: Princeton University Press.

Cronon, W. 1995. 'The Trouble with Wilderness', in W. Cronon (ed.), *Uncommon Ground: Rethinking the Human Place in Nature*. London: W.W. Norton, pp. 69–90.

Dahles, H. 1993. 'Game Killing and Killing Games: An Anthropologist Looking at Hunting in a Modern Society', *Society and Animals* 1(2): 169–84.

Dalli, C. 2006. *Malta: The Medieval Millennium*. Malta: Midsea.

D'Autun, J.Q. 1980. *The Earliest Description of Malta (Lyons 1536)*, trans. H.C.R. Vella. Malta: De Bono.

Day, J. 2019. *Homing: On Pigeons, Dwellings and Why We Return*. London: John Murray.

De Belin, M. 2013. *From the Deer to the Fox: The Hunting Transition and the Landscape 1600–1850*. Hatfield: University of Hertfordshire Press.

Deguara, Ġ. 2014. *Il-Proċess tal-insib tal-gamiem fir-rebbiegħa*. Malta: self-published.

de Saint-Exupéry, Antoine. 1991. *The Little Prince*. London: Mammoth.

Despott, G. 1917. 'Notes on the Ornithology of Malta', *The Ibis* 5(3): 281–349.

Ekers, M., and M. Farnan. 2010. 'Planting the Nation: Tree Planting Art and the Endurance of Canadian Nationalism', *Space and Culture* 13(1): 95–120.

Falzon, M.A. 1994. 'Diurnal Duck Migration over the Maltese Islands', *Il-Merill* 28: 36–37.

———. 2001. 'Representing Danger at a Mediterranean Drydocks', *Journal of Mediterranean Studies* 11(2): 355–74.

———. 2008. 'Flights of Passion: Hunting, Ecology and Politics in Malta and the Mediterranean', *Anthropology Today* 24(1): 15–20.

———. 2009. *Multi-sited Ethnography: Theory, Praxis and Locality in Contemporary Research.* Farnham: Ashgate.

Falzon, M.A., and C.M. Cassar. 2015. 'What's in a Bang? Fireworks and the Politics of Sound in Malta', *Space and Culture* 18(2): 143–55.

Fenech, N. 1992. *Fatal Flight: The Maltese Obsession with Killing Birds.* London: Quiller.

———. 2010. *A Complete Guide to the Birds of Malta.* Malta: Midsea.

———. 2016. *Kif Dieb il-Gemiem: Rakkonti dwar kaċċa u nsib mill-passat.* Malta: Klabb Kotba Maltin.

Fine, L.M. 2000. 'Rights of Men, Rites of Passage: Hunting and Masculinity at Reo Motors of Lansing, Michigan, 1945–1975', *Journal of Social History* 33(4): 805–23.

Fiorini, S. 2001. 'The Maltese Falcon: Falconry in Malta, 1239–c.1500', *Treasures of Malta* VII(2): 59–64.

Fitzgerald, A.J. 2005. 'The Emergence of the Figure of "Woman-the-Hunter": Equality or Complicity in Oppression?', *Women's Studies Quarterly* 33(1/2): 86–104.

Franklin, A. 2001. 'Neo-Darwinian Leisures, The Body and Nature: Hunting and Angling in Modernity', *Body & Society* 7(4): 57–76.

Freller, T. 2010. *Malta: The Order of St John.* Malta: Midsea.

Fsadni, M. 1999. *The Girna: The Maltese Corbelled Stone Hut.* Malta: Dominican Friars.

Fuller, E. 2015. *The Passenger Pigeon.* Princeton: Princeton University Press.

Gordon, R.M. 1987. *The Structure of Emotions: Investigations in Cognitive Philosophy.* Cambridge: Cambridge University Press.

Gutmann, M.C. 1997. 'Trafficking in Men: The Anthropology of Masculinity', *Annual Review of Anthropology* 26: 385–409.

Hahn, S., and S. Bauer. 2009. 'The Natural Link between Europe and Africa: 201 Billion Birds on Migration', *Oikos* 118(4): 624–26.

Haraway, D.J. 2008. *When Species Meet.* Minneapolis: University of Minnesota Press.

Harwood, M. 2014. *Malta in the European Union.* Farnham: Ashgate.

Heatherington, T. 2010. *Wild Sardinia: Indigeneity and the Global Dreamtimes of Environmentalism.* Seattle: University of Washington Press.

Hell, B. 1996. 'Enraged Hunters: The Domain of the Wild in North-Western Europe', in P. Descola and G. Pálsson (eds), *Nature and Society: Anthropological Perspectives.* London: Routledge, pp. 205–17.

Helm, B. 2006. 'Zugunruhe of Migratory and Non-migratory Birds in a Circannual Context', *Journal of Avian Biology* 37(6): 533–40.

Helmreich, S. 2005. 'How Scientists Think; about "Natives", for Example: A Problem of Taxonomy among Biologists of Alien Species in Hawaii', *Journal of the Royal Anthropological Institute (N.S.)* 11: 107–28.

Herzfeld, M. 1985. *The Poetics of Manhood: Contest and Identity in a Cretan Mountain Village.* Princeton: Princeton University Press.

——. 1987. '"As in Your Own House": Hospitality, Ethnography, and the Stereotype of Mediterranean Society', in D.D. Gilmore (ed.), *Honor and Shame and the Unity of the Mediterranean*. Washington DC: American Anthropological Association, pp. 75–89.

——. 1992. *The Social Production of Indifference: Exploring the Symbolic Roots of Western Bureaucracy*. Chicago: University of Chicago Press.

Horden, P., and N. Purcell. 2000. *The Corrupting Sea: A Study of Mediterranean History*. Oxford: Blackwell.

Hughes, T. 'Hawk Roosting' in *Lupercal*. London: Faber & Faber, 1960.

Hume, J.P. 2017. *Extinct Birds*. London: Christopher Helm.

Impelluso, L. 2004. *Nature and Its Symbols*, trans. S. Sartarelli. Los Angeles: J. Paul Getty Museum.

Ingold, T. 2000. *The Perception of the Environment: Essays in Livelihood, Dwelling and Skill*. London: Routledge.

Jensen, J.L. 2010. 'Augmentation of Space: Four Dimensions of Spatial Experiences of Google Earth', *Space and Culture* 13(1): 121–33.

Jasanoff, S. 1999. 'The Songlines of Risk', *Environmental Values* 8(2): 135–52.

Jerolmack, C. 2013. *The Global Pigeon*. Chicago: University of Chicago Press.

Kaltenborn, B.P., et al. 2012. 'Attitudes of Norwegian Ptarmigan Hunters towards Hunting Goals and Harvest Regulations: The Effects of Environmental Orientation', *Biodiversity Conservation* 21: 3369–84.

Kaufman, K. 2011. 'One and a Half Cheers for List-Keeping', in M.R. Canfield (ed.), *Field Notes on Science and Nature*. Cambridge, MA: Harvard University Press, pp. 49–66.

Keller, E. 2015. *Beyond the Lens of Conservation: Malagasy and Swiss Imaginations of One Another*. Oxford: Berghahn Books.

Khalfallah, M., et al. 2017. 'Reconstruction of Marine Fisheries Catches for the Republic of Malta (1950–2010)', *Mediterranean Marine Science* 18: 241–50.

Kingsnorth, P. 2017. *Confessions of a Recovering Environmentalist*. London: Faber & Faber.

Kolbert, E. 2014. *The Sixth Extinction: An Unnatural History*. New York: Henry Holt & Co.

Lanfranco, E. 2015. *Wild Flowers of the Maltese Islands*. Malta: BDL.

Leith Adams, A. 1870. *Notes of a Naturalist in the Nile Valley and Malta*. Edinburgh: Edmonston & Douglas.

Liep, J. 2001. 'Airborne Kula: The Appropriation of Birds by Danish Ornithologists', *Anthropology Today* 17(5): 10–15.

Littlefield, J. 2010. 'Men on the Hunt: Ecofeminist Insights into Masculinity', *Marketing Theory* 10(1): 97–117.

Lišková, S., and D. Frynta. 2013. 'What Determines Bird Beauty in Human Eyes?', *Anthrozoös* 26(1): 27–41.

Macfarlane, R. 2007. *The Wild Places*. London: Granta.

MacGregor, A. 2007. *Curiosity and Enlightenment: Collectors and Collections from the Sixteenth to the Nineteenth Century*. New Haven: Yale University Press.

Marvin, G. 2003. 'A Passionate Pursuit: Foxhunting as Performance', *Sociological Review* 51(2): 46–60.

Merritt, M. 2016. *A Sky Full of Birds*. London: Rider.

Mills, L.S. 2007. *Conservation of Wildlife Populations: Demography, Genetics, and Management*. Oxford: Blackwell.

Milton, K. 2002. *Loving Nature: Towards an Ecology of Emotion*. London: Routledge.

Milton, K., and M. Svašek (eds). 2005. *Mixed Emotions: Anthropological Studies of Feeling*. Oxford: Berg.

Murgui, E. 2014. 'When Governments Support Poaching: A Review of the Illegal Trapping of Thrushes *Turdus* Spp. in the *Parany* of Comunidad Valenciana, Spain', *Bird Conservation International* 24: 127–37.

Newton, I. 2007. *The Migration Ecology of Birds*. London: Academic Press.

———. 2017. *Farming and Birds*. London: William Collins.

Noss, A.J., E. Cuéllar and R. Leny Cuéllar. 2004. 'An Evaluation of Hunter Self-Monitoring in the Bolivian Chaco', *Human Ecology* 32(6): 685–702.

Pauly, D., and D. Zeller. 2016. 'Catch Reconstructions Reveal That Global Marine Fisheries Catches Are Higher Than Reported and Declining', *Nature Communications* 7(10244): 1–9.

———. 2017. 'The Best Catch Data That Can Possibly Be? Rejoinder to Ye et al. "FAO's Statistic Data and Sustainability of Fisheries and Aquaculture"', *Marine Policy* 81 (2017): 406–10. Retrieved 2 January 2020 from http://dx.doi.org/10.1016/j.marpol.2017.03.012.

Preston, A., and N. Gower. 2017. *As Kingfishers Catch Fire: Books & Birds*. London: Corsair.

Primdahl, J., et al. 2012. 'Hunting and Landscape in Denmark: Farmers' Management of Hunting Rights and Landscape Changes', *Landscape Research* 37(6): 659–72.

Raine, A.F. 2011. *A Photographic Guide to the Birds of Malta*. Peterborough: Langford.

Raine, A., J. Sultana and S. Gillings. 2009. *Malta Breeding Atlas 2008*. Malta: BirdLife Malta.

Richards, C. 2004. 'Grouse Shooting and Its Landscape: The Management of Grouse Moors in Britain', *Anthropology Today* 20(4): 10–15.

Richardson, A. 2012. '"Riding Like Alexander, Hunting Like Diana": Gendered Aspects of the Medieval Hunt and Its Landscape Settings in England and France', *Gender & History* 24(2): 253–70.

Roberts, E.L. 1954. *The Birds of Malta*. Malta: Progress Press.

Rose, G.A. 2007. *Cod: The Ecological History of North Atlantic Fisheries*. St John's: Breakwater Books.

Salazar, N.B. 2018. *Momentous Mobilities: Anthropological Musings on the Meanings of Travel*. Oxford: Berghahn Books.

Sartre, J.-P. 1962. *Sketch for a Theory of the Emotions*, trans. Philip Mairet. London: Methuen.

Schembri, P.J., and J. Sultana (eds). 1989. *Red Data Book for the Maltese Islands*. Malta: Department of Information, Government of Malta.

Schneider-Jacoby, M., and A. Spangenberg. 2010. 'Bird Hunting along the Adriatic Flyway: An Assessment of Bird Hunting in Albania, Bosnia-Herzegovina, Croatia, Montenegro, Slovenia, and Serbia', in D. Denac, M. Schneider-Jacoby and B. Stumberger (eds), *Adriatic Flyway: Closing the Gap in Bird Conservation*. Radolfzel: EuroNatur, pp. 32–51.

Selin, H., and S.D. VanDeveer. 2015. *European Union and Environmental Governance*. Abingdon: Routledge.

Sharr, A. 2007. *Heidegger for Architects*. Abingdon: Routledge.

Shiva, V. 1989. *Staying Alive: Women, Ecology, and Development*. London: Zed Books.

Shrubb, M. 2013. *Feasting, Fowling and Feathers: A History of the Exploitation of Wild Birds*. London: T. & A.D. Poyser.

Simmel, G. 1994. 'Bridge and Door', *Theory, Culture & Society* 11: 5–10.

Simpson, P. 2017. *The Gamekeeper*. London: Simon & Schuster.

Sramek, J. 2006. '"Face Him Like a Briton": Tiger Hunting, Imperialism, and British Masculinity in Colonial India, 1800–1875', *Victorian Studies* 48(4): 659–80.

Steadman, D.W. 2006. *Extinction and Biogeography of Tropical Pacific Birds*. Chicago: University of Chicago Press.

Subramaniam, B. 2001. 'The Aliens Have Landed! Reflection on the Rhetoric of Biological Invasions', *Meridians* 2(1): 26–40.

Sultana, J., and J.J. Borg. 2015. *History of Ornithology in Malta*. Malta: BirdLife Malta.

Sultana, J., and C. Gauci. 1977. 'The Situation of Birds of Prey in Malta', in R.D. Chancellor (ed.), *Report of Proceedings: World Conference on Birds of Prey, Vienna, 1–3 October 1975*. London: International Council for Bird Preservation, pp. 136–39.

———. 1982. *A New Guide to the Birds of Malta*. Malta: The Ornithological Society (MOS).

Sultana, J., et al. 2011. *The Breeding Birds of Malta*. Malta: BirdLife Malta.

Thake, M. 1985. 'Analysis of Honey Buzzard Flight Directions at Buskett', *Il-Merill* 23: 5–7.

Theodossopoulos, D. 2003. *Troubles with Turtles: Cultural Understandings of the Environment on a Greek Island*. Oxford: Berghahn Books.

Thirsk, J. 1997. *Alternative Agriculture: A History, from the Black Death to the Present Day*. Oxford: Oxford University Press.

Tillmann, J.E, M. Beyerbach and E. Strauss. 2012. 'Do Hunters Tell the Truth?: Evaluation of Hunters' Spring Pair Density Estimates of the Grey Partridge *Perdix Perdix*', *Wildlife Biology* 18(2): 113–20.

Trump, D.H. 2002. *Malta: Prehistory and Temples*. Malta: Midsea.

Tseng, S. 2008. 'Contested Terrain: Gustave Courbet's Hunting Scenes', *Art Bulletin* 90(2): 218–34.

Tsing, A.L. 1995. 'Empowering Nature, or: Some Gleanings in Bee Culture', in S. Yanagisako and S. Delaney (eds), *Naturalizing Power: Essays in Feminist Cultural Analysis*. New York: Routledge, pp. 113–43.

———. 2005. *Friction: An Ethnography of Global Connection*. Princeton: Princeton University Press.

Turner, A. 2013. *Taxidermy*. London: Thames & Hudson.

Urry, J. 1990. *The Tourist Gaze: Leisure and Travel in Contemporary Societies*. London: Sage.

Van de Roemer, B. 2018. 'Art Opens the Book of Nature: Skilfulness and Knowledge in Dutch Curiosity Cabinets around 1700', in G. Seelig (ed.), *Medusa's Menagerie: Otto Marseus van Schrieck and the Scholars*. Munich: Hirmer, pp. 127–39.

Van Dooren, T. 2014. *Flight Ways: Life and Loss at the Edge of Extinction*. New York: Columbia University Press.

Wallace, A.R. 2017. *The Malay Archipelago*. London: Folio.

Waring, G. 1843. *Letters from Malta and Sicily, Addressed to a Young Naturalist*. London: Harvey & Darton.

Watson, M. 2003. 'Performing Place in Nature Reserves', in B. Szerszynski, W. Heim and C. Waterton (eds), *Nature Performed: Environment, Culture and Performance*. Oxford: Blackwell, pp. 145–60.

Williams, S. 2001. *Emotion and Social Theory: Corporeal Reflections on the (Ir)Rational*. London: Sage.

Willock, C. 1991. *Wildfight: A History of Conservation*. London: Jonathan Cape.

Weber, N., and T. Christophersen. 2002. 'The Influence of Non-governmental Organisations on the Creation of Natura 2000 during the European Policy Process', *Forest Policy and Economics* 4: 1–12.

Wilson, E.O. 1984. *Biophilia: The Human Bond with Other Species*. Cambridge, MA: Harvard University Press.

Wilson, M.S., and E. Peden. 2014. 'Aggression and Hunting Attitudes', *Society & Animals: Journal of Human-Animal Studies* 23(1): 3–23.

Ye, Y., et al. 2017. 'FAO's Statistic Data and Sustainability of Fisheries and Aquaculture: Comments on Pauly and Zeller (2017)', *Marine Policy* 81 (2017): 401–5. Retrieved 2 January 2020 from http://dx.doi.org/10.1016/j.marpol.2017.03.012.

Zerner, C. 1999. 'Toward a Broader Vision of Justice and Nature Conservation', in C. Zerner (ed.), *People, Plants and Justice: The Politics of Nature Conservation*. New York: Columbia University Press, pp. 3–20.

Zink, N. 2014. *The Wallcreeper*. London: Fourth Estate.

Index

www.ingramcontent.com/pod-product-compliance
Lightning Source LLC
Chambersburg PA
CBHW070617030426
42337CB00020B/3829